change

Brussels
Capital of Europe

PRISME
EDITIONS

Marie-Françoise Plissart
Gilbert Fastenaekens
/
Photographers
/
/

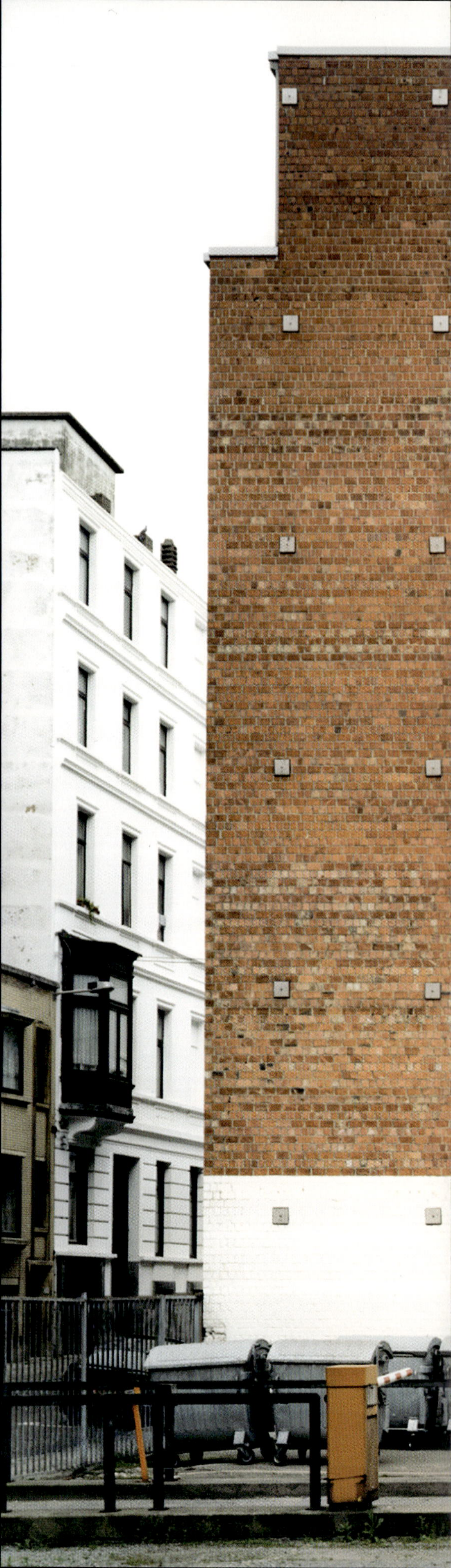

© Gilbert Fastenaekens

© Marie-Françoise Plissart

© Gilbert Fastenaekens

© Marie-Françoise Plissart

© Marie-Françoise Plissart

© Gilbert Fastenaekens

© Marie-Françoise Plissart

/
/
/
/
/
/
/
/
/
/
/
/
/
/
/
/
/
/
/
/
/
/
/
/
/
/
/
/
/
/
/
/
/
/
/
/
/

This book arose out of an important observation: the city has reached a stalemate and is running out of hope. The European city seems to have ground to a halt in its plans, the victim of oversight, suspicion or even a rejection of imagination by its architects, decision makers and residents.

/

This book arose out of words: innumerable analyses of the multiple failure of successive "Brusselisations", but also passionate discussions with architects, both Belgian and foreign, about what should be done. Some are convinced that action is required, but no longer believe in it; others have urged us to act, for us and for them.

/

This book arose from a process of reflection triggered by the trauma of devastated districts and missed opportunities and the backward-looking tinkering that followed. We have dreamt up the conditions that are necessary to cure the city's ills. We need to rediscover creativity and hope, but only if we accept to take a good look at our past. No project can be credible without awareness of one's history. That is why we are presenting the views of artists in this book, setting out concrete data and retracing the genealogy of the wounds and the strengths of this thousand year old city.

/

This book arose from a hope: taking the shortcomings or mistakes as our point of departure, the hope of rebuilding based on genuine projects. Even better, to build on the weaknesses to transform them into strengths and restore the dreams of a new urbanity which can be held up as an example for other urban therapies. After all Curitiba serves as a reference for Brazil.

/

This book arose from a challenge: with "CHANGE" we wanted to go beyond all the obstacles and restart the machine; ask architects from Brussels and elsewhere to invent projects that are possible, to risk thinking the unthinkable and with the sheath of proposals harvested, contribute to regenerating hope.

/

/

Joël Claisse, architect - Liliane Knopes, publisher

/

/

Index
/

/

Marie-Françoise Plissart
Gilbert Fastenaekens, photographers..P.2
/
FOREWORD P.22
/
HISTORY
Pierre Loze / Vincent Cartuyvels..P.24
/
A REPORT
Pierre Laconte / Lucien Kroll / Carola Hein / Francis Rambert..P.74
/
/
/
/
/
/
/
/
/
/
/
/
/
/
/
/
/
/
/
/
/
/

Naturally, the published projects in no way commit the owners of the sites in question.

PROJECTS

/

DISSEMINATE / MEDITATE

Casagrande & Rintala P.130

/

CROSS / PROLONG / REVITALISE

ACTAR Arquitectura P.138
Joël Claisse Architectures P.158
XDGA Xaveer De Geyter Architecten P.170
WEST 8 .... P.186
Odile Decq Benoît Cornette P.192
MVRDV P.198

/

ACUPUNCTURE

ARICS / MSA [Moritz & Simon Architectes] / IDOM P.212
CERAU P.222

/

URBAN STRATEGIES / MICRO - MACRO

Ti-nan Chi P.228
Luc Deleu & T.O.P. office P.232
Vincent Cartuyvels P.238
CERAU P.246
Vincent Callebaut P.250

/

CUSTOMISE

Dominique Perrault Architecte P.258

/

UNIVERSALISE / METAPHORISE

Massimiliano Fuksas P.268
Joël Claisse / Vincent Callebaut P.278
Philippe Samyn P.284
André Jacqmain P.298

/

CONCLUSION P.300

Brussels, why are you feeling down?

/

Brussels: a history of a thousand years, a city that was part of the expansion of the Middle Ages, the Renaissance movement, the metropolis of the dukes of Burgundy and Charles the Fifth of Spain, a national capital and a busy centre of creativity around 1900.

/

Today, Brussels is a wounded city where the traumas accumulate and aggravate each other, creating a centrifugal movement and a depression in the centre. It is a city that has lost touch with its roots, with the water: a buried river, the soil turned over, its inhabitants evacuated, a disrupted and fragmented urban tissue, disproportionate dimensions, a strangled city in the grasp of its institutions, abandoned by its old inhabitants, overwhelmed by offices, by architecture which is the result of marketing and that despises quality.

/

However, it is also a city of newcomers, a city with European stakes in the making, a city whose potential is felt by everyone and whose international future is gradually but surely becoming clearer…

/

So Brussels, why are you feeling down?
The architects and urban developers of Brussels and everyone who has taken pains to reflect on this city over the past twenty years, today seem to be worn out, exhausted, without projects and no longer able to imagine the harmonious development of the city.

/
/
/
/
/
/
/
/
/

An appeal to European architects

/

All interested observers have been confronted with the difficulty of probing this city in terms of urban development and especially the dislocated and contrasting character of its urban landscape, which in some areas is torn and chaotic. Indeed, one needs the keys to understand this mutating city and its special mood and to interpret this curious landscape, to decode the power play and the complex intricacy of the institutional structures that generate it and that seem to make strong and symbolic gestures, whether with regard to decision-making in general and architecture in particular, difficult or even impossible.

/

The rational procedures of architectural and urban management and studies, planning, programming, competitions, etc. which work satisfactorily in other countries, always seem to be inefficient in Brussels for some reason or another. The face of this city changes painstakingly slowly in a climate of negotiations and endless compromises between all kinds of authorities, whose powers and intentions are not always clear. However, the building of Europe itself has taken place within this very special atmosphere and climate of negotiations and compromises, of rapid advancement and unforeseen delays, and the European Union would probably not exist today were it not for this city where the expression of power has been dissipated to such an extent.

/

As a result of the fortunate coincidence of its geographic location and its historic and cultural background, Brussels, which is situated at the heart of a country which itself consists of two countries and lacks a strong identity, turned out to be the ideal breeding ground for the gradual and prudent development of the European Communities, which ultimately led to the single currency in Europe. However, since the great European adventure began, major decisions and strong gestures, radical, simple and efficient procedures, as well as an overtly demonstrative architecture that risked to offend the susceptibility of the individual nations, have always been avoided.

/

Europe in the making Capital or Capitol?

/

It was only with the Treaty of Nice that Brussels, which until then had only been the provisional location of a string of European institutions, was appointed the official seat of the European Union. However, will Brussels ever become the "capital" of Europe? Who shall say? None of the European nations want to see a demonstrative, symbolic and strong expression of a central decision-making authority. What are the particular characteristics of this city, which have made it the ideal location for bringing nations together, a place where confrontations are resolved through negotiations and discussions? Is the city better than others at welcoming heads of state, public officials, representatives, demonstrators, pressure groups and lobbyists, conference guests, etc.? Is Brussels in a position to improve its urban development and the quality of its buildings? To fulfil its needs, will the city set up urban spaces or organisations to meet the specific requirements of the European democracy? Will the city evolve in order to provide the various components of European society with the opportunities to meet and express themselves. Will the Eurocrats isolate themselves in their privileged areas or shall we see the entire city evolve and participate in the European future? Will the city and its inhabitants accept the concentration and the centralisation of European institutions? Shall we witness the creation of a monumental "European district" which is closed off and secured, accessible only to ministers, civil servants and members of Parliament – the ultimate expression of the power of the European Union? Brussels, capital or Capitol? What will Europe look like?

/

To implement relevant and suitable measures for this gigantic construction site that will continue for several decades, we must first take a closer look at the early and recent history of this city. We need to understand its environment, its mentality, its characteristic procedures, which have allowed it to play host to Europe's construction without assuming the role of capital and without offending national feelings that can revive unexpectedly.

/
/
/
/
/
/
/
/
/
/
/
/
/
/
/
/
/
/
/
/
/
/
/
/
/
/
/
/
/
/
/
/

HISTO

/

The history and symptoms of a constantly evolving city…

/

/

Pierre Loze
Vincent Cartuyvels

/

/

RY

/
/
/
/
/
/
/
/
/
/
/
/
/
/
/
/
/
/
/
/
/
/
/
/
/
/
/

/
/
/
/
/
/
/
/
/
/
/
/
/
/
/
/
/
/
/
/
/
/
/
/
/
/
/

I. From its foundation to the XVIII century

/

The roots

/

A crossroads
Valleys and hills
The medieval framework
The balance of power
An uncertain status

A country between two others

/

/

Who would have believed it? Founded in the aftermath of the collapse of the Carolingian Empire, Brussels has always weighed in the balance of Europe. It owes its birth to relations between the Germanic Empire and France. In 977, in the face of the feudal influence that came from France and spread across Lower Lorraine, Emperor Otton II decided to make Brabant a defence against the encroachments and conquering habits of his cousin, the king of France. He satisfied the claims of the latter's brother on these territories and consequently made him Duke of Lower Lorraine. He did not succeed in winning obedience nor in tightening relationships with the Holy Empire and he also failed to contain the rise of the burgeoning feudal system.

/

However, the manoeuvre did succeed beyond expectations in creating at the meeting place between these cultural and political entities, which differed in so many ways, a curious country which belonged to neither of them and alternated allegiances to maintain its independence, and which over the centuries would determine its own destiny based on this strange and ambiguous position.

A castle on the crossroads

/

/

The new duke of Lower Lorraine established his fortified castle on an island in the river Senne, on the site of an old Roman farm, in an area where Latin had been replaced by the Germanic language. The valley was wide and the slopes to the west rose gradually while the steeper slopes to the east had an old Roman road running along them. The site provided no entrenchment and only a nearby forest formed a natural barrier with the Germanic world. A chapel dedicated to Saint Michael had already been built on one of the hills to the east for the farming inhabitants of the area.

/

From then onwards, Brussels followed the typical pattern of development shared by all medieval cities in Europe. Merchants, attracted by the presence of the duke and the riches of a small court, set up within the scope of his protection at the foot of the castle. As mercantile activity developed further, the Grand' Place market square was established nearby, together with the Saint Nicholas church, built for the inhabitants of the market town while the castle had its own chapel, dedicated to Saint Géry. The dukes had the relics of a local martyr, Saint Gudula, brought to the chapel, as at the time the possession of holy relics was an indispensable sign of power.

/
/
/
/
/
/
/
/
/
/
/
/
/

/
/
/
/
/
/
/

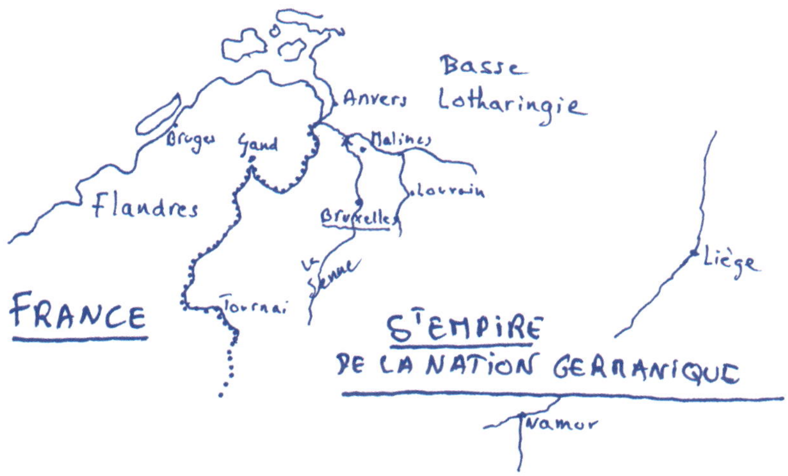

/

Somewhere between Flanders and Liege, on a secondary, just about navigable river: the Senne.

/
/
/
/

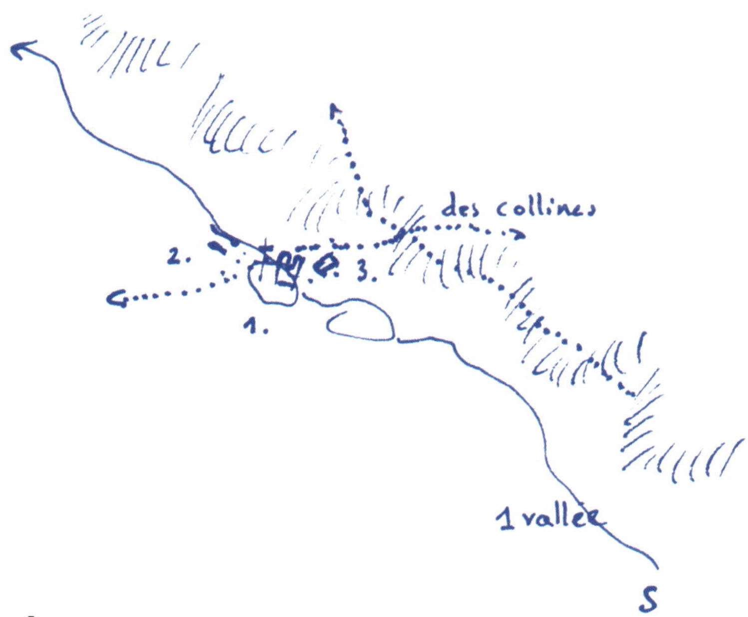

/
/

The Senne:
It flows northwards towards Antwerp
Therefore: the sea
Foundation:
1. the island of Saint-Géry: a castle, a church
2. a port
3. a market

A bipolar city

/

/

In 1047, only a few decades after the founding of the castle, the dukes abandoned it and chose to move to a higher location. They transported the relics of Saint Gudula to the church of Saint Michael, which was located on one of the higher hills and they set up their new residence and court nearby on one of the neighbouring hills and in a spacious environment: the Coudenberg. Thus and to this day, the bipolar urban configuration of the city was created: a lower-town area for the working class craftsmen and merchants and a higher-town area where higher aristocracy and nobles resided. Over the years, a series of buildings made their mark on the landscape and perpetuated this contrast of urban values and powers that came and went: dukes, followed by emperors and nobles, and later the bourgeois, members of parliament and today the European institutions.

/ /

/ / / / / /

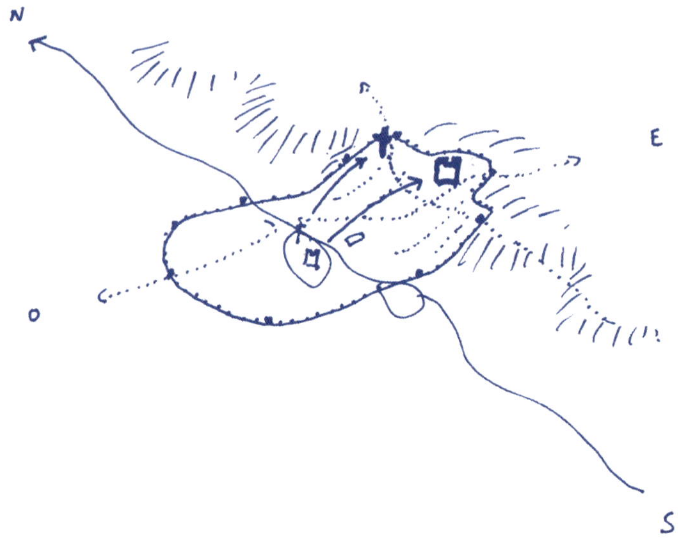

/

A bipolar city
The castle was therefore the starting point, which was followed by a church, a port, merchants and inhabitants - and a village at the foot of the hills, a crossroads.
It quickly became bipolar, and remained so. The church and castle moved to the higher town, 2 hearts: one in the centre, in the valley and the other to the east, on the hill. The first city wall was on the west/east axis from the lower town to the higher town, while the second city wall paved the way for the current pentagon.

/ /

The two city walls

/

/

A first city wall, which was exceptionally long for the time, was built in the XII century. It contained the higher town and the lower town, the old castle and the church of Saint Géry, the Grand' Place and the church of Saint Nicholas, with a detour to include the church of Saint Michael and Sainte Gudula as well as the royal palace and the surrounding aristocratic districts. Remnants of the wall can still be seen today, spread across the city centre, its fragments lost between more recent constructions.

/

In the XIII and XIV centuries, the bourgeoisie of craftsmen and merchants began to develop. Brussels was ideally located on the east-west axis between Cologne - Liège - Bruges and on the north-south axis between Antwerp, Nivelles and the cities of Northern France. To this day, the street names keep alive the memory of the activities of the craftsmen and of relations with neighbouring towns, and bear witness to the role played by Brussels in the exchanges with various wool production centres and metal industries, but also its commercial role beyond its own borders, with countries such as England, Germany, France and Italy. As a result of this prosperity and the demographic growth, a second much larger city wall was built from 1357 to 1379 to contain the new districts that had formed outside the city. This gave Brussels its oval shape which later with the strongholds at Vauban and the ring-road boulevards resulted in today's pentagonal form.

/
/
/
/
/
/
/
/

/
/
/
/
/
/
/

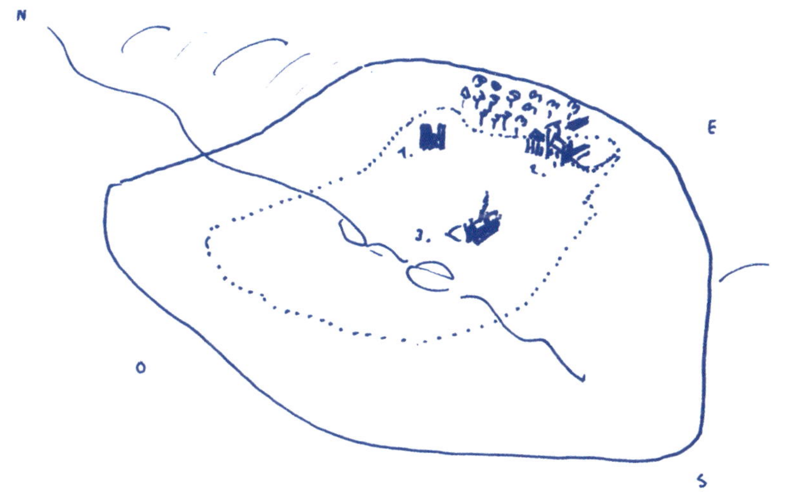

/

The end of the Middle Ages and the balance of power. The church and the nobility in the higher town: the bourgeoisie in the lower town. Each had its own structure… and tower:

1. the cathedral
2. the ducal palace
3. the town hall

/
/
/
/
/
/
/
/
/
/
/
/
/
/
/
/
/
/
/
/
/
/
/
/
/
/
/

Prosperity and the balance of power: a culture of negotiation…

/

The industrial and mercantile bourgeoisie dominated the common people. Jealously guarding its prerogatives, the bourgeoisie controlled the crafts and reigned over public life, founding its authority on the protection of the duke.
The town hall, which was built in 1421, reflects a happy period in the history of the city, following a period of social conflicts and pitiless repression. A balance was struck between the powers of the reigning princes, the bourgeoisie and the power of the crafts and from then onwards these parties were represented in the town hall. As such, the custom of mutual negotiations between the different players of society developed with no single party dominating the other completely.

/

In the meantime, the other cities of Flanders and Brabant had become its rivals. Brussels cunningly benefited from the uprisings of Louvain and Ghent against their prince and established itself as residence of choice for the dukes of Burgundy and later Charles the Fifth of Spain. Brussels also benefited from the rising trade in luxury goods that resulted. To encourage the permanent presence of the court, the city even decided to pay for some of the costs involved in expanding the duke's palace. Brussels had become a splendid sight: at the beginning of the XVI century it became the capital of the Habsburg Empire with a magnificent and ornate town hall, churches filled with treasures and paintings, dominated by the immense palace of Charles the Fifth which was decorated with endless pinnacles. The city welcomed the ambassadors of every court and acquired a taste for the cosmopolitan life which it had succeeded in attracting: a host of languages were spoken within its walls, and it embraced the intellectual and artistic influences of Italy, France and Germany.

© Speltdoorn

/

Brussels before the bombardment by Louis XIV.
Jan Baptist Bonnecroy, View of Brussels [1664-1665], 165 x 300 cm.
Fondation Roi Baudouin, on loan to the Royal Museums of Fine Arts of Brussels.

The network of the bourgeois city

/

/

The first panoramic plans of the city date back to the XVI century. They show the city as an extremely dense network of winding streets that widen at regular intervals to form a square.
The network of roads from east to west, which cross the hills on which the city had established its patrician districts, clearly dominate.
In the XIX century, this layout of the city was modified by the north-south connection. A canal, created in the XVI century to provide a maritime connection with the port of Antwerp and the river Scheldt, led to the establishment of a port inside the walls of the city. This infrastructure for transport by inland waterways resulted in a spectacular increase in trading and manufacturing capitalism and the influence of the bourgeoisie grew together with the considerable progress of science and the spread of Protestantism.

/
/
/
/
/
/
/
/
/
/
/
/
/
/
/
/
/
/
/
/

/
/
/
/
/
/
/
/
/
/
/
/
/
/
/
/
/
/

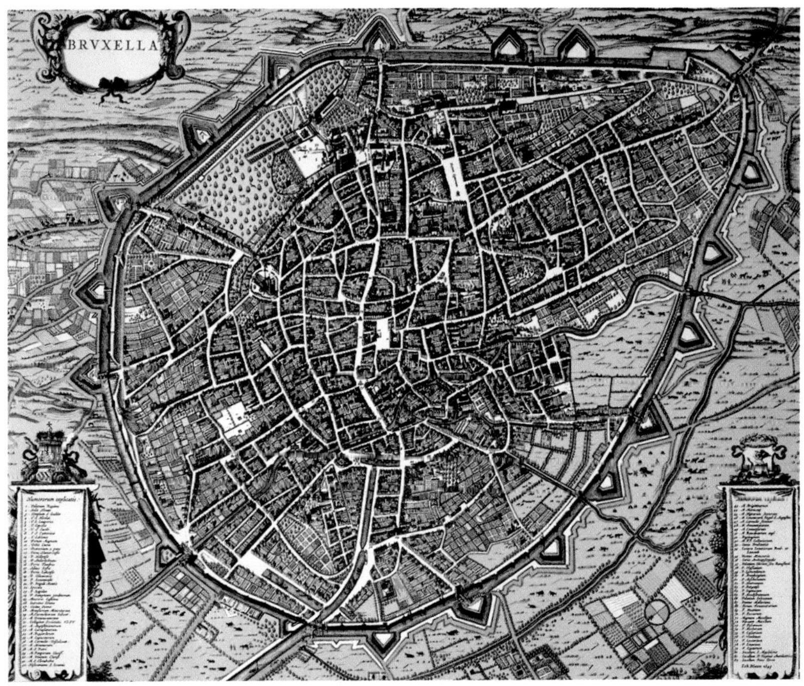

© C.I.D.E.P. asbl

/

Capital of the Dukes of Brabant, then of the Dukes of Burgundy, then of Charles the Fifth of Spain: this modestly sized city grows into an imperial residence.

/

1st divide: the palace and the aristocracy set up home to the east in the higher town while the canal and the inner city definitively attract the mercantile and industrial activities to the lower town, in the centre and to the west.

/
/
/
/
/
/
/
/
/

Social and religious confrontations: massacres and burning at the stake

/

/

Sanctified by the church, since the end of the reign of Charles the Fifth the Habsburg monarchy had anticipated to which point the economic and ideological rise of this individualist bourgeoisie, that was beginning to demand the secularisation of church property, more power, religious freedom, as well as commercial freedom, would begin to threaten the established order. The ambitions of this bourgeoisie risked compromising the central authority of the monarchy, which was making considerable headway. The confrontation ultimately came during the following generation with Philip II who wanted to rule this remote province of his immense empire from Madrid, without discussions.
The systematic and general levying of taxes as well as the rigorous application of the religious laws provided the pretext for the Protestant uprising. The King immediately sent the duke of Albe with soldiers and the ruthless massacre of ten thousand people followed. Brussels and Antwerp were the main targets of this bloody repression. The survivors fled to the north where they formed the first modern nation, the Northern Netherlands. The rebels' demands, formulated in religious terms, were in fact social issues with the same objectives as those of the French Revolution: free movement of goods, the sale of the church's possessions and property, the abolition of all restrictions on work, industry and commerce.

/
/
/
/
/
/
/
/

Europe's battlefield

/

/

The last catholic bastion in the face of the Protestant world, this territory which had been the ideal location for commercial exchanges due to its proximity to the major political actors, also became the battlefield of Europe during the XVII and XVIII centuries. The Southern Netherlands, with Brussels as their capital, had become the place of residence of Spanish governors who led a relentless war against the heretics and at the same time opposed another organisation of the mercantile, materialist and individualist society that was emerging and threatening the old order. This war against former subjects and discretely backed by France, slowly weakened Spain and eventually took on a European dimension with consequences in Germany, during the Thirty Years War, and was subsequently waged further, leaving behind it the same trail of massacres and destruction within the context of rivalling Spanish and French monarchies and then between the Austrian and French monarchies.

/
/
/
/
/
/
/
/
/
/
/
/
/
/
/
/
/

Pragmatic pacifism and weakening nationalism

Fear of these European wars which had raged in the region and the territorial stakes from then onwards up to the XX century, has consequently become a fundamental component of the country's identity. This fear of war has clearly marked the local mentality and particularly that of Brussels, which served as the capital of successive governors without ever identifying completely with their cause. The capacity to support foreign powers, the will to maintain the neutrality of the country, a deep mistrust of grand ideologies, a prunounced pragmatism and preference for short-term solutions which are satisfying from a materialistic point of view, and also ongoing pacifistic trends all come together and are combined with a weak sense of nationalism and patriotism and always a good dose of scepticism. These character traits explain the extremely active involvement of Belgium, and Brussels in particular, in the European project from the outset, its ongoing contribution to its construction and its unreserved adherence to the ultimate objectives of Europe despite the implications in terms of loss of local identity.

Traumatic experiences: a bombardment, a fire

/

/

During the wars waged by Louis XIV against Spain, a time of territorial bickering that ultimately drew the borders of modern France, Belgium was devastated several times. In 1695, Brussels was even completely shelled by the troops of Field Marshal Villeroi in reprisal for the resistance he met when approaching the neighbouring city of Namur. These terrible episodes have left deep marks and the events are remembered in paintings and etchings. The town hall and the ducal palace as well as a handful of churches were the only buildings to escape this terrible military campaign which destroyed nearly four thousand houses and buildings, sixteen churches and convents, including works of arts. In less than five years, the craftsmen of Brussels rebuilt the Grand' Place and created the magnificent buildings that we can see today. The city rose from its ashes and left behind all regrets of its lost beauty. Besides this disaster, which deeply marks the collective memory of the city, Brussels also remembers a second calamity which dealt the final blow to its medieval and renaissance past. In 1731, the old palace of the dukes of Brabant and Charles the Fifth of Spain, which had been restored and refurbished on several occasions, went up in flames because of the carelessness, as the story goes, of a palace cook who was preparing jam. Despite the efforts of the city's fire fighters, the fire could not be contained and the buildings were reduced to ashes. With the exception of the Grand' Place, the Hôtel de Ville [town hall] and a few churches, Brussels had lost all the vestiges of its past. It would be interesting to know to which extent the lack of respect that Brussels would repeatedly show with regard to its heritage of the XVIII and XIX centuries, can be explained by a loss of identity which is linked to these two events and their impact on the collective culture.

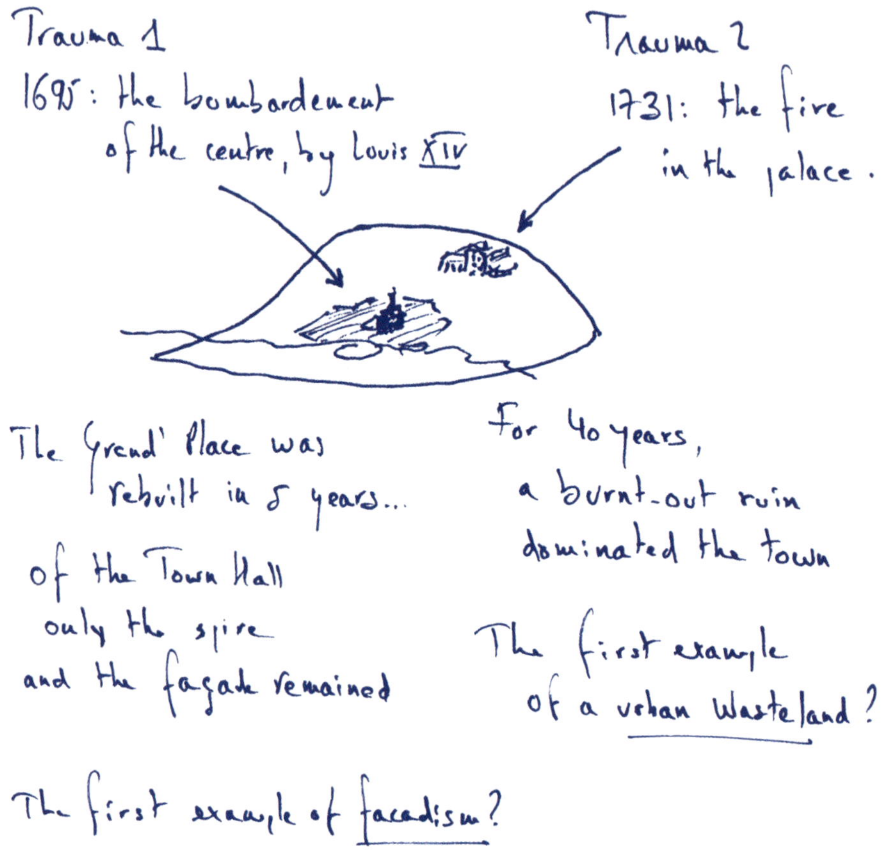

The loss of identity syndrome: a city à la française

/

Under the Austrian Habsburg monarchy, the Netherlands and their capital Brussels experienced an unprecedented rise of the French influence among the nobility and upper middle classes. French replaced Flemish and Spanish as the language of the ruling classes but in the streets people continued to speak their local dialect which mixed up words and expressions from the three languages in a droll colloquial manner. Having let the desolate ruins of the palaces dominate the appearance of the city for thirty years, the Austrian governor Charles of Lorraine finally decided to refurbish his palace, transforming the old Nassau mansion which opens towards the Place Royale and was built on the site of the old court, as well as the Park of Brussels where the old gardens of the Palace were once situated. This vast project in Louis XVI style was designed by a French architect. Emperor Joseph II thought it was a very provincial style. Once again, the signs of power appeared in the city: this time, those of the enlightened monarchy. This project, on the edge of the medieval city, ignored for the first time the existing elevation by working with terraces. Forming a succession of squares bordered with façades in the same style, the whole Place Royale and the park were later, at the beginning of the XIX century, opened up, by removing the main arched entrances of the enclosure, in order to extend the main thoroughfares [Rue Royale, Rue de la Régence, Rue Belliard, Rue de la Loi] into the new neighbouring districts. In a way, this project provided the matrix and model for the expansion of a neo-classical modern city.

/
/
/
/
/

© Archives de la Ville de Bruxelles

/
The old palace seen from the park

© Archives de la Ville de Bruxelles

The new royal palace: an enclosure

/
/
/
/
/
/
/
/
/
/
/
/
/
/
/
/
/
/
/
/
/

© Prisme Editions

Today, a crossroads

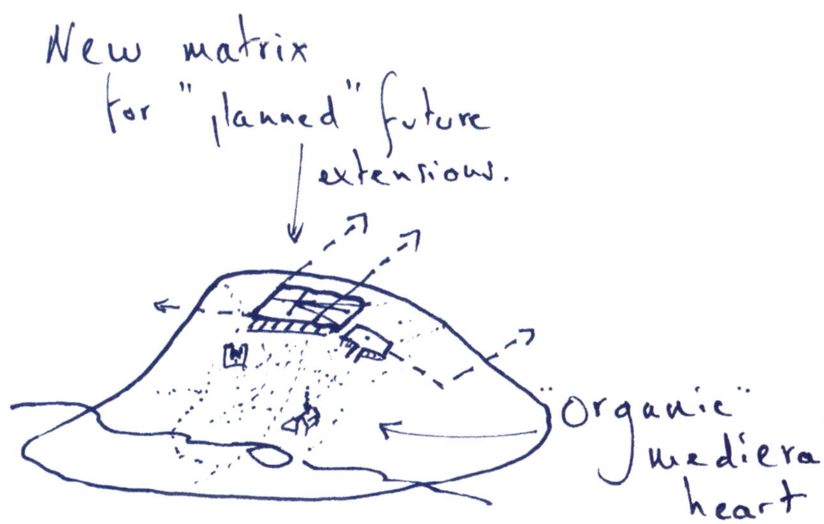

/
A geometrical complex, as if stamped on a flattened relief, encrusted in the medieval tissue, precariously balanced on the slope that it denies. It is the last heart of the city, a new matrix for the modern bourgeois extensions.
/
/
/

II. The XIX Century

/

Expansion

/

The industrial and bourgeois city

The capital of a new state
Urban coherence
The first frenzies

Provincial town or capital?

/

Voltaire acerbically described Brussels as a city with backward ideas where Casanova stayed one night only to find that few women were gracious and dignified enough to be conquered, unlike Venice, Paris, Dresden and Saint Petersburg. However, Brussels made every effort to keep up with fashion. While Paris stirred in 1789, the small capital was experiencing its own Branbançonne revolution, which was an uprising against the enlightened monarch but also to demand independence and a return to the privileges of the corporations and crafts of the Middle Ages! A faction of these "revolutionaries" were however inspired by Paris and the ideas of the Enlightenment, yet the reactionary movement dominated and would have triumphed were it not for the invasion of the Sans-Culottes who annexed the country to France and subjected it to the laws of the Republic, then the Directoire, and subsequently the Consulat and the Empire.

/

The Belgian states, which in fact constituted a mosaic of independent provinces, were transformed into nine French administrative departments for twenty years. They were reorganised in a rational manner and administered very strictly by the new bourgeoisie who took on board the ideas of the Enlightenment against the backdrop of the secularisation of religious property. Children were educated in French secondary schools and universities while commerce and industry flourished.

/
/
/
/
/
/
/
/

The ring-road boulevards, the neo-classical city

/

Under the regime of Napoleon, the fortifications of the old "feudal" city were pulled down and large ring-road boulevards were built. Neo-classical mansions were erected in the higher-town area and new districts were created around the park and Place Royale. In the lower-town area, the façades of numerous baroque houses were modernised and stripped of their gables, which were replaced by straight cornices decorated with simple bands and coverings. This white city set out to be modern and dreamt of competing with Paris or London. The city built a theatre and set up the Grand Hospice, a workhouse where the poor and beggars were locked up. The bourgeoisie of Brussels started to take an interest in applied sciences: the arrival of new cultural and geological methods marked the discovery of new resources above and below ground and paved the way for an industrial revolution which was to be extremely successful in this country. In addition to the development of historic sciences, human sciences applied to population control, statistics and criminology were also booming. Lawyers and accountants were abundant, though thinkers and philosophers rare.

/

After the battle of Waterloo and the treaty of Vienna, Belgium was united with the Northern Netherlands. The founding by the king of Holland of the Société Générale, the first Belgian industrial holding, encouraged the development of modern capitalism. However, the Belgians were not too pleased with this reunion with their former Protestant compatriots. Nor were the English happy with the combined influence of a naval power and a prosperous industrial country. The presence of French exiles who had fled during the restoration of the Bourbons in France, and numerous English tourists who wanted to see the site of the glorious battle or visited the continent after the blockade was lifted, restored the cosmopolitan mood of Brussels.

1830 : a buffer state by English appointment

/

On a summer's evening at the Théâtre de la Monnaie, the tenor sang "Liberty, Liberty…" during the performance of the Mute Girl of Portici, rousing the excited audience that stormed out of the theatre to show its enthusiasm. The idle masses joined the group, triggering a revolution against their new rulers. The Dutch failed to break the uprising and after a few days the bourgeoisie set up a temporary government and proclaimed independence for their country with the approval of England.

/

Once again, concerns regarding the balance of power in Europe created a buffer state on the borders of the major powers. Brussels became the capital of this new state thanks to the role it had played during this uprising. The English hoped that without the French and Dutch markets to sell their products, Belgian industry would waste away. However, the bourgeoisie, who were full of new ideas and who successfully imitated the industrial methods of the English, surprisingly managed to make Belgium the second largest industrial power after the United Kingdom. A railway network was already established in 1834 and together with the network of canals, Belgium had one of the densest infrastructures in Europe. Thanks to the alliances of dynasties, diplomatic and commercial relations with neighbouring countries had a favourable impact on industrial activity. Belgium coped easily with the events of 1848 and the war of 1870, which even brought more exiles and capital to the country.

/
/
/
/
/
/

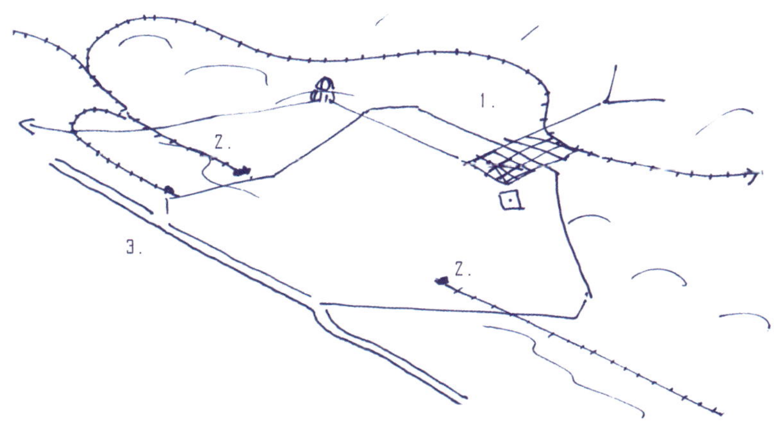

After 1830 :
1. the extension towards the east : the Leopold district for the nobility
2. the structuring influence of the train : 2 stations : north and south
3. the Charleroi canal for industrial activity

Just like London…

/

/

Brussels was in the grasp of renovation: the refurbishing and redevelopment of the old city became an obsession of the bourgeoisie, driven by the rush of speculation but also by the wish to emulate the neighbouring capitals. The modification of streets to accommodate trams, the removal of blind alleys, the creation of north-south connections, the modernisation of buildings in neo-classical style gradually began to change the appearance of the city centre. The working classes were pushed back to the outskirts of the city or to the industrial areas developing to the west of the pentagon formed by the exterior boulevards. On the other hand, in 1838 a new district earmarked for the upper middle classes was created to the east of the pentagon. It was situated beyond the exterior boulevards, running on from the major axes of the Park of Brussels, a fashionable venue for leisurely strolls, and along which the Parliament and the Palace of the King [Palais du Roi] had sprung up. This new district adjacent to the Palace of the King has two squares inspired by London's Belgravia square, near Buckingham Palace, as well as a railway station, in analogy with Victoria Station. For the construction of the Court of Justice, the liberal bourgeoisie commissioned the services of the fashionable architect Joseph Poelaert. His intention was to raze to the ground the entire working-class district of the Marolles and to build on the higher part of the city the largest building in Europe as a symbol of the all-powerful Justice. He was also responsible for the monumental design of the route from the Court of Justice to the Royal Church and Chapel of Laeken, via the Park and along the Colonne du Congrès and for the construction of the main architectural highlights along this route. This emphasised the opposition between the higher town, dedicated to the powerful and rich, and the lower town with its mercantile and industrial activities. The old layout, passed down over the centuries was inherited and further reinforced.

/

/

/

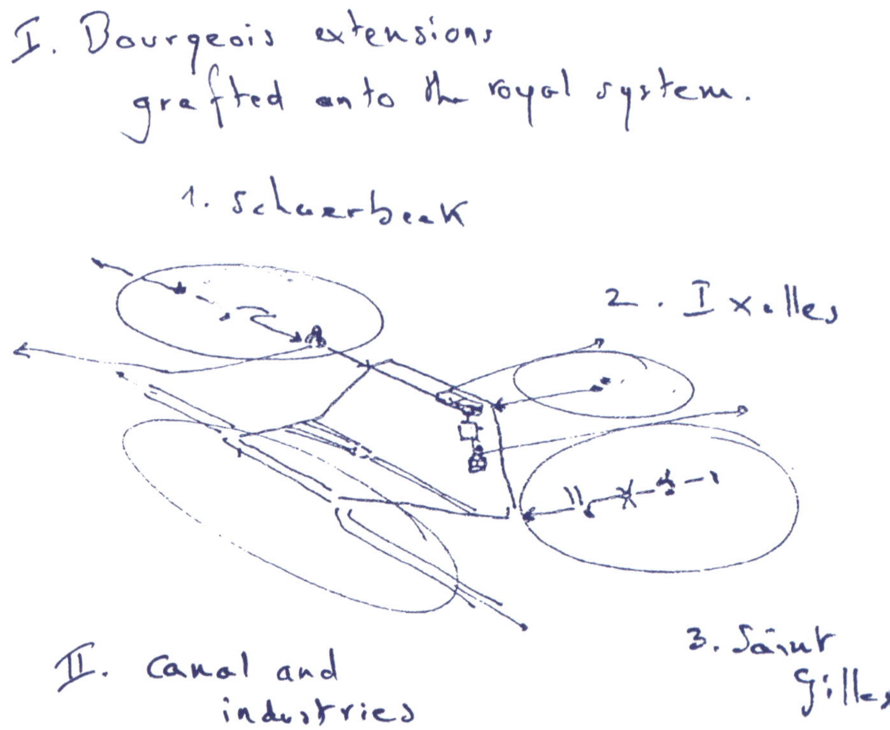

/

/

Grafts and divides:
I. Bourgeois extensions: the communes of Schaerbeek [1], Ixelles [2] and Saint Gilles [3] graft their urban system [roads, communal houses] onto the royal system.
II. Working class districts: along the canal, industries and working class homes in an extremely dense network

/

Today these districts have become working class. The bourgeoisie have moved out further towards the east.

/

/

/

/

/

/

/

/

/

/

/

/

/

/

/

/

/

/

/

And like Paris…

/

/

Around 1860, despite the ongoing modernisation of the historic centre, the Rue de Laeken and the old district of the Beguinage in particular, and despite the building of the Rue Neuve, the Rue du Midi, the Rue Blaes and the new Nord and Midi stations and the opening of indoor shopping galleries, the old heart of Brussels was still extremely depressing. The river Senne with its decrepit buildings along its banks, flowed through the city and around two islands. The river was in effect an open sewer, a situation made worse by the increasing population. In 1866, after a plague epidemic, mayor Anspach decided to undertake far-reaching public works: from 1868 to 1871, hundreds of houses were expropriated and pulled down and the Senne was deviated to flow into an enormous sewer covered by Haussmann-style boulevards. Real-estate promoters who had been driven away by the Paris Commune, participated in the projects alongside the Belgians, while sculptors under the direction of Carrier-Delleuze provided sculptures for the Bourse de Bruxelles, a monumental building that was erected at the centre of the boulevards. The building is in the same style as the Paris Opera and glorifies money and speculation, and together with the Court of Justice bears witness to the pride of the ruling bourgeoisie who knew how to get rich and avoid revolutions. The liberal ideology was in full swing and the figures sculptured on the Bourse depict puttis pushing the coal-mine trolleys.

/ / / / / / / / /

/ /

To renovate and develop the centre, Brussels built itself a Haussmann-style boulevard, stretching between the 2 stations, Nord and Midi, along which it erected a Bourse and a prestigious square. It hoped to attract the bourgeoisie to new Parisian-style apartments. But the middle classes preferred the single-family homes of the suburbs. Yes, even back then…

/ / / / / / / / / / / / / /

/ / / / / / / /

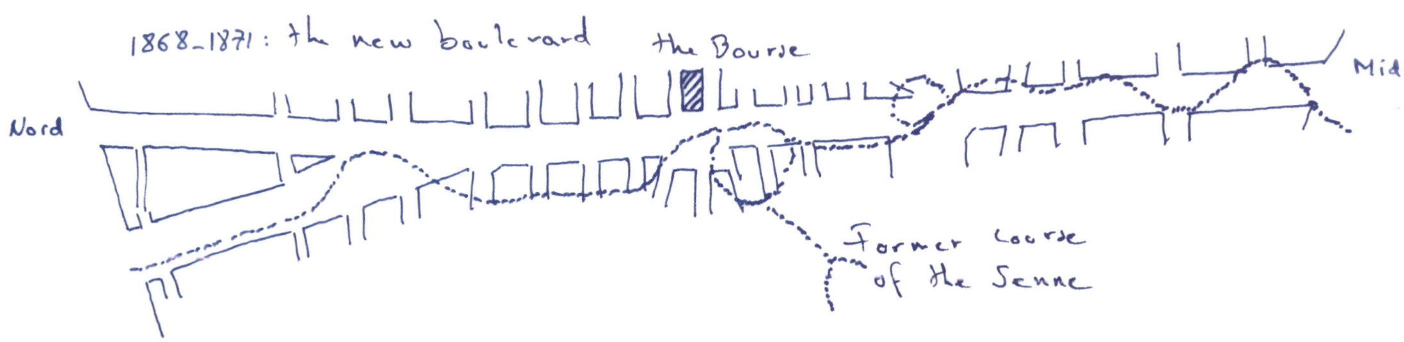

The slippery slope

/

/

While these building projects were being carried out in the old historical centre, forcing out the inhabitants, the surrounding communes were continuing to grow and new communities were built. An emulator of Joseph Poelaert, Victor Besme, designed the plan for all the roads around the pentagon which in effect form a coherent network with the dome of the Court of Justice as a focal point. With the support and approval of King Leopold II, over the next forty years, the roads inspector designed and executed the necessary works for all the streets, avenues, boulevards and parks which laid the foundations for the quality and charm of greater Brussels in the following century. However, the slow progress of the work on the Court of Justice [1866-83] and the construction of the access roads [1883-1895] and the laborious completion of the boulevards in the centre [1871-1880], especially combined with the bankruptcy of the French promoters and the fact that the various elements did not fit together as nicely as initially planned, revealed the limitations of this method of remodelling a city. At the same time, another district which was being developed within the confines of the pentagon, on the site of the old Notre Dame aux Neiges district [1874-1885] and which included homes, theatres, covered galleries and public baths, was also in disarray as the result of poor sales and financial difficulties.

/

The legendary scepticism of the people of Brussels, only too ready to poke fun at all figures of authority, had a field day scoffing at these grand urban development projects and their political and financial promoters. Other adventures in the same vein echoed these failures in the XX century and proved once again that Brussels cannot measure up to those cities that it seeks to emulate.

/

/

/
/
/
/
/
/

/

A coherent network of prestigious avenues structure the bourgeois extensions towards the east and the south east, linking a series of monuments [domes, pediments and spires] designed to symbolise royalty and the nation.

/
/
/
/

The Mont des Arts
a phase of megalomaniac follies

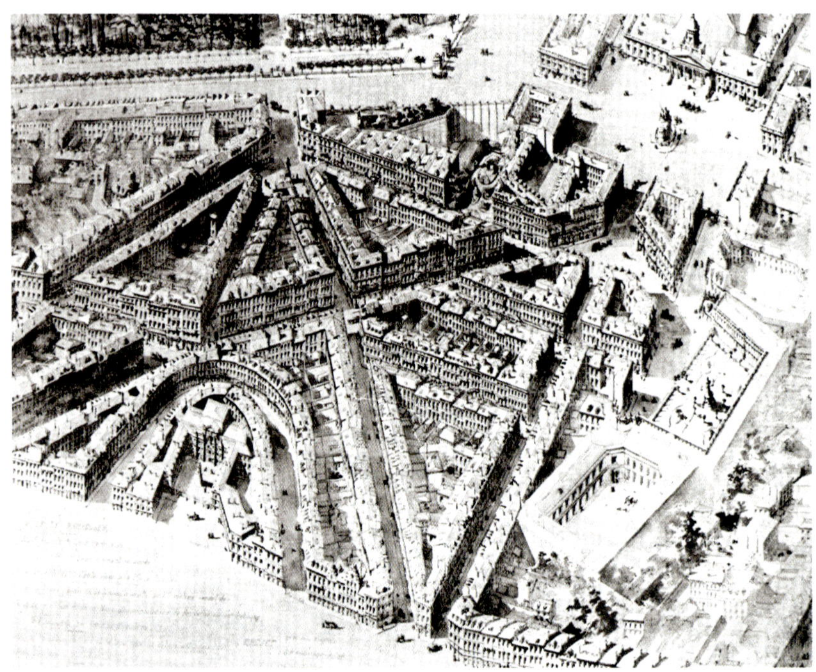

© Archives de la Ville de Bruxelles

/
/
/
/
/

The Mont des Arts and the Nord-Midi Junction

/

These construction sites had not yet been completed when someone had the bright idea of creating an underground railway junction that would link the Nord and Midi stations. This junction would cross the east side of the pentagon along a series of working-class districts and also demolish the remnants of the old aristocratic district of the Middle Ages that used to surround the ducal palace.
At the foot of the Place Royale, a monumental Mont des Arts was planned for development. This project would house the extensions of the Museum of Fine Arts created in 1883 along the Rue de la Régence and together they would create a vast museum complex.

/

This time, the mayor Charles Buls fiercely opposed the project. He was behind the restoration work on the Grand' Place and an enlightened defender of the city's remaining traditional architecture. However, Charles Buls finally resigned when preparations for this major construction project began. Demolition work that took place at the end of the XIX century mainly resulted in the pulling down of the Ter Arken and Saint Roch districts that bridged the higher and lower parts of the city, i.e. between the Place Royale and the Grand' Place. Alphonse Balat, followed by his pupil Charles Maquet, both studied the possibility of building a vast neo-classical complex despite the extremely steep slope that hardly lent itself to such an enterprise. Several other architects also tried this approach but to no avail.

/

For the Universal Exhibition of 1905, public gardens with a waterfall and surrounded by shops were designed by the French landscape gardener Vacherot and quickly built and soon became a favourite haunt of many inhabitants of Brussels. It survived… for half a century.

/

/

/
/
/
/
/
/
/

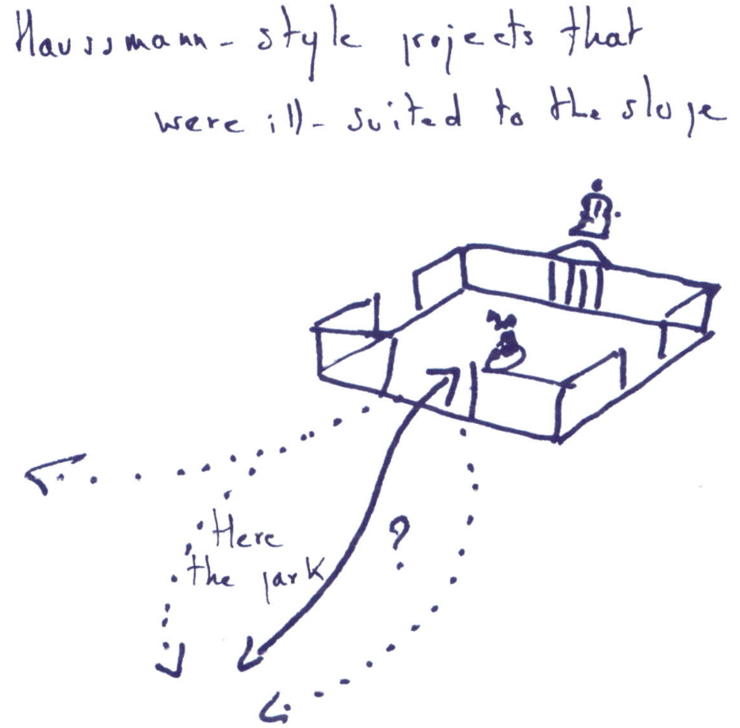

/
/
/

/
1905, improvised at the last minute, a picturesque park that simply yet effectively sets off the slope: steps, waterfalls, rocks, statues and shrubs offer intimacy and are warmly received by the inhabitants of Brussels.

The royal arc de triomphe

/

/

In 1880, for the celebrations of the fiftieth anniversary of the Independence of Belgium, a national exhibition was organised in the vast halls built specially for the occasion in a large park on the other side of the Léopold district. During the exhibitions that were held in the same halls in 1885 and 1888, the idea was born to erect a monumental arch at the centre of the complex. Gédéon Bordiau, a pupil of Joseph Poelart, was commissioned to build the arch which had to be completed with pasteboard each time an exhibition was held. King Léopold II was eager to see this monument finished, however, financial reasons, unwillingness and a lack of interest in these kinds of monumental projects caused delays. In the end, for the exhibition of 1905, the king ordered the destruction of the arc de triomphe with a single arch which Bordiau had started and he commissioned at his own expense the architect Girault, who had built the Grand Palais in Paris, to build a new monument with three equal arches decorated with sculptures depicting the glory of Belgium.

/
/
/
/
/
/
/
/
/
/
/
/
/
/
/
/
/
/

/
/
/
/
/
/
/
/
/
/
/
/
/
/

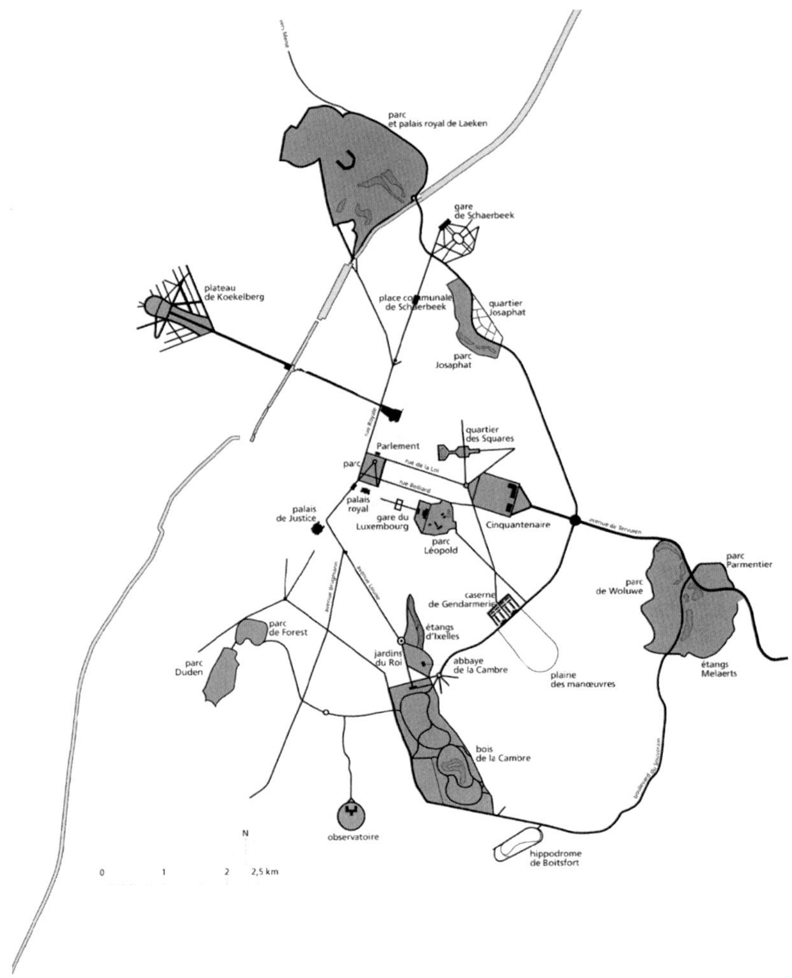

/

In 1880, Brussels was a hive of international intellectual and artistic activity. The country's largest industrial city, its centre (the pentagon: 2 x 2.5 km) was home to around 160,000 inhabitants.

/

Numerous islands of single family homes with gardens and a coherent network of boulevards and parks, of streets and squares gave it - and still gives it today- an exceptional charm.

/

The incredible variety of eclectic facades, Art Nouveau and even Art Deco, means that each street in Brussels has its own unique personality.

Brussels' broad avenues

/

/

The royal entrepreneur grew weary of Belgian architects and fell out with Balat for example, whom he replaced with his pupil Maquet to complete his palaces in Brussels and Laeken. He also commissioned Girault once again to draw up the plans of his palace in Tervuren which was located at the end of a very long succession of avenues lined with trees and parks starting at the arc de triomphe. The inhabitants of Brussels looked upon these grand urban projects of the king with much irony: he then commissioned Victor Besme and used all his influence to ensure the projects were completed with obsessive perseverance. The megalomania of the king was criticised: the width of the streets and avenues which the king deemed extremely important was considered to be too excessive. On the other hand, the king's stipulations determined the appearance of the southern outskirts of Brussels. It is true that today, these suburbs of Brussels have a clear and coherent structure. The presence of parks and squares has facilitated the development of new districts which can be accessed easily and provide pleasant living conditions for the family houses with their gardens. This type of dwelling which is part of a network of hierarchic streets is one of the features that still mark this city despite the ongoing disruptive construction work.

© Marie-Françoise PLISSART

The rules of town planning: aestheticism, features, variety, space
A "text book city" that can still be made out today.

But, this city
with its provincial size

was being promised the status
of an international capital

↳ fabulous projects were pouring in

first of all
Like Paris

outside...
in side...

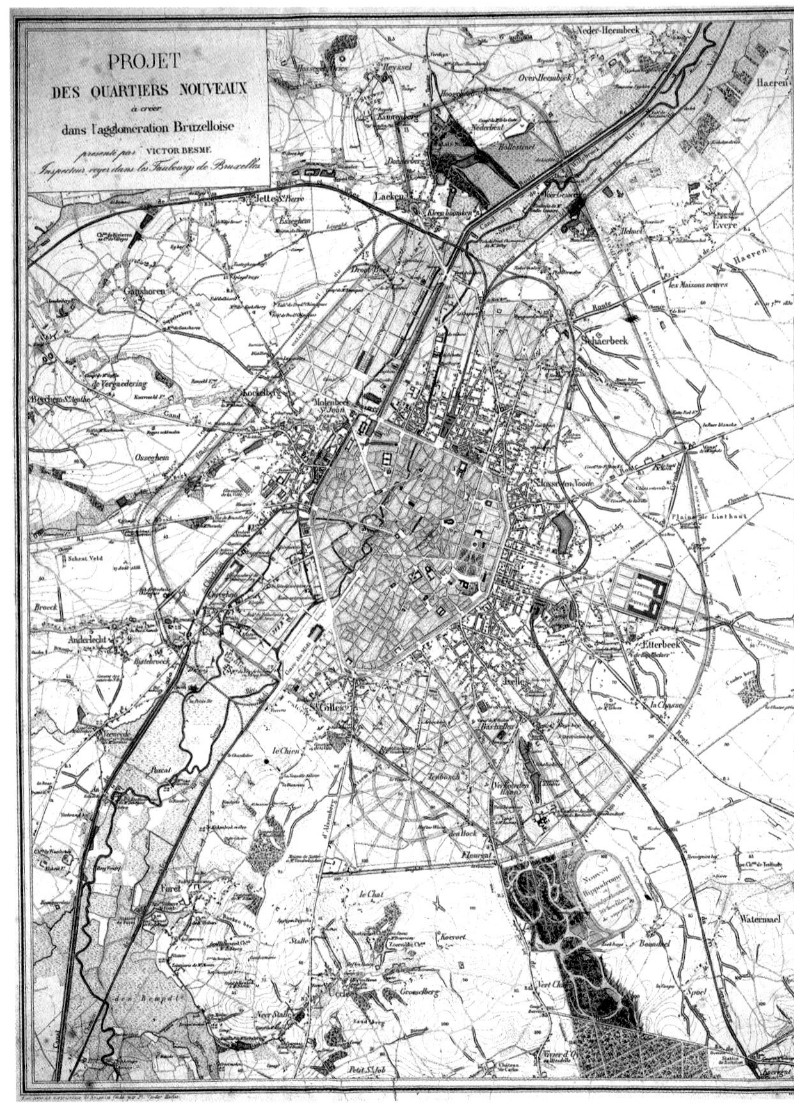

© Archives d'Architecture Moderne, Bruxelles

Then,
like New York…

How far is it ready to go
to play in the major league?

Go on, Bruxelles ma belle,
Be a devil!

III. The XX Century

/

A pact with the devil

/

Amnesia and traumatic experiences
A deserted city
Resistance or enactment?
The European challenge

Problematic inheritance

/

/

The destruction of the more medieval districts, which connected the higher and lower city, the setbacks that plagued the Mont des Arts project and the Nord-Midi junction programme together constituted a serious urban problem that future generations would have to struggle with.

/

On the eve of the First World War, Brussels had the appearance of a large but unfinished city with green suburbs, already boasting houses in a variety of eclectic and art nouveau styles among the numerous building plots, and a city centre full of construction sites where entire districts had been pulled down. The development of the suburbs and the abundance of plots for building undoubtedly contributed to the slowing down of construction work in the centre, to the loss of interest, to its depopulation and to its gradual impoverishment. The ruins were left untouched and the districts ravaged by wars and real-estate crises were ignored for decades or used as car parks during more prosperous periods, giving foreign visitors the deceptive impression that this city had recently been bombed. It has become embedded in the collective consciousness and generated the idea of a permanent building site to serve the short-sighted intentions of real-estate developers and the economy in general. Gradually, the fundamental representation of the city as a place of conviviality and identity has faded away.

/

/

/

/

/

/

/

/

/

/

/

/

/

/

/

The axes: turned around, superimposed

On the medieval network, oriented west east, carried by the flow, the slope and the stream.

/

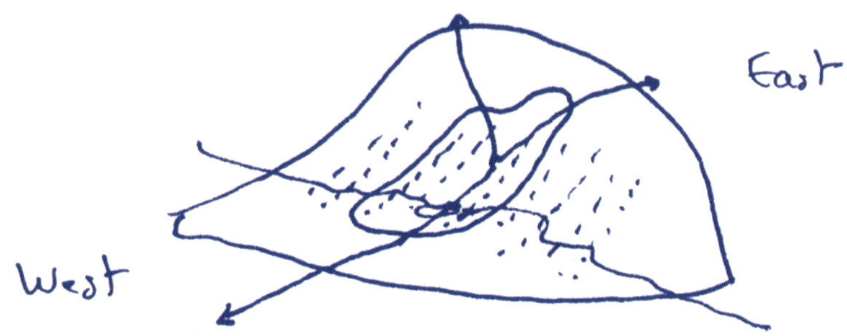

/

/

/

A modern network was superimposed, leading from the north to the south, structured by the symbolism of the royal axes, by the Nord and Midi stations and, later, by a boulevard on the underground railway junction.

/

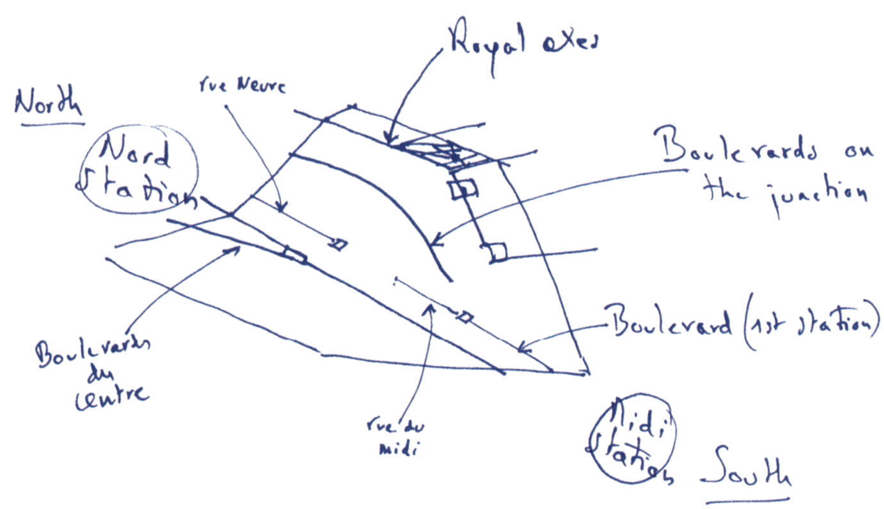

/

These axes, earmarked as prestigious traffic arteries, were often to be deserted, and still are today.

/

Paradoxically, it is along the medieval axes that the new commercial and cultural currents are appearing.

/

/

/

/

/

Where's the river?

/

/

The covering of the river Senne turning it into a sewer and the construction of the boulevards Adolphe Max, Lemonnier and Jacqmain in 1869-71 had already deprived the city centre of a large part of its medieval character. However, the city still had its port which had been built in the XVI century. Boats could moor in the Saint Catherine dock which was only a few hundred meters from the Bourse and this was a pleasant feature of the districts west of the centre. During the first years of the XX century, the port was moved outside the city and the docks were filled in. This changed the appearance of these districts and the relationship of the city with water profoundly. The absence of this river, which has been replaced by a straight canal along the west side of the pentagon, is something the inhabitants of Brussels are not consciously aware of. In addition, the population's lack of awareness of the natural environment of the city is affected by the negation of the hill which rises to the east of the pentagon and this means that the centre of the city has become an historic non-event without any natural reference points.

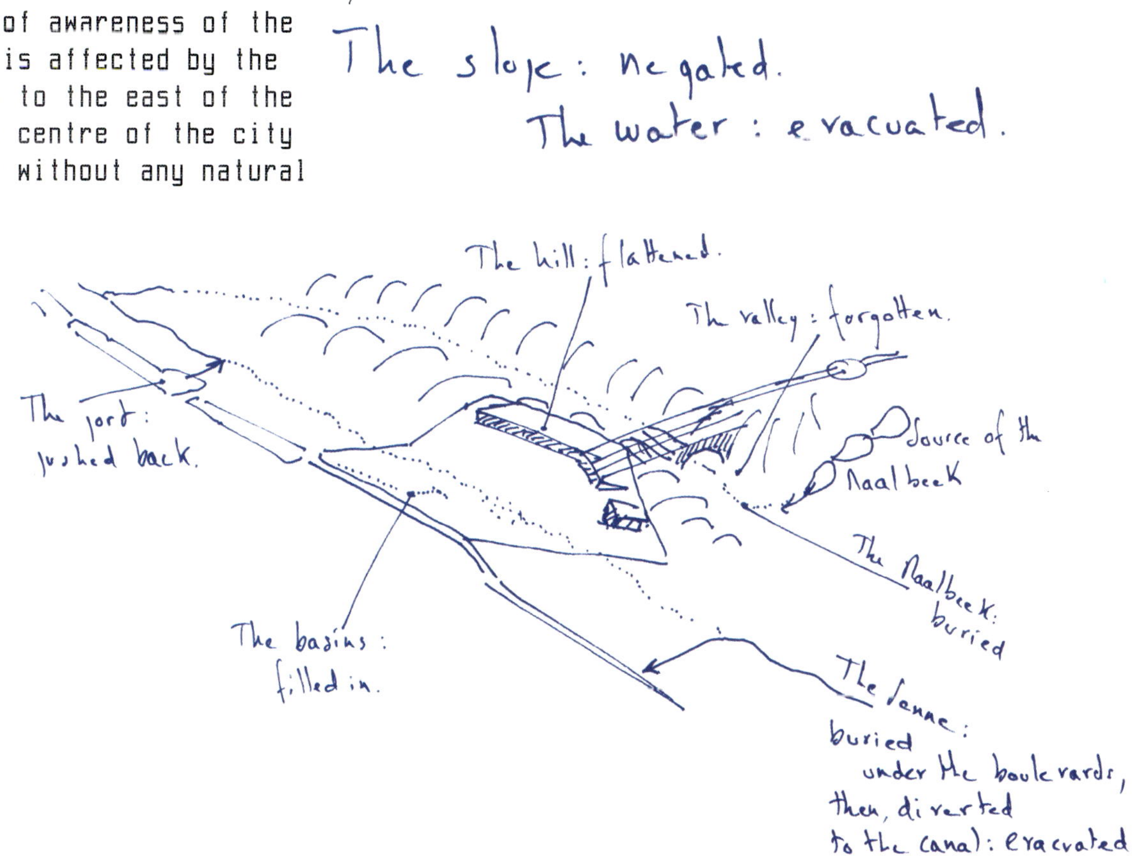

The negation of the hill

/

/

On the eve of the First World War, the majority of the sites expropriated for the Nord-Midi junction had already been cleared. The line of a series of streets in S-shape from the Place Royale or the Parc Royal was clearly drawn for use by cars. Along these streets, classic French-style buildings gradually appeared, reminiscent of the ones you can see in Paris, and these were occupied by large financial institutions and insurance companies [Rue des Colonnes and Rue Ravenstein]. The imposing building site for the Nord-Midi junction was started between the two world wars. Victor Horta, who built the Palais des Beaux-Arts on Rue Ravenstein, had several ideas for the Mont des Arts and was also approached for the Central Station.

/

However, once again the sluggishness of the works in progress and the Second World War postponed the completion of the station until 1949 and by another architect. This extreme slowness ultimately jeopardised the Mont des Arts project. It was finally built in 1954 according to a design by Ghobert and Houyoux in a simplified neo-classical style. The new extensions to the National Bank were built during the same period along the Boulevard de l'Empereur according to a design by Van Goethem. All of these buildings, whose architecture is reminiscent of the styles used in totalitarian regimes, turned out to be immediate failures and they were to generate an unequivocal aversion among the inhabitants of Brussels. The architects in question, most of whom never lived to see their work completed, had failed to find the correct proportions and the appropriate style for this location.

/

/

/

/

/

In 1903

The junction ripped open the hill between the cathedral and the Grand' Place and from the North to the South, as if a bomb had landed there.

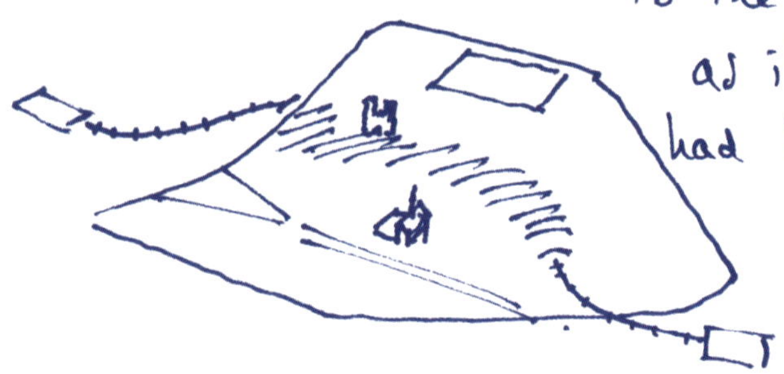

/

/

Brussels, with its fragile identity, set itself up as a city on the crossroads with a promising future. This was the excuse it needed for a project that was unique in its kind in Europe: the eradication of central districts to make way for an underground railway junction. In fact, over the next hundred years, a 80 year construction site [50 underground, 30 above ground] ended up disfiguring the city, erasing the history of its hill, putting off inhabitants and scaring them away.

/

Disproportionate architecture

/

The link with what remained of the medieval city centre had not been resolved at all: at the Mont des Arts, French-style gardens were created which led to the Palais des Congrès, the underground conference facility which was built under a set of staircases in a bizarre manner. This was further accentuated by the last minute conservation of the old Nassau chapel, placed under disproportionate propylaea which serve as the entrance to the Albert I Library. However, we should not forget that it was under these stairs that Maurice Schumann, Jean Monnet and Paul-Henri Spaak met to start the negotiations that ultimately led to the creation of the European Communities. The pseudu-baroque constructions housing offices and hotels that were later built opposite the Mont des Arts and the Central Station were meant to create a link but have not succeeded in re-establishing the coherence of this disfigured area.

/

Above the railway tunnel, the Boulevard de l'Empereur and the Boulevard de l'Impératrice (nobody knows to whom these names actually refer) do not really lead anywhere, except to bottlenecks and impractical crossroads and they are mainly used to access the underground car-parks which are embedded in the original hills of medieval Brussels.

/

Even more signs of the city's lost identity were created as the Universal Exhibition of 1958 approached.

/
/
/
/
/
/
/
/
/

/
/
/
/
/
/
/
/
/
/
/
/

The fifties / sixties
On the junction, an architecture inspired by Mussolini, then, modernist
And, a useless boulevard ?

© Hubert Isselée

/

The centre: crossroads of Europe. Central Station. Albertine.

/
/
/
/

New York and Brasilia

/

To prepare for this grand event, Brussels began to modernise as it had never done before. American values were the planner's inspiration and the customs from the other side of the Atlantic were often imitated in the form of grotesque caricatures. Access by car was a major focus of attention and even the Grand' Place was transformed into one of the prettiest car parks the world had ever seen. New roads and tunnels were built along the main avenues to speed up the flow of traffic while many trees were cut down to accommodate these new facilities: Avenue Louise, the ring-road boulevards and later Avenue de Tervuren all became urban motorways. The city of Léopold was adapted for "modern traffic" and no compromises were made. A special viaduct was even built over Boulevard Léopold II to avoid traffic lights and to make sure people could drive to the Exhibition even faster. The Atomium and a series of "modern style" buildings reflected the new-found flavour of the month. Although most of these disfiguring works could not be reversed, except for the viaduct which was pulled down twenty years later, they did turn Brussels into a city fit for driving and until recently traffic jams were rare.

The Sixties / Seventies

Everywhere

Anywhere

Any how ...

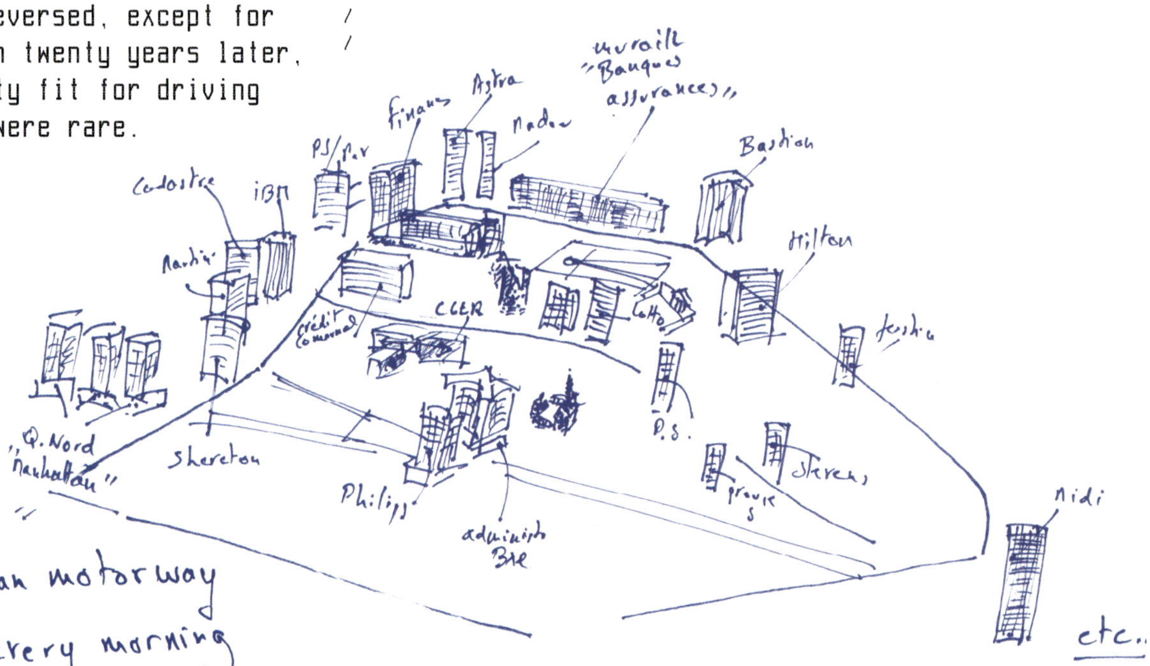

Not forgetting the urban motorway to invade the city every morning and desert it every evening

/
/
/
/
/
/
/
/
/
/
/
/
/
/
/
/

© Vincent CARTUYVELS

Towers…

© Vincent CARTUYVELS

out of all proportion…

© Vincent CARTUYVELS

© Vincent CARTUYVELS

Casual modernism, the city at a crossroads

/

In the following years, wheeling and dealing architects who until now had continued with great caution in the neo-classical strain, suddenly became casual modernists. The so-called "Martini Building" with its conspicuous sign appeared on the skyline of the city centre boulevards, on the spot where the old Nord station was located before it was moved for the Nord-Midi junction. Adjacent to the central station, the Sabena building which looked more like a service station, and the Westbury Hotel, an ugly renovation of the Lever House, were flanked by the Telephone company [RTT] building which housed its equipment in a functional architecture that closely resembled its phone boxes. The centre of the city was designed as a crossroads, a communication hub. The wasteland area between Rue de la Madeleine and Rue Montagne aux Herbes was leased to the Car Park Consortium that managed the car park which they pompously baptised the "Crossroads of Europe". The Grand' Place and its immediate surroundings were christened the "îlot sacré" [the sacred island] and were gradually to become an historic Disneyland.

At the heart of the city and on the summit of the hill, a 600m long wall, and a 140m high tower for the Civil Servants of the Central State.
A 25 years construction site to end up with a building that was already obsolete.

© Régie des Bâtiments

/
The Administrative City of the State : 1958-1983

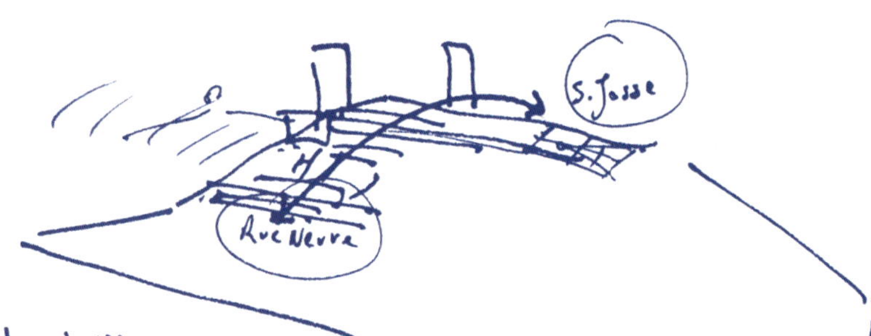

Embankments, walls, ramps, plateaux, overhangs, cantilevers, and underground passages massacred the hill, eradicated its history, wore away the soil.
A stony desert was created at the heart of the city.

Concrete landscaping, towers and mono-functional zones

/

Below the Colonne du Congrès and along the Boulevard de l'Empereur, the administrative City of the State has been built on an enormous horizontal concrete slab that covers the car parks. The Tour des Finances [Finance Tower] is the vertical counterpart to this "composition" which has created a lifeless and impassable zone between the higher and lower parts of the city. Extensions to the National Bank and the new buildings of the CGER and Crédit Communal banks below this zone in the old Meiboom quarter, eventually succeeded in transforming this part of the city into a real desert.

/

At each of the old city gates, on the outer boulevards, the PS, Madou and Midi towers and on Avenue Louise, the Treiste and ITT towers appeared simultaneously on the skyline to the naive delight of some and for the financial benefit of real-estate developers and politicians. The grand mansions along these boulevards and avenues were demolished and then gradually replaced by insipid office buildings with six or seven floors. The upper middle classes were the first to capitalise on their property, leaving these neo-classical mansions which had been built along the major axes and in the Léopold quarter to settle outside the centre in the green suburbs towards Waterloo, Ohain, Genval and Wavre. This resulted in a loss of identity and culture at a time when the prospect of profits from the European Communities were beginning to emerge.

/

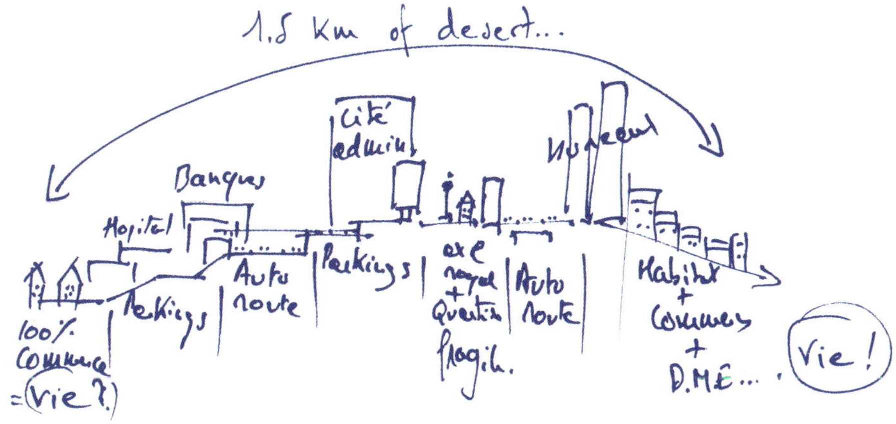

/

[side section of the hill, from the rue Neuve to St Josse across the Administrative district].

/

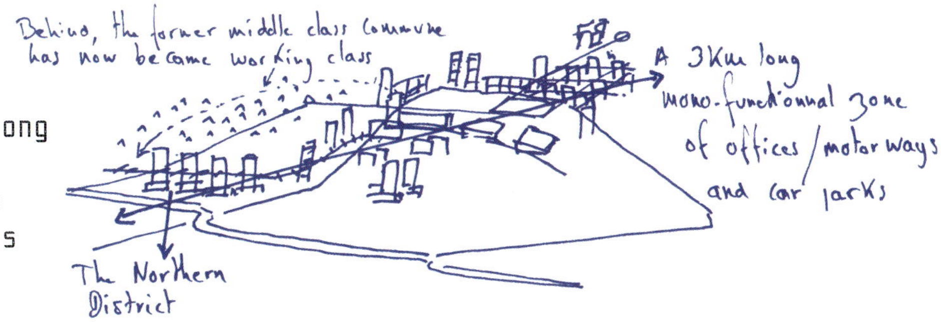

This desert crosses the city: from the Northern District to the European District, a "continuous 3Km strip" of offices.

/

The city loses its unity

/

/

The city of king Léopold, with its country houses and villas in neo-classical, eclectic and art nouveau style, were characterised by a unity of scale which was respected by the art deco and modernist styles of the period 1920-1930. With the construction fever of the 60s, the fashionable apartment buildings, which indeed could already be seen between the two world wars on a relatively marginal scale, conquered the market and triggered a real urban boom. On the remaining plots of land and also on sites where the "unfashionable" houses and villas of the previous century were demolished, a considerable number of apartment buildings were erected in Le Corbusier style which emulated the master's ideas in a hasty and mediocre manner. Less obvious than in the city centre, a disparity of scale was now also created in the suburban communes of Brussels. The housing development on the old Brugmann property in Uccle, or the construction of "Brusilia" in Schaerbeek, are just two examples among many striking instances of architecture without quality and without careful urban planning which mushroomed nearly everywhere in the city in order to satisfy demand and keep the construction industry happy. The result was a multitude of contrasting neighbourhoods. This abundance of new buildings, which were generally of mediocre quality and situated at haphazard locations, did however ensure that Brussels would never have a shortage of homes.

/
/
/
/
/
/
/
/
/

Motorways

+

Car parks

+

Offices

=

exodus of inhabitants.

The pentagon:

in 1900: 160,000 inhabitants

in 1980: 40,000!

The Northern District

/

/

The area around the Chaussée d'Anvers and the North station, with its tiny neo-classical houses, had become disreputable. At the end of the 60s, a clever real-estate developer who was a self-made man strongly influenced by American ideas, succeeded in acquiring most of the property. He devised a project together with the politicians of the time in Brussels, to establish a new district consisting of a forest of forty high-rise towers. The buildings would be erected on concrete slabs at various levels to accommodate car parks and underground traffic and be linked to the Place De Brouckère, and as such create a new city centre - with Manhattan as its model. This ambitious project began while at the same time the city authorities were building their own administrative complex along the boulevards in the centre and at the same time granting permits to build the Philips tower. These new high-rise buildings undoubtedly disrupted the unity of the French Haussmann-style boulevards. Proposals for the demolition of the Marolles district below the Court of Justice were also being investigated.

© Régie des Bâtiments

No comment…

Urban conflicts and local residents' committees

/

At the end of the 60s, young people began to protest against the greedy real-estate developers and politicians who had set their sights on the Northern District and the Marolles area. The demonstrations were successful and during the 1973 crisis many of these projects were abandoned. However, the Northern District had been entirely razed to the ground and Brussels once again had a new stretch of wasteland, only a stone's throw away from the city centre. On this barren terrain, the five "Manhattan" towers were erected.

/

To this day, the battles of the Marolles and the Northern District are still remembered as the "urban conflicts of Brussels" by pressure groups and local residents' committees. The halting of the systematic destruction of the city by real-estate developers and contractors was certainly necessary. No other city had neglected its heritage and identity to such an extent. Their vows to reconstruct the city were based on an ambitious programme. However, the spokesmen of the local residents' committees did not succeed in proposing a rigorous methodology to achieve these aims. Their alternative solutions consisted of vague images without architectural content and were not supported by feasibility studies into societies consisting of a mixed economy and partnerships between the private sector and the authorities.

/

And yet, Brussels had only recently been the stage of Lucien Kroll's social ecology experiment "Mémé", which was to be the starting point of ecological urbanism in practice and theory which he went on to develop abroad. However, the spokesmen of the pressure groups in Brussels preferred to play the role of judges of architectural good taste. But their actions could never hope to defeat the financial reality which since then has continued to determine the evolution of architecture in the city.

The seventies: finally, a debate
But, to end up
with this?

© Archives d'Architecture Moderne, Bruxelles

© Vincent CARTUYVELS

or this?

© Prisme Editions

or that?

Brusselisation

/

/

The movement which began in the XIX century was stepped up: the alliance of speculation and the short-term interests of private and institutional property owners continued to define the map of Brussels. This led to a city conceived as a commercial, administrative and entertainment crossroads which has evolved towards the development of zones for each of these activities: offices, shopping centres and entertainment areas, living zones. The city has been transformed haphazardly without urban reflection or planning, at the mercy of random events and opportunism and with the sole concern of pleasing all parties involved: shopkeepers, car owners, commuting civil servants and corporate employees and even the so-called Ligue Esthétique Belge that foreshadowed the pressure groups, but above all property owners who were eager to attract investors to their property. It is a city which is designed as a tool of progress, as an instrument of enrichment, a labour market area, and to a far lesser extent, if at all, to satisfy the needs of conviviality, memory, social vision, identity or culture. This phenomenon is not at all exceptional in the USA, however, on the Old Continent it is quite unacceptable. The phenomenon is referred to as "Brusselisation". It is even more disquieting because it is taking place in a city that is home to the institutions of the European Union, itself under construction.

The Seventies : inventory of a disaster:

© Prisme Editions

© Prisme Editions

2 faces with the same violence !

© Michel Michiels

The Agglomeration
/
/

Since the seventies, Belgium has been through a number of institutional reforms which have resulted in three distinct Regions within the federal state. Throughout the transformation, the status and territorial borders of Brussels have been a bone of contention. The Flemish Region and the Walloon Region were first created and a provisional institution was set up for Brussels which lasted for seventeen years and was referred to as the Agglomeration. As such, for almost twenty years, Brussels was designated as the phenomenon it was actually becoming: an institutional, human, social and urban patchwork, an entity with an elusive and multifaceted identity, gradually losing hold of its self, which has had an impact on the social tissue and cultural experience of the traditional city. In 1979, the so-called Agglomeration produced for the first time ever a planning document which defined activity zones in the city and protected the residential zones against the advancing tertiary sector. However, the reduction of the levels of authority, the slowness, the restricted margin of manoeuvre and the general political weakness had an adverse effect on decision-making with regard to urban affairs throughout this period.
/
/
/
/
/
/
/
/
/
/
/
/
/
/

Saved by the European identity
/

The Brussels-Capital region was indeed only created ten years later and also obtained its own regional Parliament just like the other regions. During this long process of institutional mutations, whereby Brussels lost its supremacy as a capital and part of its financing to the other regions, the rise of the European Communities and the city's affinity with the European cause replaced the national identity and provided new perspectives and hope for the future. Certainly, the development of Europe throughout this period had to endure several episodes of acute scepticism. After all, Brussels was still only the provisional seat of the institutions. However, the enlargement of Europe and the arrival of increasing numbers of civil servants were the inevitable confirmation that this city would play an essential role in the gradual unification process as a privileged meeting place.
/
The complacency of the authorities with regard to investors who were attracted by the development opportunities within the context of the European Union and the inability to channel these opportunities in a coherent framework had become so self-evident that the first government of the Brussels-Capital Region immediately published a Regional Development Plan [RDP] which was intended to provide a solution for the inadequacies of the past. In the meantime much damage had been done.
/
/
/
/

A RDP to bring in a social mix...
and to go back to town planning?

/
/

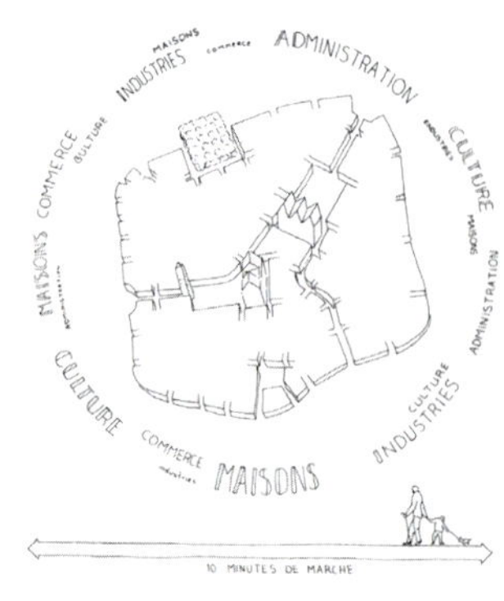

© Archives d'Architecture Moderne, Bruxelles

The RDP and new directions
/
/

Diversity was the key word in this RDP: without hampering the tertiary sector, it laid down town planning practices which would force investors to become more involved in the renovation or construction process of housing in the city. In this respect, the regional authorities called for the rapid development of the Northern District with "reasonably-sized" office buildings and homes. There was also uncertainty with regard to the buildings along the canal through the west part of Brussels, which needed to be widened to accommodate barges weighing 2000 tons. In the end, the Region officially cancelled the project. Subsequently, several office buildings and a few houses were built along the canal while the Boulevard Léopold II, which had been left derelict for more than a quarter of a century following the construction of a viaduct, was renovated and redeveloped as a tertiary zone. And last but not least, the arrival of the TGV high-speed train in Brussels had also aroused the interest of the real-estate developers: they had acquired the majority of land and like Belgian National Railways they planned a number of grand building projects. The constraints of the so-called special planning scheme (PPA), the reduced availability of parking space and the size of the buildings all limited the opportunities for development in this area. Fear of a new failure similar to that of the Northern District combined with the varying level of demand and the influence of pressure groups and local residents' committees left their stamp on these developments.

/
/
/
/
/
/
/

Architecture and building permits
/

In response to the building permits that were granted practically everywhere for hotels and office buildings, the pressure groups and local residents' committees wanted to have their say and demanded aesthetically sound developments with buildings that reflected an "urban" character. These artificial conditions, with which the real-estate developers readily complied, generally produced architecture with false pretences and without any sense of quality. The political and administrative negotiations became the driving force behind all architectural designs: the architects of Brussels were ultimately the decorators of bitterly negotiated office and hotel projects. The collusion between real-estate developers and businessmen, and their preoccupation with the rules of the market, resulted in a lack of interest in the actual construction methods. On the other hand, the pressure groups failed to produce a valid action plan to influence these projects.

/
/
/
/
/
/
/
/
/
/
/
/
/
/
/
/
/
/
/
/

Supply and demand

/

/

Confronted with the arrival and the growth of the European institutions, the Belgian State, which was responsible for providing office and other space, began the construction of the first buildings in an inefficient, slow and expensive manner. The state reforms and the linguistic and institutional quarrels of the 70s and 80s subsequently kept everyone busy. A Flemish wave, full of hostility towards the increasing influence of the French-speaking population and the expansion of its suburbs, and which curiously confused this phenomenon with the arrival of foreign institutions in the city, contributed to the lack of interest and further highlighted the incompetence of the Belgian state in these matters. The detection of asbestos in the Berlaymont building and the slow response to this problem even demonstrated the inability of the Belgian state to perform this task effectively. This disinterest began to cast doubt on the choice of Brussels as permanent seat of the European institutions. Consequently, private contractors were given free rein to manage the renting and leasing of office buildings to the various European institutions. Belgian private investors, insurance companies, real-estate developers and contractors alike responded, discretely and on a needs basis, to the rising demand for offices as a consequence of the European enlargement. The federal and regional governments of Belgium were aware of the economic benefits that the country could reap from this situation and were desperate to keep the institutions in Brussels. The withdrawal of Europe from Brussels would be an economic catastrophe. They consequently refrained from intervening in these issues in order to avoid a clash of Flemish and Brussels politics in these matters and also to avoid unfavourable decisions with regard to the ambitions of the city to become the European capital.

/

/

As you are offering me the possibility of doing it the "Belgian way", how can I say no?

Seat of the European Parliament.

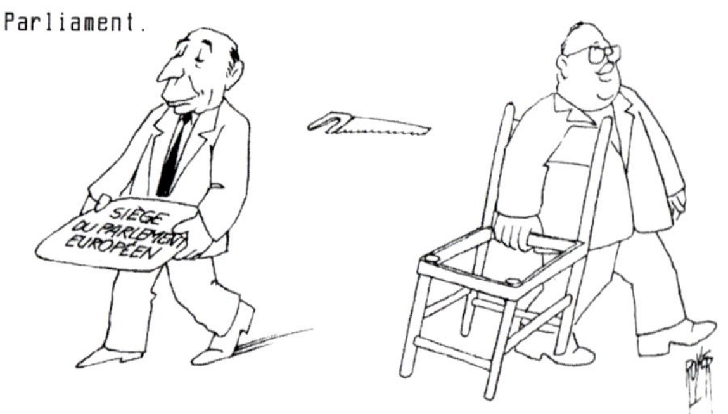

© ROYER

And Europe: a "Belgian-style" patchwork

Europe at all costs
/
/

The appearance of the Léopold District and the area surrounding the Schuman roundabout is clearly a product of these circumstances. This step by step approach, the absence of a clear vision, the fear of upsetting the various parties involved obviously could not give rise to the harmonious and programmed development of an area that would meet the needs of the staff of the European institutions nor to the construction of buildings through architectural design competitions. A balanced policy whereby these various offices would be spread evenly across the entire city according to a co-ordinated plan was also unthinkable. It was in fact only by coincidence, as result of the need to remove asbestos from the Berlaymont building and the relocation of its occupants to offices situated near the Beaulieu station, that the authorities found that it was possible to spread the offices of the European institutions along the metro line that stops at the Schuman roundabout. The role of private investors in providing the necessary buildings for the European institutions was emphasised once again in this respect.
/
The opening of the markets from 1992 onwards and the acquisition of numerous Belgian insurance companies and businesses by major conglomerates has attracted more real-estate investors with a pronounced international profile to Brussels. However, these acquisitions have disrupted the investment policy of the traditional actors and have given rise to the reappearance of urban wastelands and a very confusing situation following the speculative frenzy in the run-up to 1992.
/
/
/
/
/

A second Brusselisation
almost as disastrous as that
of the sixties and seventies

The eighties and nineties

In the European District,
but also everywhere.

after the traumas, the placebos!

Loans, summonses, collages,
pastiches and postiches...

Kitsch shapes,
Kitsch names!

A European Parliament

/

/

The construction of a European Parliament in Brussels at the same time as the French state was building one in Strasbourg is probably the most striking example of the conditions under which certain European institutions have been established. In the beginning, several construction firms had acquired the land of an old brewery behind the station of the Léopold District, beyond the open railway tracks. Their project initially consisted of building an International Conference Centre [ICC] located near the European institutions which they could rent out to them.

/

The European Parliament premises in Rue Belliard were much too small: they were interested in the new location and in the end decided to buy the premises while they were still being constructed. While it was still under construction, they even modified the plans and adapted the complex to their own needs. As negotiations progressed with the financial and administrative department of the Parliament, it soon dawned that more premises, more amphitheatres, more offices for the members of parliament and their assistants, a library, an IT centre, more parking space, etc. would be required. However, the code name for these premises which were meant for the work sessions of the members of parliament in Brussels would continue to be the ICC because the various member states were still divided with regard to the question of where the Parliament should be based: in Brussels or in Strasbourg?

/
/
/
/
/
/
/
/

© Photo: Airprint - Infographie: AEL

Europe on a quest for symbols

The utmost discretion

/

/

The regional authorities were not opposed to this project. They provided the necessary permits as long as the project remained discrete and did not rouse the public opinion of the inhabitants of Brussels and the pressure groups that represented them. The five companies behind the ICC project were backed by one of Belgium's major banks [Cob-Bacop]. Subsequently, as the project began to grow, they received the support of the Société Générale de Belgique which however demanded the consortium of architect firms that were involved in the project to appoint a project manager who would be in charge of the aesthetic aspect of the complex.

/

The first extension projects to the building that housed the main amphitheatre of the ICC required the covering of the railway tracks so that offices for the members of parliament could be built. However, the implications for the overall cost of spanning the tracks as well as the safety considerations made the developers opt for buildings along the winding railway track and not on top of them. As a result, the going real-estate market rates could be used and the lease contracts could be drawn up quickly. The SNCB [Belgian Railways] built the tracks and an underground railway station. As the construction work on this imposing complex was well under way, the pressure groups and the press, who couldn't see the forest for the trees, were preoccupied by the issue of conserving the old station and the listing of its facade as a national monument and fuelled public opinion on this issue.

/

/

/

/

/

/
/
/
/
/
/
/

© Marie Françoise PLISSART

chaotic, closed, opaque, hostile ?

© Marie Françoise PLISSART

colossal, mutistic, absent, anonymous, empty ?

A flexible architecture adapted to current needs

In effect, a "second Parliament" was gradually being born, discretely and without evoking any serious debate among Belgian or international public opinion with regard to its existence in Brussels or the impact of its proximity to the other institutions on the democratisation of the European institutions. The complex was made to measure and to meet the wishes of the members of parliament, facilitating their everyday work in Brussels while the official meetings required by protocol were held in Strasbourg. In stark contrast to the rational planning à la française of the amphitheatre in Strasbourg, the complex in Brussels continued to grow according to a flexible programme which could be changed at all times. This flexibility obviously made the architects' task more challenging and hindered the development of a technically interesting design of symbolic importance but in the end it met the needs of its users perfectly. Today, the complex is adapting once again to the enlargement of the Union which now has twenty-five countries. The aesthetics of the exterior is dominated by façades consisting of bluestone slabs and reflecting glass that merge with the grey sky and as such blur the gradual rise of the building on the city side. On the Parc Léopold side, the building is fourteen floors high, which is not a common sight in Brussels.

© Marie Françoise PLISSART

How many aborted symbols?

Towards more transparency?

/

/

We now have a better understanding of why international competitions are so rare when it comes to these controversial developments. Today, it is difficult to consider intervening in the architecture of the European buildings or attempting to remedy their lack of character and the concatenation of circumstances that replaced their urban planning without being aware of the context in which they were created. These very same conditions underlie the creation and growth of the institutions of the European Union itself and the sometimes difficult relationship among them and with the national authorities. Moving the Parliament from Brussels would have weakened the institution and slowed down the development of its role as overseer of the Council of Ministers. Besides the interests of real-estate developers and investors, other more profound political questions were at stake. It is unlikely that the creation of other institutions will be more transparent. The discussions at the Laeken summit regarding the location of the European Water Agency are another example of the difficulties of reaching consensus on these matters and the Belgian Prime Minister concluded the summit with a proposal for the "temporary" establishment of some of these institutions in… Brussels.

/
/
/
/
/
/
/
/
/
/
/
/

Is there still hope? Just like Europe and any city worth its name, diverse and identifiable areas. An architecture created by very different personalities capable of inserting symbolism into the truth of today's forms. Different scales creating a link between the historical, collective dimensions and the human, intimate scale. A hybrid and mutant district: clearly multifunctional, colourful, transformable, which can be appropriated by its inhabitants. A porous place: crossed, open, irrigated by a plethora of networks. A city that merges into the city and feeds it!

/
/
/

© Vincent CARTUYVELS

A Brussels "movida"?
The new commercial and cultural currents are following the east-west axis, and in fact breathing new life into the old medieval "organic" trajectory.

/
/
/
/

Brussels: the open city

/

/

Of course, Brussels has ambitions beyond its European role, however, the presence of these international institutions is a godsend, generating wealth and triggering development that is unheard of for a city of this size. The city's territory harbours a huge potential, whose long-term perspectives have only partially been exploited. Its population will have changed completely over the next twenty years. An increasing number of rich European immigrants and not-so-rich non-Europeans will come to this city and define its contrasting social character. A unique feature that distinguishes Brussels from other cities is the fact that the poorer inhabitants live in the centre while the wealthier people live on the outskirts or even in neighbouring regions. As a consequence, fewer run-down areas can be found in the suburbs of Brussels. As foreigners have not yet been granted the right to vote, the influence of the new population on decision-making cannot be felt, however, the second generation may quickly reverse this situation. Although some twenty languages are spoken, the Flemish minority is still fighting for its identity in order to ensure its cultural and economic supremacy. The Flemish continue to fear the invasion of the French-speakers who are gaining ground on the outskirts of Brussels. The French-speaking bourgeoisie, who are more easy-going from a cultural point of view and lack the awareness of an identity, have a propensity for the east and are gradually moving towards the Brabant Walloon region. The establishment of the university of Louvain-la-Neuve in Ottignies, near the town of Wavre, has created a new centre "in the country" which they seem to like very much. Claimed by some, abandoned by others and inhabited by increasing numbers of newcomers, the identity of Brussels with its weak roots in the past continues to fade away.

/

/

Initial signs of mutation

/

/

The Bruxelles 2000 event which promoted the city to "European Cultural Capital" for a year revealed how difficult it was for the city to play a role that does not come naturally to it, and only the Zinneke parade, the celebration of social and racial mix, succeeded as an original and innovative happening. More so than the initiatives taken by the authorities, there is no doubt that the driving force behind the new identity of this city are the numerous and diversified cultural associations and communities in Brussels and their wide range of often competing activities. The multiplicity and diversity of this microcosm is in fact the only hope for the old city centre to revitalise its urban substance and subsequently recreate the urban character of a traditional city in the various districts. It is curious that this partial renaissance is taking place along the pedestrian axes of the old medieval roads, as shown by Claire Billen. Our use of the car, which has saturated our roads, is changing along with our relationship and expectations with regard to the city. Thanks to the new communication technologies combined with the evolution of the democratic society, whose powers are breaking up, moving around physically no longer has the same significance and there is no need for the central authority to express itself as it did before. Our society is gradually turning away from the grand images of authority and rationality which the ruling powers of the bourgeois and popular democracies were so keen to emulate in order to imitate the princes and the church of the ancien régime. In the old days, the city was meant to reflect the institutions and their power but nowadays there is no longer a need to emphasise their spatial and architectural rhetoric.

/

/

/

Great expectations: an appeal to all European architects

/

What will the architecture of this city look like tomorrow now that it no longer has to worry about expressing the role of a capital and can focus on the construction of a Europe of regions that seeks the ideal balance of expression, facilitating the coming together of these regions in dialogue and agreement? The expectations in this respect are considerable. Architects from all corners of Europe must be urged to participate in this adventure that Brussels will experience over the next few years: this challenge consists of welcoming new institutions and members of parliament from the twenty-five countries of the enlarged European Union and embracing their formidable cultural contributions.

/

/

/

/

/

/

/

/

/

/

/

/

/

/

/

/

/

/

/

/

/

/

Text: Pierre Loze and Vincent Cartuyvels
Sketches, choice of illustrations and captions: Vincent Cartuyvels

A REP

/

ORT

THE WORLD

/

/

For the first time in the history of humanity, people are being federalised by law and not by force.
The eyes of the WORLD are upon us.

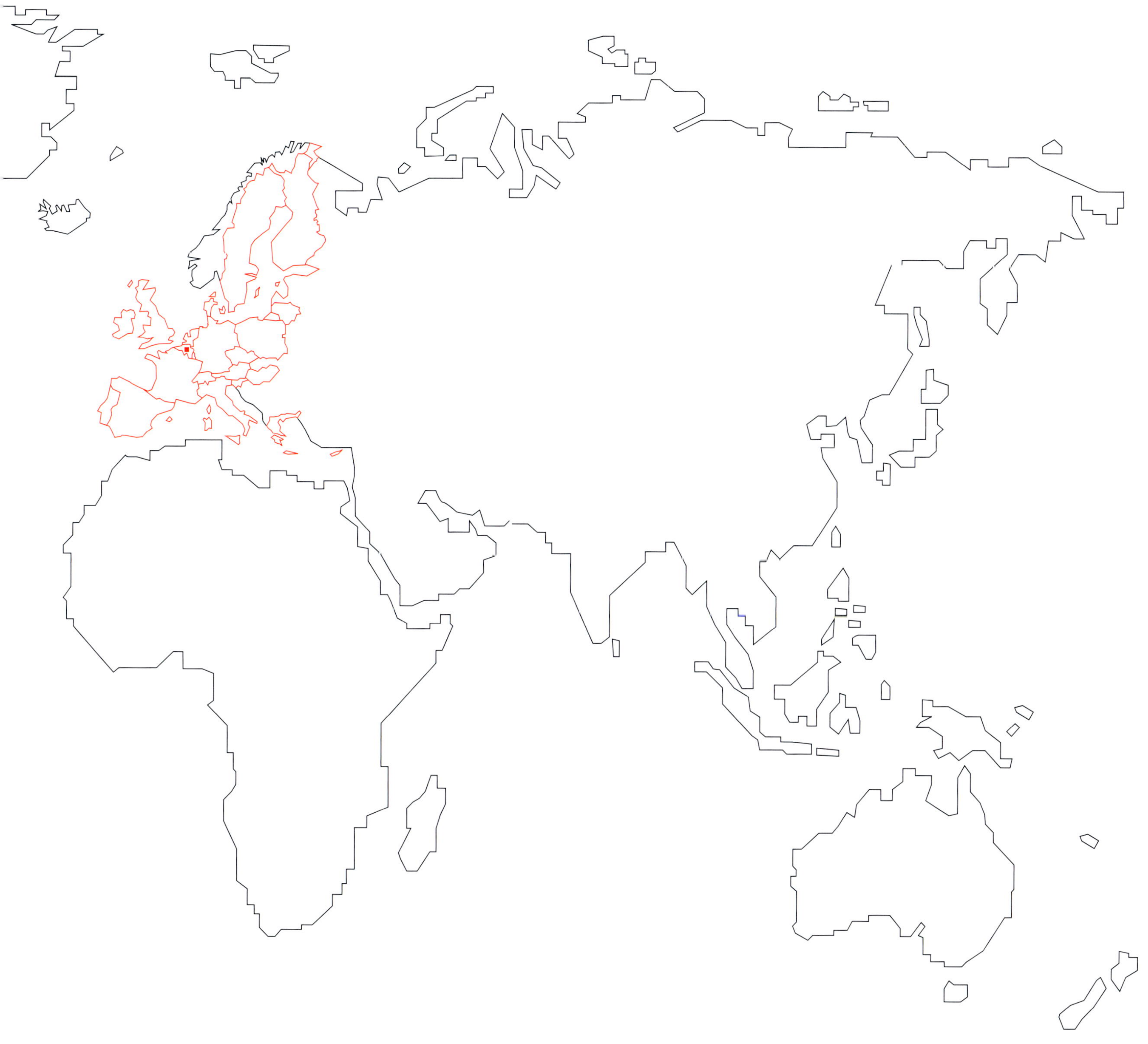

EUROPE 2004

/

/

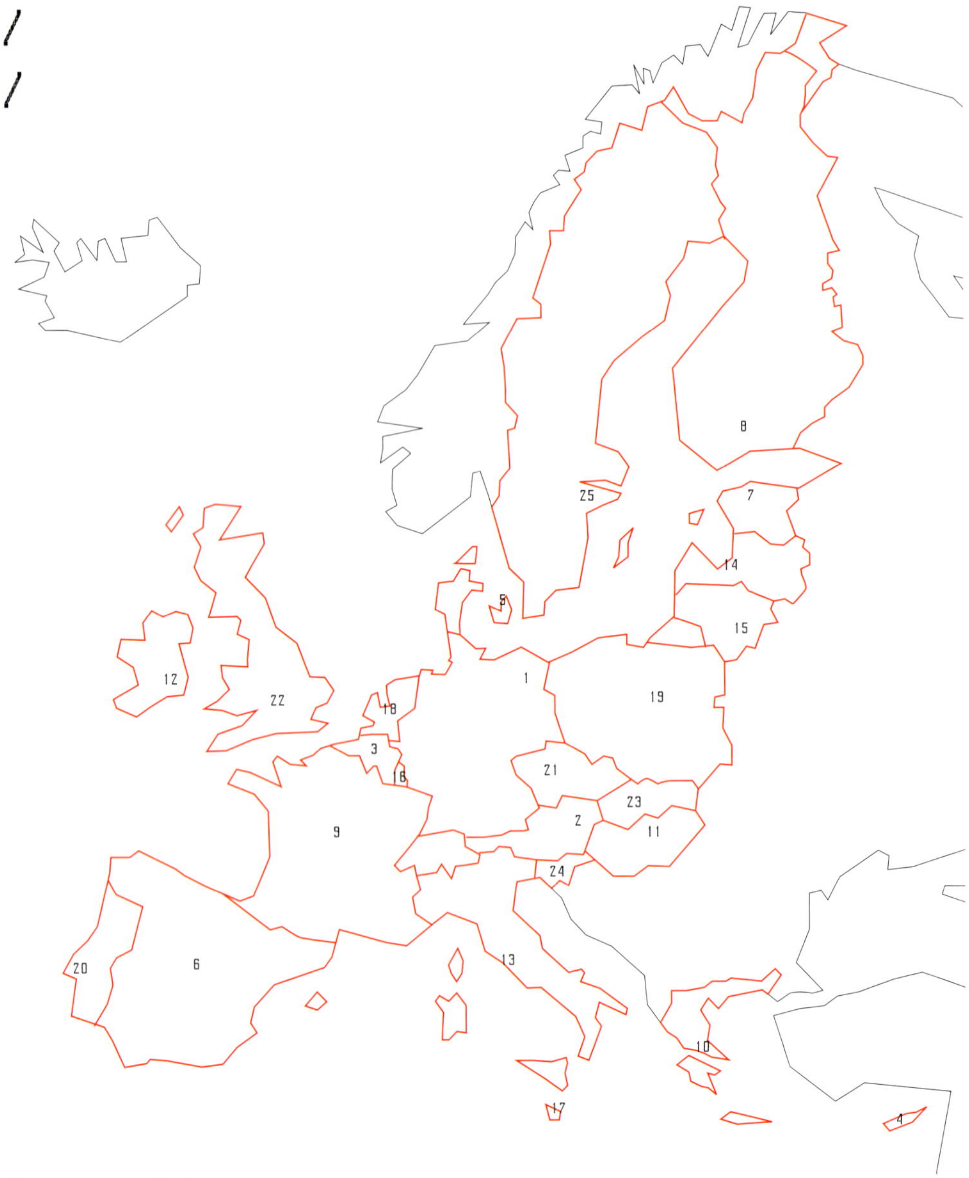

European Union

/

/

Germany / 357,021 km^2 / 83,725,920 inhab / 234.52 inhab./km^2
[1] Berlin / 3,317,000 inhab.

/

Austria / 83,858 km^2 / 8,210,007 inhab / 97.91 inhab./km^2
[2] Vienna / 1,562,700 inhab.

/

Belgium / 30,510 km^2 / 10,310,530 inhab / 337.94 inhab./km^2
[3] Brussels / 1,004,239 inhab.

Cyprus / 9,250 km^2 / 776,459 inhab / 83.95 inhab./km^2
[4] Nicosia / 185,708 inhab.

/

Denmark / 43,094 km^2 / 5,402,078 inhab / 125.36 inhab./km^2
[5] Copenhagen / 1,075,900 inhab.

/

Spain / 504,782 km^2 / 40,161,967 inhab / 79.57 inhab./km^2
[6] Madrid / 2,894,100 inhab.

/

Estonia / 45,266 km^2 / 1,398,851 inhab / 30.91 inhab./km^2
[7] Tallinn / 397,150 inhab

/

Finland / 337,030 km^2 / 5,200,674 inhab / 15.44 inhab./km^2
[8] Helsinki / 566,800 inhab.

/

France / 547,030 km^2 / 61,313,639 inhab / 112.09 inhab./km^2
[9] Paris / 9,640,000 inhab.
/
Greece / 131,940 km^2 / 10,690,759 inhab / 81.03 inhab./km^2
[10] Athens / 759,100 inhab.
/
Hungary / 93,030 km^2 / 10,007,536 ha / 107.58 inhab./km^2
[11] Budapest / 1,864,000 inhab.
/
Ireland / 70,280 km^2 / 3,971,581 inhab / 56.52 inhab./km^2
[12] Dublin / 986,600 inhab.
/
Italy / 301,230 km^2 / 57,816,319 inhab / 191.94 inhab./km^2
[13] Rome / 2,646,700 inhab.
/
Latvia / 64,589 km^2 / 2,326,146 inhab / 36.02 inhab./km^2
[14] Riga / 779,600 inhab.
/
Lithuania / 65,200 km^2 / 3,579,872 inhab / 54.91 inhab./km^2
[15] Vilnius / 580,000 inhab.
/
Luxembourg / 2,586 km^2 / 459,721 inhab / 177.78 inhab./km^2
[16] Luxembourg / 81,200 inhab.
/
Malta / 316 km^2 / 403,322 inhab / 1,276.34 inhab./km^2
[17] Valletta / 221,180 inhab.
/
The Netherlands / 41,526 km^2 / 16,249,177 inhab / 391.31 inhab./km^2
[18] Amsterdam / 719,100 inhab.
/
Poland / 312,683 km^2 / 38,597,579 inhab / 123.44 inhab./km^2
[19] Warsaw / 1,611,800 inhab.
/
Portugal / 92,391 km^2 / 10,120,316 inhab / 109.54 inhab./km^2
[20] Lisbon / 556,800 inhab.
/
Czech Republic / 78,866 km^2 / 10,240,311 inhab / 129.85 inhab./km^2
[21] Prague / 1,200,100 inhab.
/
United Kingdom / 244,820 km^2 / 60,056,768 inhab / 245.31 inhab./km^2
[22] London / 10,500,024 inhab.
/
Slovakia / 48,845 km^2 / 5,435,880 inhab / 111.29 inhab./km^2
[23] Bratislava / 448,900 inhab.
/
Slovenia / 20,253 km^2 / 1,937,749 inhab / 95.68 inhab./km^2
[24] Ljubljana / 290,600 inhab.
/
Sweden / 449,964 km^2 / 8,881,056 inhab / 19.74 inhab./km^2
[25] Stockholm / 1,226,200 inhab.
/
/
/
/
/
/
/
/

Total Europe of 25 countries :
3,976,360 km^2 / 457,278,557 inhab.

London
/
/
/
/
/
/
/
/
/
/
/
/
/
/

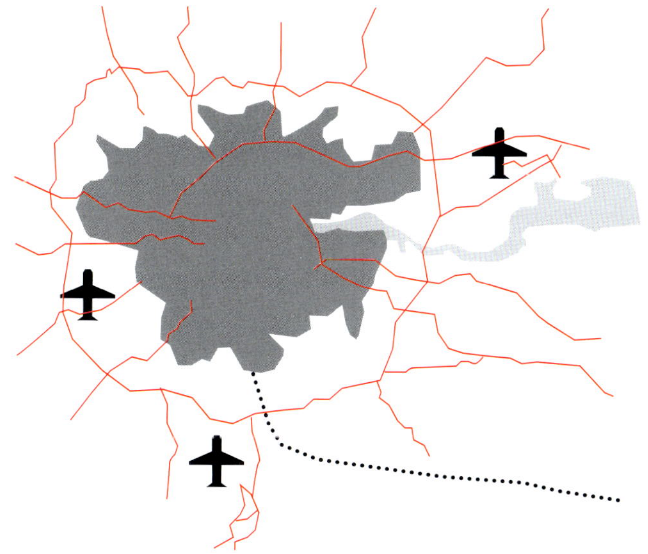

Paris
/
/
/
/
/
/
/
/
/
/
/
/
/
/
/

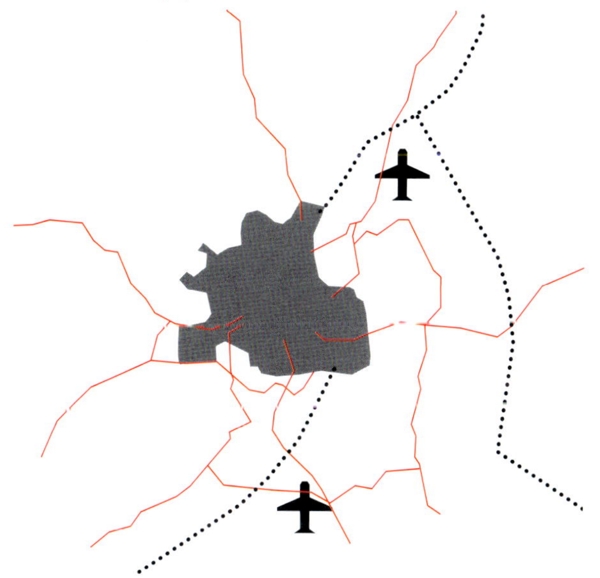

Brussels
/
/
/
/
/
/
/
/
/
/
/
/
/

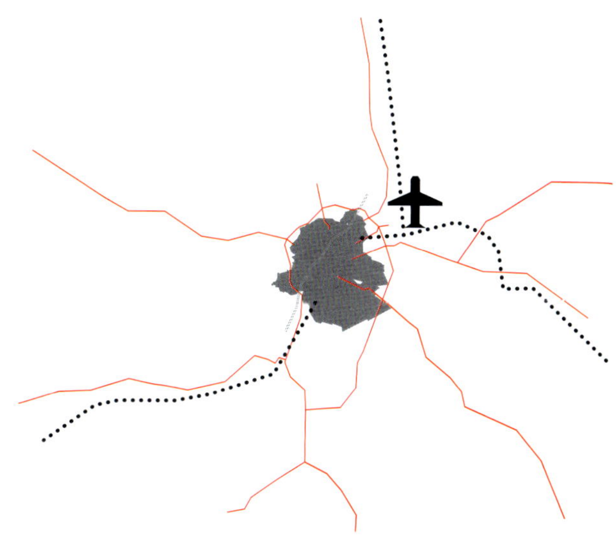

Distances from Brussels

/
/
/
/
/
/
/
/
/
/
/
/
/
/
/
/
/
/
/
/
/
/
/
/
/
/

/
/
/
/
/
Germany / Berlin = 652 km
/
Austria / Vienna = 917 km
/
Cyprus / Nicosia = 2,909 km
/
Denmark / Copenhagen = 764 km
/
Spain / Madrid = 1,315 km
/
Estonia / Tallinn = 1,602 km
/
Finland / Helsinki = 1,649 km
/
France / Paris = 266 km
/
Greece / Athens = 2,086 km
/
Hungary / Budapest = 1,135 km
/
Ireland / Dublin = 776 km
/
Italy / Rome = 1,183 km
/
Latvia / Riga = 1,455 km
/
Lithuania / Vilnius = 1,728 km
/
Luxembourg / Luxembourg = 205 km
/
Malta / Valletta = 1,850 km
/
The Netherlands / Amsterdam = 171 km
/
Poland / Warsaw = 1,168 km
/
Portugal / Lisbon = 1,713 km
/
Czech Republic / Prague = 720 km
/
United Kingdom / London = 321 km
/
Slovakia / Bratislava = 974 km
/
Slovenia / Ljubljana = 890 km
/
Sweden / Stockholm = 1,284 km
/
/
/
/
/
/
/
/
/

/
/
/
Brussels has always been a hub.
/
/
/
/
/
/
/
/
/
/
/
/
/
/
/

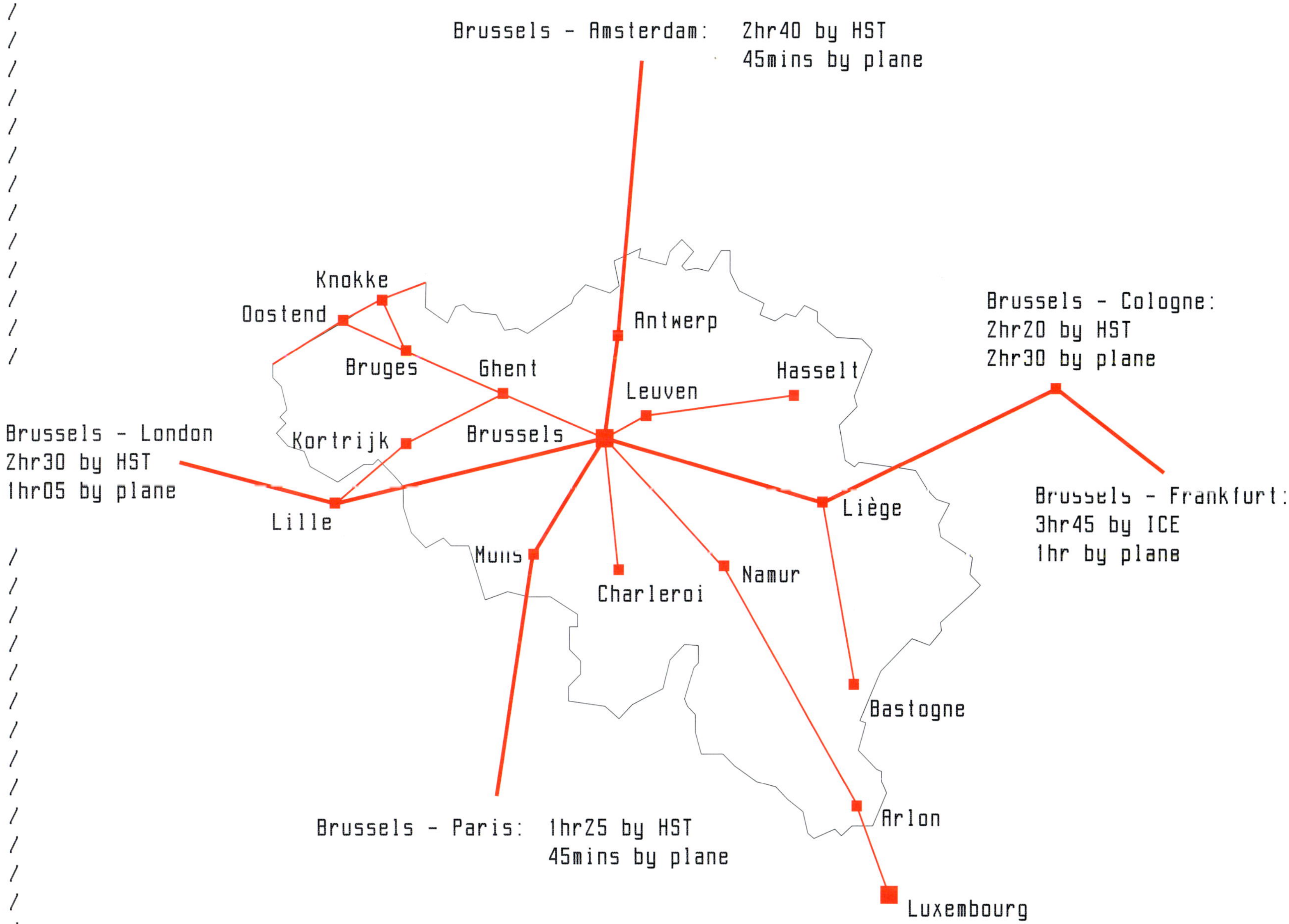

/
/
/
/
/
/
/
/
/
/
/
/
/
/
/
/
/
/
/
/

BELGIUM
The fragmentation of power

Belgium

The federal state

The Communities

The Flemish Community

The French Community

The German-speaking Community

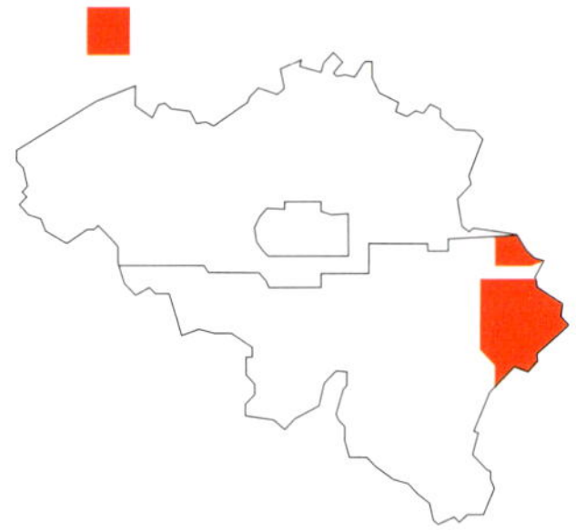

The Regions

The Flemish region

The Brussels-Capital Region

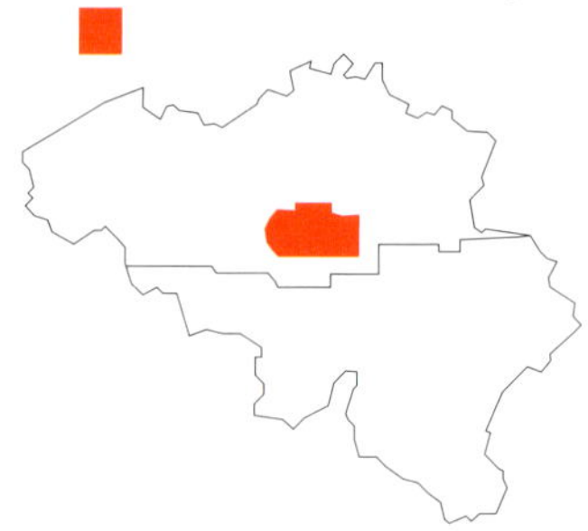

The Walloon Region

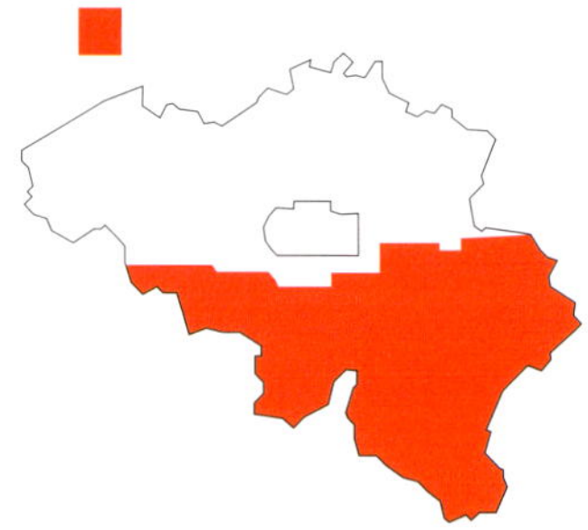

A City torn between the Flemish Dutch-speaking Community and the French-speaking Community: Reflections

/

The increasing influence of the political parties

/

The increasing influence and power of leaders and senior members of the main political parties in Belgium since the sixties, has made it possible for them to exercise all three powers which should, according to Montesquieu, remain separate.

/

The executive power

It comprises the members of the seven current executives [only one in 1960] whose first task is to designate the party leaders. These leaders are the "mother-in-laws" of the executives until the time comes when they choose to nominate themselves as the head of one of them. It is therefore in the interest of every potential minister to "invest" in his party and chairman rather than in managing public affairs. It is also the senior party members who designate the most important positions in ministerial cabinets. Consequently, these officials are often tempted to report to the senior party members rather than to their minister.

/

The legislative power

The composition of the legislative power, i.e. that currently in office in Belgium, is determined by the same top party members. Again, they are also responsible for their own proliferation as a result of the successive State reforms. Who would dare suggest that there are too many of them?

/

/

/

/

The judicial power

The third power is of course also subject to the influence of the parties, not so much from the point of view of initial appointments but rather with regard to advancement and empowerment.

/

The rise of the parties is certainly a common feature of many democracies and especially those that adopt the proportional system, which favours coalitions of parties. However, the Belgian situation is very special as a result of the centrifugal bipolarity and its capital which is trapped between two poles.

/

Centrifugal communities and parties: an adverse effect on the central State

/

In Belgium, each community has its own political parties, which is the opposite to the situation in other federal countries such as Canada, Germany or Switzerland, and each party answers only to the electorate of its own community. In fact, they no longer have a national objective and they continue along their path of power conquest with only their respective Communities in mind. Their leaders aspire to giving them the status of State, to the detriment of the Belgian State.

The control of the federal State is the result of a "dialogue between the communities", in other words between groups of parties, that ultimately decide which aspects shall remain federal.

For the Flemish parties, this quest for "the common well-being of Flanders" is reflected in the Resolutions of the Flemish Parliament of 1999 that demand the status of federal States for the federal entities, i.e. the replacement of federalism by a confederalism with two states. These resolutions continue to underpin their demands regarding autonomy.

/

/

The weakening of the Belgian State in the international context

/

Defending "Belgian" interests has become very difficult within the context of today's Belgian State. For example, the regionalisation of the waterways and ports have made it impossible for Belgium to negotiate an acceptable proposal with the Netherlands, i.e. the deepening of the western section of the river Scheldt which is indispensable for the port of Antwerp, in exchange for the supply of "Belgian" water, which the Dutch need so badly. On its own, Antwerp, which is only supported by the Flemish government, has nothing to offer in exchange for the vital co-operation of the Dutch.

/

New perspectives for political parties

/

The elections of 2003 [federal Parliament] and 2004 [other Parliaments] opened new perspectives for political parties and changed the political landscape drastically. As a result, CD&V [formerly CVP], the Flemish Christian Democrat party, remains essentially "client-oriented" [stability]. However through its alliance with the separatist party N-VA has now taken a more confederal stance [change].

Important changes have also affected the French-speaking Parti Socialiste. Elio Di Rupo who in a significant gesture chose to become leader of the party instead of president of the government of the Walloon Region has stressed the limitations of Walloon regionalism and the necessity to move closer to Flanders and not to ignore Brussels.

/

/

/

Brussels-Capital: a region in its own right?

/

The division of the country directly affects the central bilingual region called Brussels-Capital, which in principle is a region in its own right but whose resources are endangered by the actions of the two communities.

For example, its share of the national personal income tax revenue is calculated exclusively in proportion to the number of inhabitants and the level of income because the tax is levied at the place of residence. The capital's share continues to fall.

On the other hand, tax on real estate constitutes nearly half of regional income. The Flemish government has in fact implemented favourable real-estate taxation and this has an adverse effect on fiscal revenue from real-estate in Brussels.

Inheritance tax is also more favourable in Flanders and this may also result in the draining of funds to the Flemish region.

/

Perspectives on civil society

/

In fact, only a regional development programme in favour of a population with medium or high income will make it possible to increase.

Such a residential development objective will require an effective urban development and crime prevention programme as well as more accommodation facilities, including social housing. This implies the recycling of "urban wastelands", zones located near the city centre, which are excluded from the residential market. Cities all around the world are rediscovering the potential of their waterways and river basins. These kinds of projects also exist in Brussels.

/

/

/

However, they are not on the political agenda. The territory of the 19 communes of Brussels [160 km^2] accommodates less than one million inhabitants while the 20 administrative districts of Paris [87 km^2] have twice as many, i.e. half the area for twice as many people. These figures speak for themselves! The urban wastelands, the mono-functional office districts, the warehouses and large shopping centres with their car parks which generate little added value, hamper to a great extent any efforts with regard to residential development.
/

Assets still to be exploited
/

Despite its political isolation, Brussels-Capital is in an ideal position to play an active role as a truly multicultural European region: the link between the Belgian communities and the European regions alike. The city should assume this new status rather than fall into the custodian supervision of the federal States.
Each of these options will require the regional governments to finally make a choice. Will the opinions of the various political party leaderships prevail: they all have their own radically different visions on the future of Brussels. Nothing could be less certain. The Brussels section of the French-speaking Parti Socialiste has developed conflicting opinions. One option reflects the regionalist vision: common defence of the Region by all of Brussels' political parties, French-speaking as well as Flemish; the other option reflects the more radical community-driven vision, in other words an ever-growing osmosis between Walloon and Brussels socialists within the French-speaking Community with the intention of positioning themselves in the context of future supervision by the Communities and Regions over Brussels.
/
/
/
/

Conclusion: from civil society to political activity in favour of a European city
/

Perhaps the time has come for civil society in Brussels to opt for the project of the open European city. Brussels already has a great track record:
- its international community which is generally quite attached to Brussels,
- its cultural and artistic protagonists: bi-community public institutions, private foundations and multilingual associations,
- private sector players and economic associations from both communities,
- the defenders of its heritage and urban environment, and last but not least
- its inhabitants, irrespective of whether they are born in Brussels or elsewhere.

Considering the ongoing enlargement of the European Union, the multicultural potential of the city can only grow.
The eligibility and voting right of foreigners opens important new perspectives and provides opportunities for the representatives of the multicultural civil society on the lists that will be presented by the political parties for the next communal elections in 2005. This requires strong and organised action which still has to be put in place.
/
/

Pierre Laconte
Foundation for Urban Environment, Abdijdreef 19, B-3070 Kortenberg, pierre.laconte@euronet.be
/
/
/
/
/

Note: This contribution for CHANGE, Editions Prisme, Brussels, is an edited and abridged version of the article "Partis communautaires et perspectives bruxelloises: quelques pistes de réflexion" [Community parties and perspectives on Brussels: reflections], which was published in La Revue Générale, Brussels, issue 6-7-2003.

BRUSSELS
The fragmentation of power

/
/
/
/
/
/
/
/
/
/

1. Anderlecht
2. Auderghem
3. Berchem Ste-Agathe
4. Brussels
5. Etterbeek
6. Evere
7. Forest
8. Ganshoren
9. Ixelles
10. Jette
11. Koekelberg
12. Molenbeek St-Jean
13. St-Gilles
14. St-Josse-ten-Noode
15. Schaerbeek
16. Uccle
17. Watermael-Boitsfort
18. Woluwe St-Lambert
19. Woluwe St-Pierre

/
/
/
/
/
/
/
/
/
/
/
/

/
/
/
/
/
/
/
/

/
/
/

An average city divided into 19 baronies

/
/

/
/
/
/
/

© photo AirPrint

/
The heart of the city: the Grand' Place
/
/

BRUSSELS
Growth and density

13th century
25,000 inhabitants

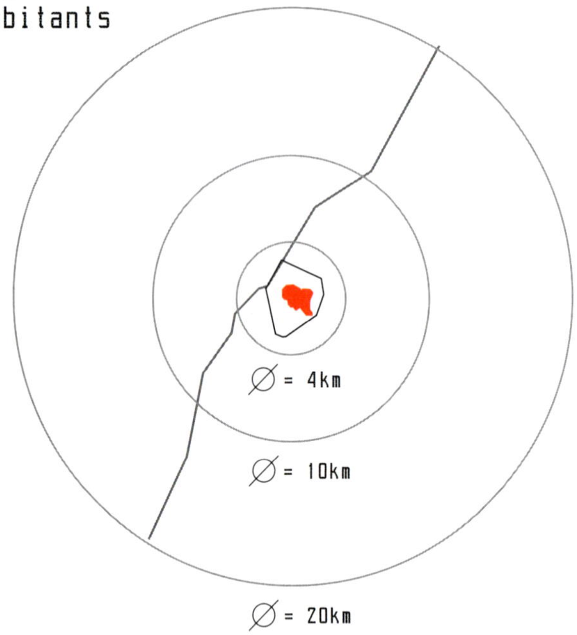

19th century
80,000 inhabitants

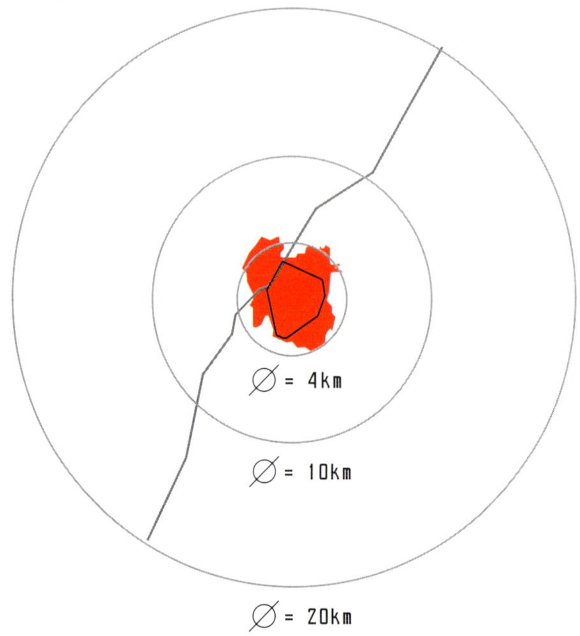

15th century
45,000 inhabitants

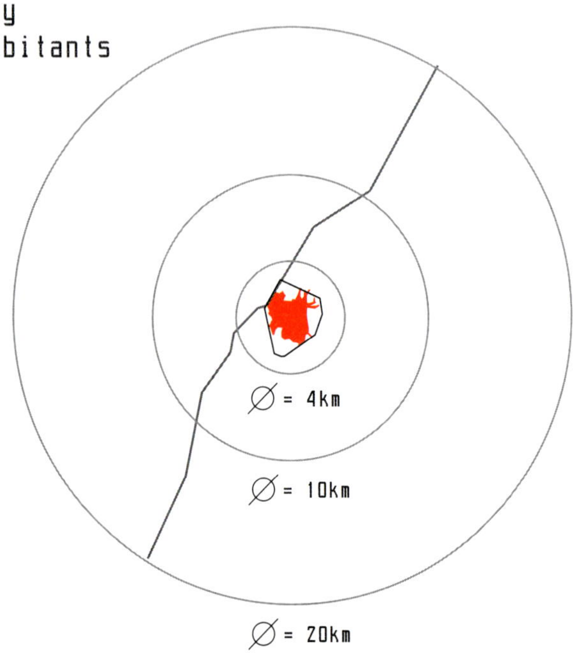

21st century
1,004,239 inhabitants

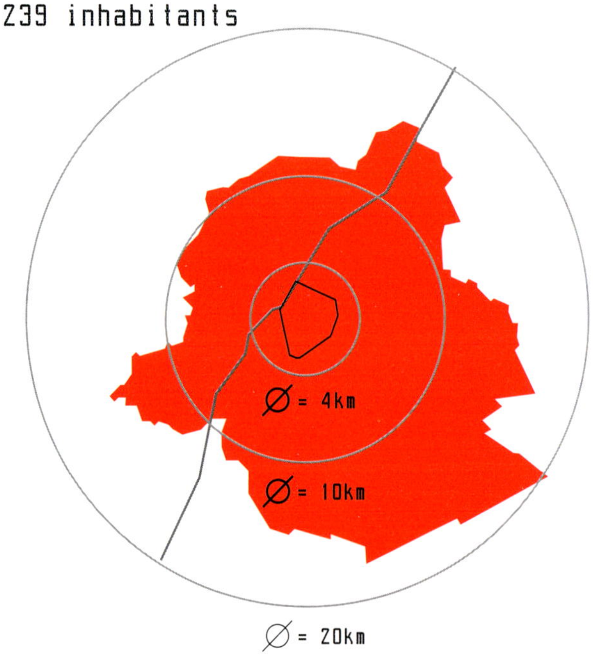

The centre was made for pedestrians but is overwhelmed by cars.

Brussels - Capital

/

/

Surface area: 161km^2

/

Number of inhabitants: 1,004,239

/

Density: 6,238 inhab./km^2

/

Working population: 413,187 [2003]

/

Commuting working population: 322,000

/

/

Employment breakdown by sector:

Industry	11.6 %
Services	88.3 %
Agriculture	0.1 %

Unemployment rate 15.74 % [2003]

68,484 job seekers [+11.4 % in 1 year] of which:
35,344 men
33,140 women
25 m office space/pers.
12,000,000 m of office space in 2005
1,500,000 m of hidden office space.

/
/
/
/
/
/
/
/
/
/
/
/
/
/
/
/

AND MORE...

/

/

4 universities
48 institutes of higher education

/

61 museums

/

religions:
Catholic
Protestant
Anglican
Jewish
Orthodox
Islamic

/

monuments and listed sites in 2004:
209 complexes
681 monuments
182 sites
[a total of 2,834 buildings]
5 archaeological sites

/

18 parks in Drussels that
occupy ca. 53 % of the total area of Brussels

/

19 cinemas

/

Brussels-Capital has some 4,000 restaurants in total

/

46 hospitals and clinics

/
/
/
/
/
/
/
/
/
/
/

Population density per commune
Population as at 2004.7.1

/
/
/

	inhab	inhab/km²	km²
Anderlecht	93,234	5,180	18
Auderghem	29,152	3,239	9
Berchem-Sainte-Agathe	19,734	6,578	3
Brussels	143,056	4,335	33
Etterbeek	41,103	13,701	3
Evere	32,878	6,576	5
Forest	47,435	7,906	6
Ganshoren	20,633	10,317	2
Ixelles	77,119	12,853	6
Jette	42,045	8,409	5
Koekelberg	17,573	17,573	1
Molenbeek-Saint-Jean	78,312	13,052	6
Saint-Gilles	43,733	14,578	3
Saint-Josse-ten-Noode	23,088	23,088	1
Schaerbeek	110,629	13,829	8
Uccle	75,006	3,261	23
Watermael-Boitsfort	24,317	1,871	13
Woluwe-Saint-Lambert	47,481	6,783	7
Woluwe-Saint-Pierre	37,711	4,190	9
/			
Brussels Capital	1,004,239	6,238	161

/
/
/
/
/
/
/
/
/
/
/
/
/
/
/
/
/

A city whose inhabitants have fled from
the centre.

Population living in the Brussels-Capital Region
/
/
/
/
/
/
/
/
/
/
/
/

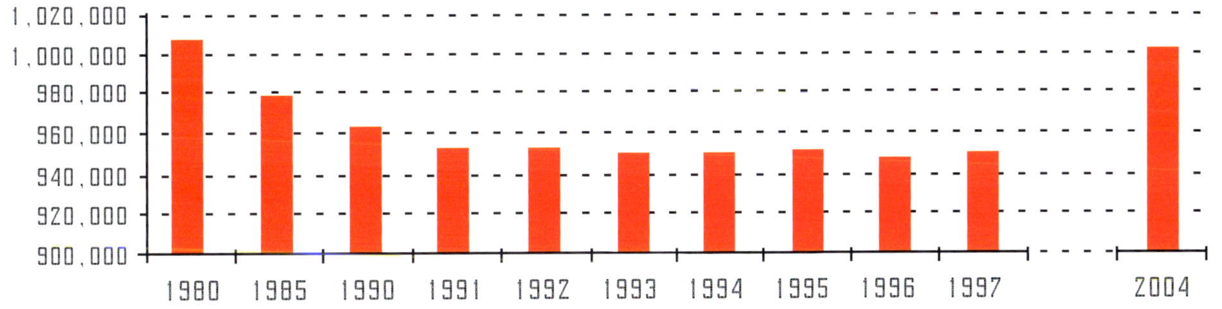

As figure 1.1 illustrates, the population embarked on a downward spiral in the 1980s.
However, this trend stopped in 1995, and the population level has stabilised at around 1,000,000 inhabitants.
/
/
/
Population density for the Brussels-Capital Region.
/
/
/
/
/
/
/
/
/
/
/
/
/
/
/
/
/

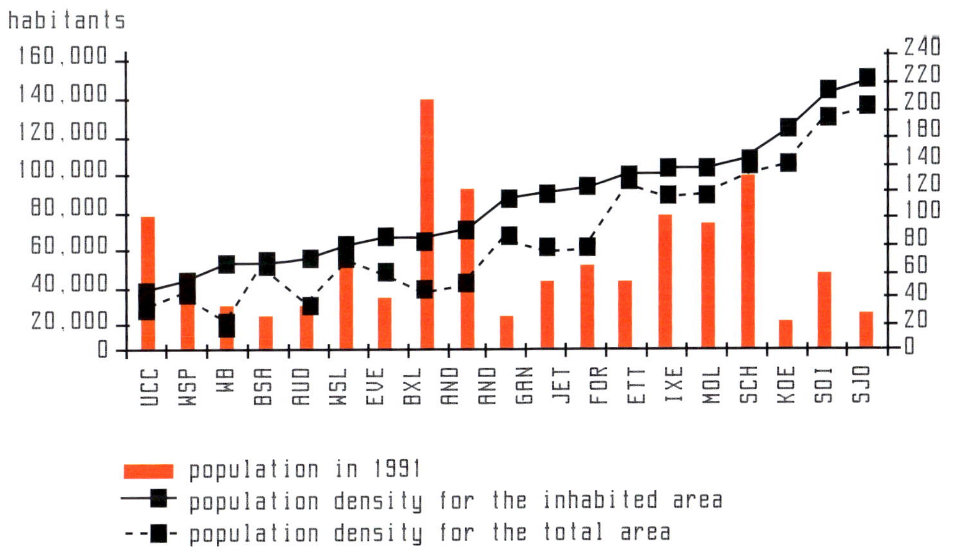

The average density for the region is 59.2 inhabit./ha [compared with the density for Belgium which is 3.4 inhabit./ha] and varies between 19 inhabit/ha [Watermael-Boitsfort] and 180 inhabit./ha [St-Josse].

/IN/General remarks
/

/
XIV - XVII century = city enclosure
2 km average diameter,
4 km of main roads,
9 tunnels,
13 urban access roads
/
 = 59.9 % of travel activity

M = 3.6 % of activity

 = 5.4 % of activity
/
Car + metro = 5.1% of activity
Not defined = 2.1%
/
24% do not travel
In the Brussels-Capital Region,
76% travel an average of 3 times a day
= 32.8 km/day
/
18 km/h = commercial speed of trams and 24 km/h in reserved lane,
17.3 km/h for buses,
28.3 km/h for the metro.
24.9 km/h for cars.
/
Brussels has 1,300 taxis.
/
/
/
/
/
/
/
/
/
/
/
/
/

Transportation Data
/

/
Why do the inhabitants of Brussels travel?
/
To drop off or pick up someone: 15 %
Return home: 66.4%
Business travel: 3.7 %
Go to work: 22.8%
Go to school: 9.8%
Go to dinner: 6.1%
Daily groceries and shopping: 27.9%
Personal reasons (visit doctor, bank,...): 11%
Visit relatives/friends: 17.2%
Walks and strolls: 7.1%
Entertainment, sports, culture: 15.4%
Other reasons and undefined reasons: 0.6%
/
366,000 commuters/day in Brussels in 1999
of which 207,000 by car
Only 50,000 cars carry more than 1 person
/
57% of business travel is by car.
/
/
/
/
/
/
/
/
/
/
/
/
/
/
/
/
/
/
/
/

Belt Data

/

/

Percentage of daily traffic during rush hours:
1955 : 28 %
1985 : 32 %
1999 : 50 %
/
Number of trips using public transport in Brussels:
1945 : 478 million
1970 : 175 million
1989 : 188 million
2003 : 220 million
/
/
/
/
/
/
/
/
/
/
/
/
/
/
/
/
/
/
/
/
/
/
/
/

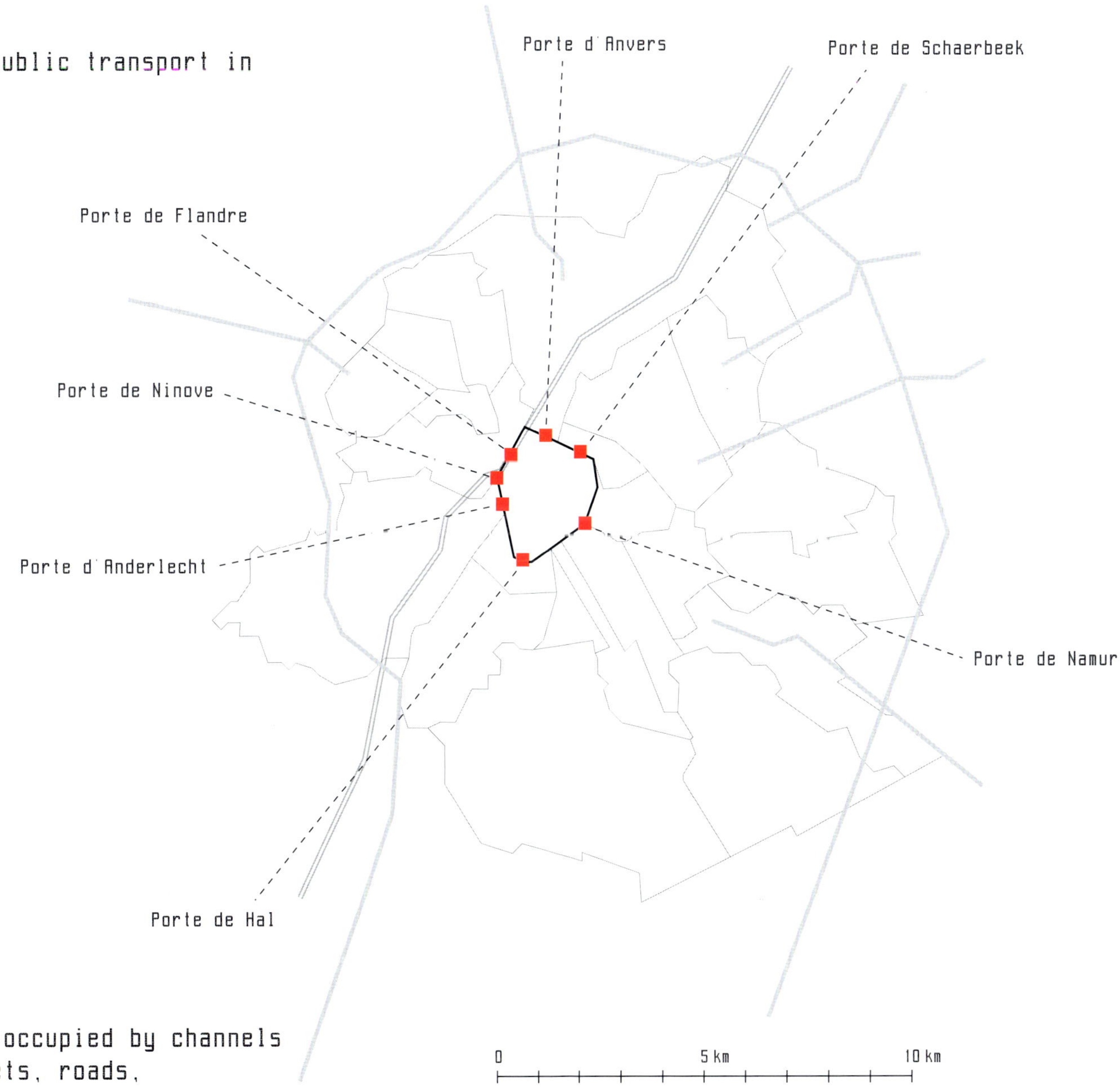

In Brussels, the space occupied by channels of communication (streets, roads, waterways and railways) amounts to 19.5 % of the territory. This is only 5.8 % on average for the rest of the country.

/
/
/

© Marie-Françoise Plissart

/
/
/
/
/

/
/
/

© photo AirPrint

/
The major avenues have been transformed into main roads to provide rapid access to the city.
/
/

Ring Data

/

/

80 km of asphalt

/

4 hours of traffic congestion/day

/

552,700 vehicles/day

/

Connections with 6 motorways

/

3,000 vehicles/hour/traffic lane during rush hours

/
/
/
/
/
/
/
/
/
/
/
/
/
/
/
/
/
/
/
/
/
/
/
/
/
/
/
/
/
/
/

/
/
/
/
/
/
/
/
/
/
/
/
/
/
/
/
/
/
/
/
/
/
/
/
/
/
/
/
/
/
/
/
/
/
/
/
/
/
/
/
/

Brussels is isolated in two ways: politically [a French-speaking island and a Flemish zone] and physically: access roads from the motorways are congested along several kilometres each morning.

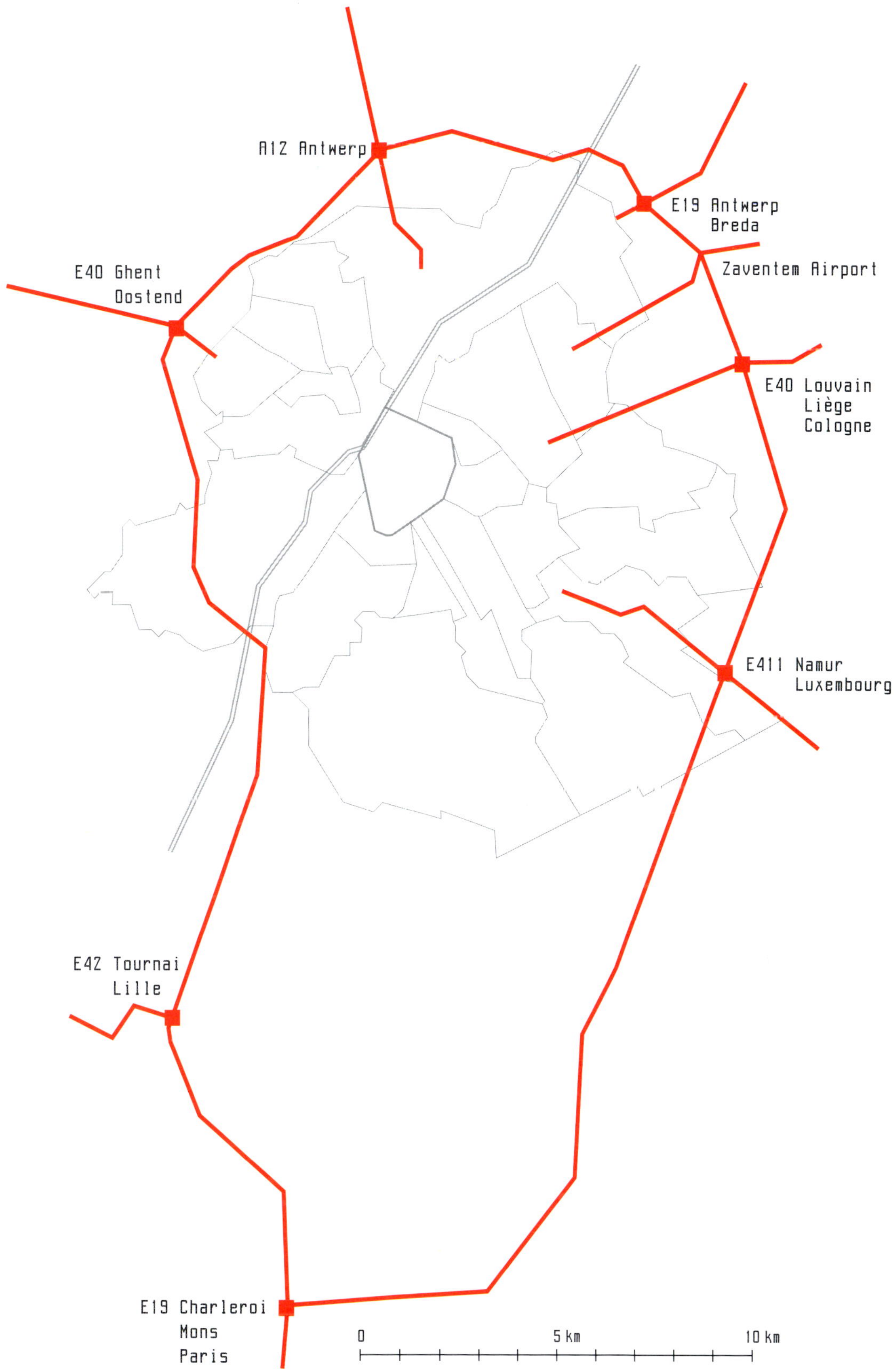
A12 Antwerp
E19 Antwerp
Breda
Zaventem Airport
E40 Ghent
Oostend
E40 Louvain
Liège
Cologne
E411 Namur
Luxembourg
E42 Tournai
Lille
E19 Charleroi
Mons
Paris
0
5 km
10 km

Metro Data

/

/

1892 = first metro project in Brussels
1954 = STIB transport company established
17 December 1969, pre-metro station Schuman - De Brouckere operational
20 September 1976 = inauguration date of metro line 1
1988 = metro line 2 operational
/
2003: 4 new metro stations, including 1 at Erasme, all with lifts for persons with reduced mobility. Additional 3 km of metro network.
/
43.10 km network [heavy-duty metro]
128.3 km network [total distance of the pre-metro + tram lines
/
3 metro lines:
line 1A: 27 stations / line 1B: 30 stations
line 2: 14 stations
611 m = average distance between stations
/
28.3 km/h = average speed
/
580 escalators
/
314,226 travellers daily
/
1 carriage = 70 cars
/
Zaventem Airport to administrative districts takes 30 minutes
/
From 1999 to 2003: number of travellers increases by 7.6%.
/
/
/
/
/
/
/

/
/
/
/
/
/
/
/
/
/
/
/
/
/
/
/
/
/
/
/
/
/
/
/
/
/
/
/
/
/
/
/
/
/
/
/
/
/
Small trams everywhere and at all times
And/or
A more comprehensive metro network
And/or
A RER [regional express train service]
/
Which option will be chosen?

Gare du Nord
De Brouckère
Roi Baudouin
Bockstael
Arts-Loi
Simonis
Schuman
Gare de l'Ouest
Stockel
Gare du Midi
Mérode
Erasme
Herman Debroux
metro
pre-metro
0
5 km
10 km

/OUT/Station Data

/

/

1926: Belgian Railways [SNCB - NMBS] established,
99.8 % of shares owned by the Belgian state

/

340 lines
3,521 km of tracks of which 83 %
are electric,
300 km/h cruising speed
for high-speed trains

/

700,000 travellers per day

/

Transports 55 million tons/year

/

160 to 200 km/h maximum speed
limit for domestic traffic

/

€ 6.4 billion investments earmarked
over 4 years [2004 - 2007]:

/

€ 703 million: extension of capacity
€ 1,206 billion: maintain current capacity
€ 308 million: mixed infrastructure for
high-speed train/domestic networks
€ 1,016 billion: high-speed train infrastructure
€ 944 million: rolling stock
€ 379 million for stations
€ 624 million for logistics
€ 624 million for pre-financing
€ 612 million: RER project
[regional express railway]

/
/
/
/
/
/
/
/
/
/

/
/
/
/
/

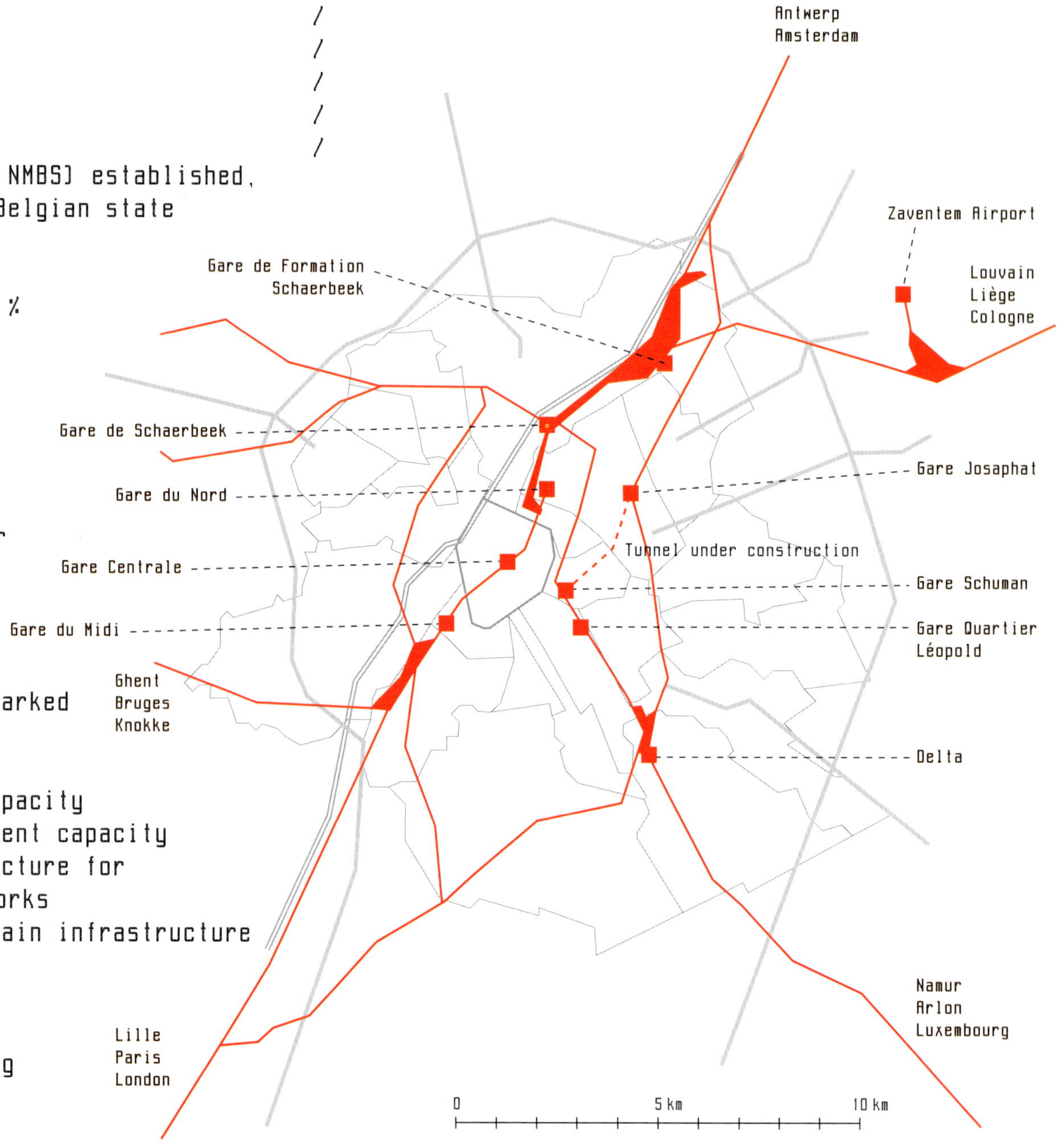

/
/
/

A city divided by the trains: there's no way
around it!
So why not make the most of them.

/
/

RER Data

/

/

The RER is on track...
120 stations
Frequency of trains: every 15 minutes during rush hours
640 trains per day for the entire RER
Work started in 2004
1st Brussels line: connection with Schuman - Meiser station [work starts: 2005]

/
/
/
/
/
/
/
/
/
/
/
/
/
/
/
/
/
/
/
/
/
/
/
/
/
/
/
/
/
/
/
/

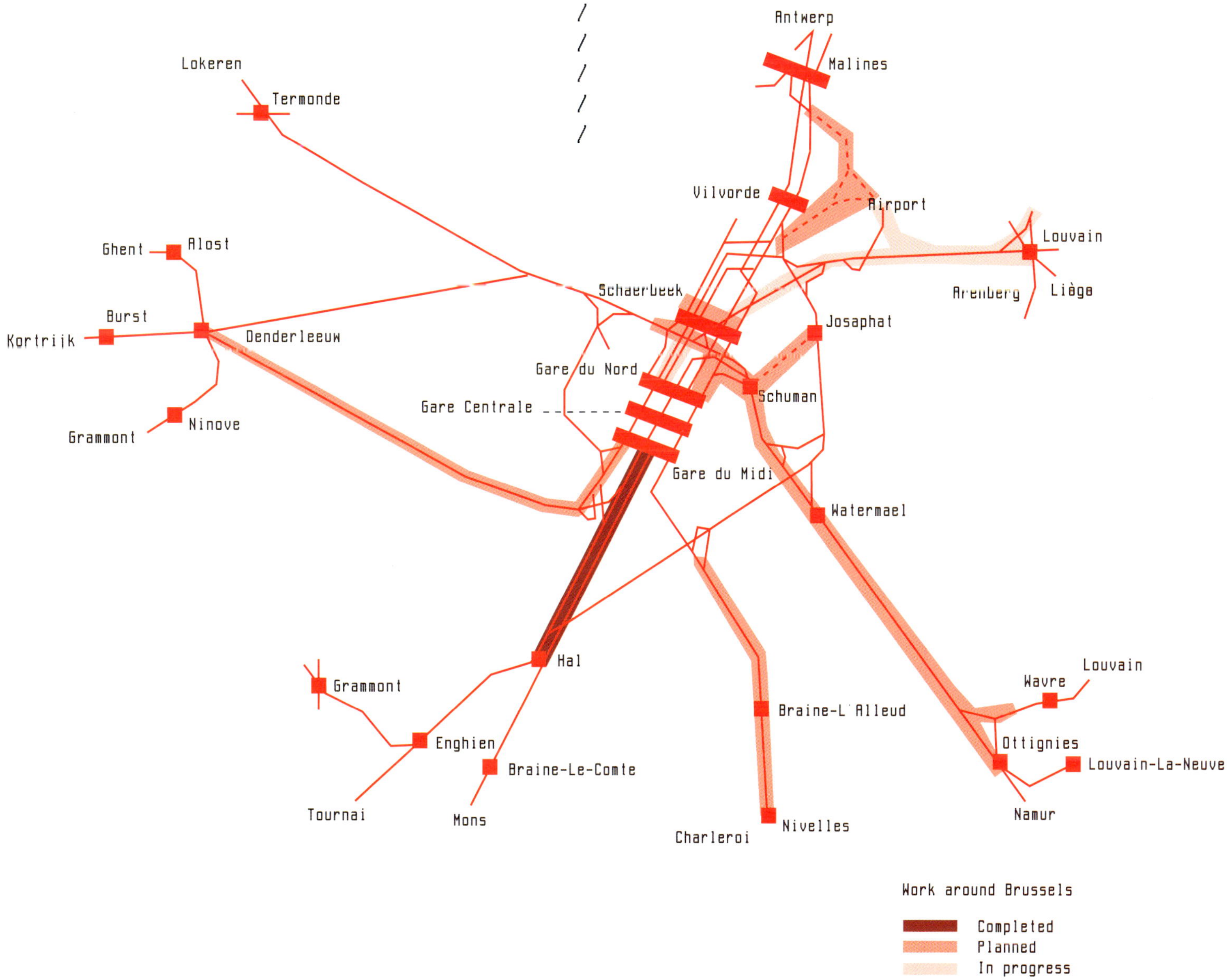

/
/
/
/
/

© Marie-Françoise Plissart

/
Tour du Midi : a high tower as a positive beacon.
Bruxelles-Chapelle Station : injury
/
/

/
/
/
/
/

@ photo AirPrint

/

Northern District:
A ghetto of office buildings enclosed between
the railway and the canal.
Prototype of the disruption of scale.

Airport Data

/

/

50''54'08 NORTH,
04''29'09 EAST

/

1,245 ha total area,
109 ha total area for Brucargo

/

2,984 metres for runway 02/20,
3,638 metres for runway 07L/25R,
3,211 metres for runway 07R/25L

/

32 docking spaces for passenger aircraft at maximum capacity

/

24/24 = opening hours

/

15,000,000 travellers every year

/

Connection planned with RER

/
/
/
/
/
/
/
/
/
/
/
/
/
/
/
/
/
/
/
/
/
/

/
/
/
/
/
/
/
/

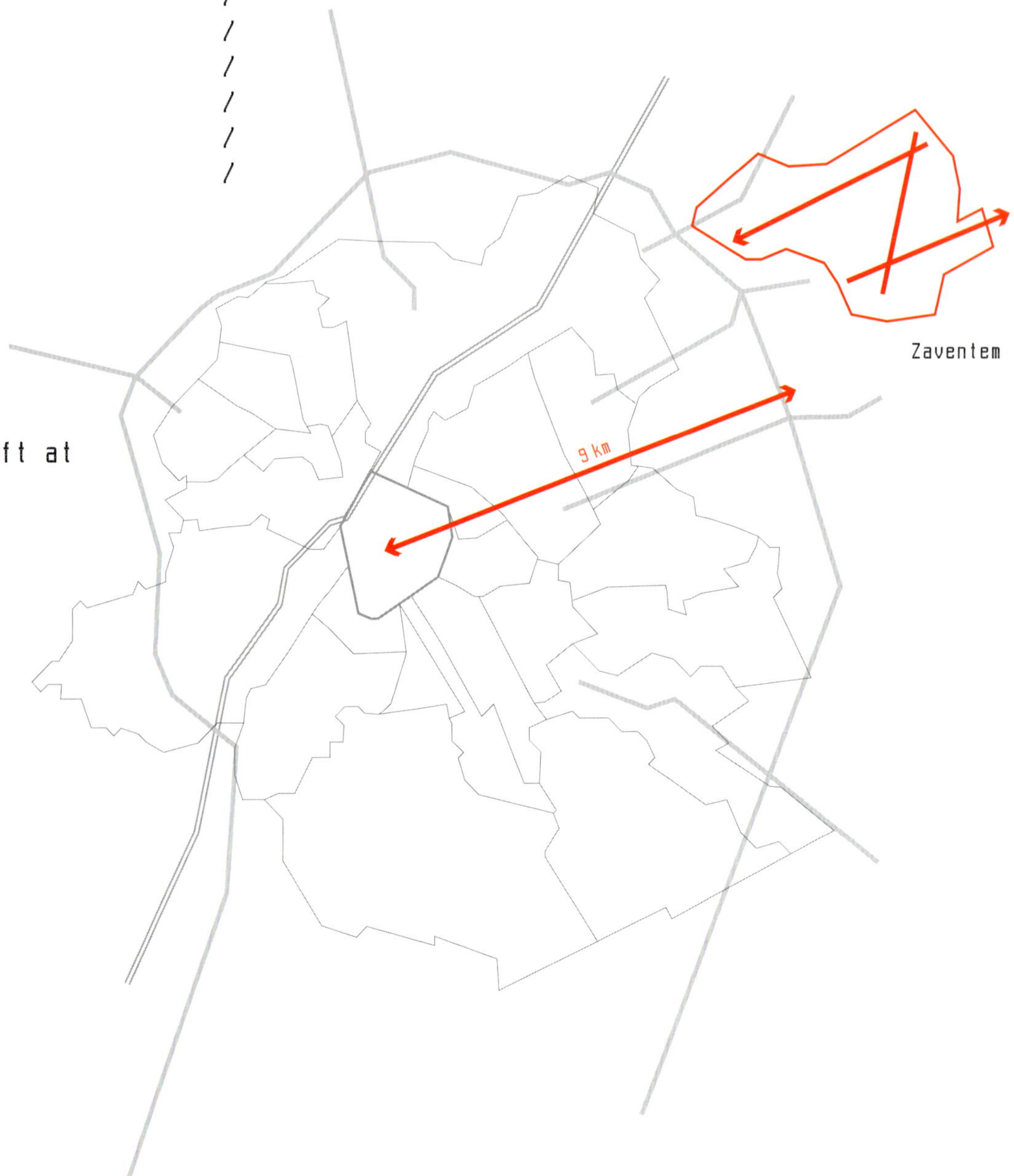

/

An airport which is too close to the city

/
/
/
/
/
/

© photo AirPrint

/
Only 8 km from the historic centre.
/
/
/
/
/
/

Port Data

/

/

5 hours by boat to Antwerp

/

9,000 jobs
6,000 direct jobs
3,000 indirect jobs

/

70 ha useful area
14 km of waterways in Brussels Region
12 km wharf

/

20,000,000 tons/year of goods are handled by the port:
7,000,000 tons/year arrive by waterway,
300 companies, max. 4,500 tons/ship.

/

1 barge = 40 lorries

/
/
/
/
/
/
/
/
/
/
/
/
/
/
/
/
/
/
/
/
/
/
/
/

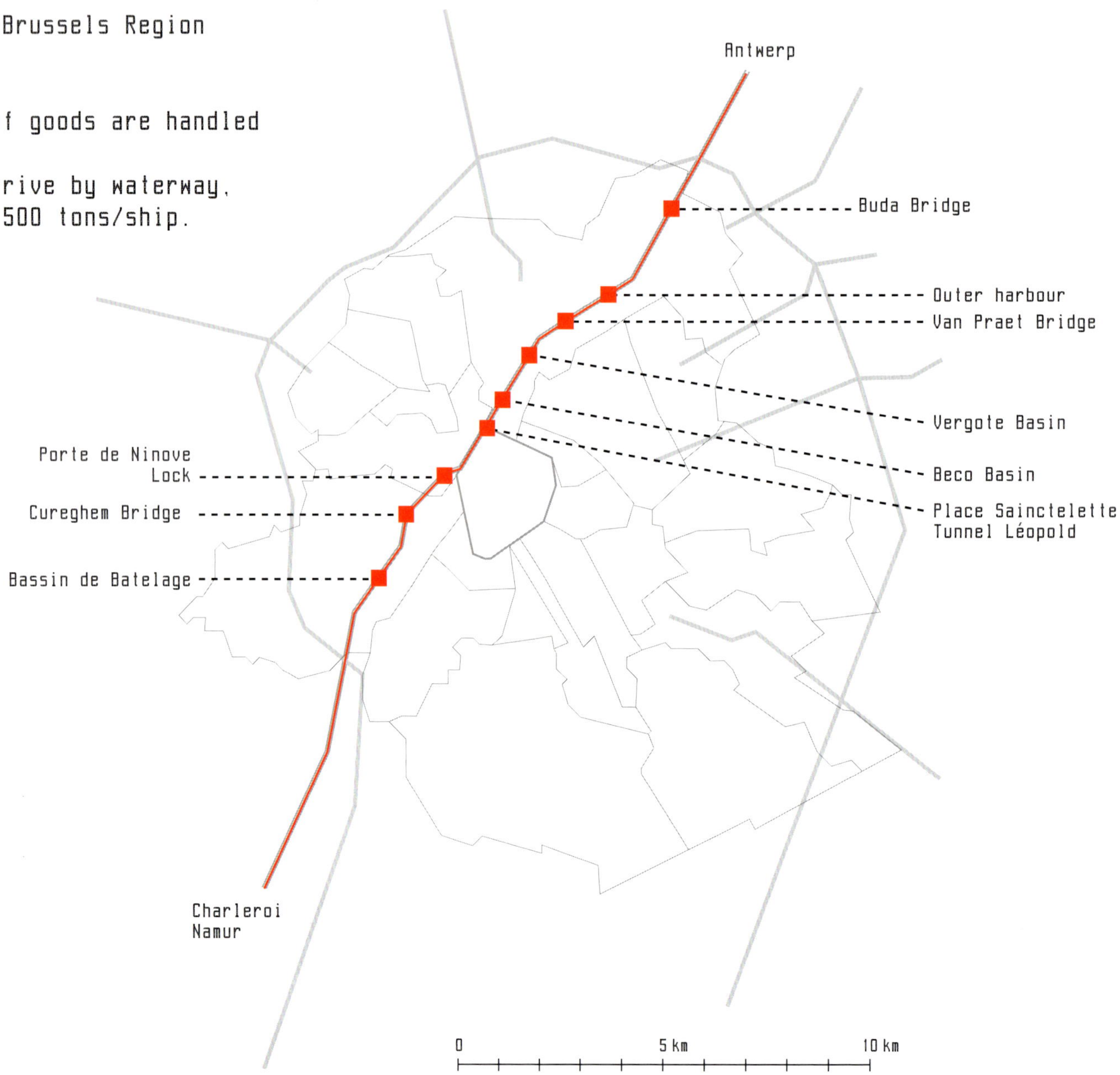

/
/
/
/
/
/

© Port de Bruxelles - Airprint

/
A sea port. And a yachting harbour opposite a garbage incinerator.
/
/
/

/
/
/
/
/

© Port de Bruxelles - Airprint

/
Green borders - towpaths - boathouses.
A pastoral scene and a forgotten place.
/
/
/
/

/
/
/
/
/

@ Port de Bruxelles – Airprint

/
A bottleneck which hampers major development works
in the south.
Expansion maybe… Past projects never materialised.
/
/
/

The water is there: chasm or link?

© Port de Bruxelles – Airprint

Data Europe

/

/

10,396,421 inhabitants in Belgium,
including 964,990 foreigners

/

Number of inhabitants in Brussels: 1.004.239,
including 263,451 foreigners [2004]

/

The 2003 census of foreigners resulted in the following figures:
144,162 nationals from the European Union,
158,936 nationals from other European countries,
62,484 nationals from Africa,
25,208 Asian nationals,
8,485 nationals from the Americas,
328 nationals from Oceania,
5,828 refugees and stateless persons.

/
/
/
/
/
/
/
/
/
/
/
/
/
/
/
/
/
/
/
/
/
/
/
/
/

/
/
/
/

1. European Commission
2. Council of Ministers
3. Parliament

/
/
/
/
/
/
/
/
/
/
/
/
/
/
/
/
/
/
/
/
/
/
/
/
/
/
/
/
/
/
/
/
/
/
/
/
/
/

© Photo Airprint

BRUSSELS NEW TOWN

/

/

Now, Europe is starting to worry about the image that the Belgian capital is reflecting upon it: not exactly glorious and rather narrow to fit its ambitions. So it has decided to organise a consultation exercise of "experts" carefully chosen from among the most abstract or those least knowledgeable about the meaning of architecture or urban planning. Apart from demagogy, which is always possible, precisely what assignment have they been given?
Ministers, Europeans, Intellectuals, Architects and Invited Guests have been requested to lay the foundations of an overall critique of town planning in Brussels, with the unmentioned aim of ceasing to live in a provincial city, and proposing more virile alternatives.

/

/

To consult

/

This is new: until now, any official debate on urban planning in Brussels was quietly smothered. Or perhaps nobody was interested and probably nobody was capable of running or initiating the debate. Belgian sociological studies are either contemplative and never active, or have sold out, or just deal with everyday trivia. There are few urban sociologists and they often only mumble innocuous banalities or spout statistics; few in the press [paper or electronic media] are really interested. Except ARAU, of course, initially in a heroic protest, and once they came closer to power, in a quiet, romantic tone. At best, they are dealing with archaeology, though always with the best intentions; at worst, they show a rather questionable leaning towards "new urbanism".

/

/

/

/

Sterility!

/

Of course, one may fear that the guest advisers may favour illustrations of power and structural rigidity and models of administrative cities [Canberra, Washington, New Delhi, Twin Towers, Brasilia, etc.] whose boring sterility is soothing for the institutions, but in no way lends itself to the expression of service for a population of nearly half a billion cultivated people, who are all different. They would deny that, but …
However, a few voices were raised, in a piecemeal way [and my text here is deliberately random, totally partial and incomplete!].

/

/

Ita Gassel

/

First of all, the wonderful Ita Gassel, my friend, who died discreetly one fine summer day in Treignes, his village sanctuary in Wallonia. The work that we carried out together in Belgium and in France showed us how much his method [his attitude?] was able to produce intentions and create an active consensus: "Action, research and participation that reflects them". Always eager to "do", he had not taken the time to "say" anything about it: there is no serious work to bear witness to his completely unique and lone activity, despite the many friends who pleaded with him to get down to it.

/

/

A few analysts

/

There is Pierre Puttemans: loyal, always lucid but sometimes disillusioned and lonely. Pierre Loze had experienced Belgian architecture during his childhood and was very familiar with it. The philosopher Karel Elno lived in Flanders, took refuge in a Dutch university and then he too disappeared amid general indifference, eclipsed and replaced by his opposite, Professor Geert Bekaert, who spent the first half of his life debating violently and intelligently about socio-

political motives and the second half reduced to architecture as the art form of the elite, trapped in its narcissism. Wim Kennis, a sociologist, was quite promising but eventually became bogged down in trivia. Evert Lagrou is a gentle, perceptive lecturer [at Sint-Lucas] rather than a polemicist or an activist. Jean Rémy, professor of sociology at UCL, is an innocent and meticulous contemplative of minor events. But at present, Iwan Strauven looks to have the same curiosity and inventiveness that his father Francis had at the same age.
/
/
A few active people
/
Maurice Culot and his courageous team fought hard to conquer the governing circles where an urban culture could still be discussed. They succeeded in imposing their model of a European city, sensitive, appealing but outdated, and they rendered the debate sterile.
As for myself, I am only writing after having experienced the reality of project supervision [whether a success or a failure] or a case study [these are mainly reports or projects]. The reasoned accounts of these studies were never published in Belgium, but many of them were published abroad, and in many languages; "La Mémé" went around the world, but was never published in Belgium: is that symptomatic?
/
/
Urban culture
/
The Green Party, the new interlocutors, often want to adopt a purely quantitative vision of town planning : their participating concern is often theoretical when they want to plan the city. Unfortunately, they are not open to the possible issues at stake in participative architecture and its ecology. Henri Simons and his small team are toiling away effectively, but only in well-managed and sensibly minor operations.
The rare curiosity of local intellectuals and that of the "run of the mill" public is limited, at best, to the Belgian scene. Foreign authors are not widely read here, not widely known, rarely invited to broadcasting programmes hardly ever appear in discussions; popular architects can only be seen in coffee-table books. The rare conferences that are organised are restricted to the brilliant platitudes from the stars: they are a pleasure to listen to, like the stories of great long-distance travellers. Invitations to foreign architects to undertake exemplary work in Belgium is extremely rare: often it is only an alibi [the competitions in Antwerp for example] or for decorative purposes [Roland Castro in Liège].
/
/
What about the colleges?
/
Despite their freshness, any underground or violent debates that could nurture new generations are concealed from them and, automatically urban planning and architecture are presented as entertainment art or media wheeling and dealing. Often, this is done with a great deal of goodwill.
/
/
Answers?
/
So this call for opinions is new.
What was the response from those invited by the Prime Minister in the introductory report? More brilliant platitudes, a few plays on words, jokes and visions carefully detached from the Brussels context. Discussions [albeit almost inaudible] could tear apart the beautiful image that they are preparing to depict for us.
Then, subliminally, a frightening vision of demonstration of power by urban planners is concealed behind some wishful thinking about the mixtures of Euro-Belgian populations and their conviviality, passing over in silence the cultural and financial divide which is already impossible to bridge between the "Eurocrats" and the "ordinary Belgians": what will it be like when a whole part of Brussels has been sacrificed to that ideology? Who will analyse and synthesise that?

Power?
/
I am looking for a comparison with the attempts to reconcile universal equity with the free unfettered capital markets: there is a case of water and fire. So far, it has been prohibited to criticise or evaluate the impact of capital on national economies [and first and foremost the weakest economies]. Nevertheless, for some time now, discretely, it has been noticed that pension funds hold enormous sums for investment, and the giant financial companies are trying to "look their best" to deserve those investments.
So we then saw the emergence of a number of independent groups, who devote their energies to certifying the social responsibility of firms which are asking people to invest in them: these groups of analysts are becoming increasingly influential. That is already the case in the United States [they certainly need them], while in France, ARESE is being knocked back into shape under Nicole Notat's leadership.
Miraculously, they are the ones who are going to put the market on their guard, making them more honest [they certainly have their work cut out]. However, it is well known that in normal companies, care for the environment [and social responsibility] is left to the advertising department.
I am thinking about that, because in parallel with our town planning activities, what argument other than morality [which does not count for much in free markets] could provide a balance? Am I being pessimistic? The state, at best, issues prohibitions through cumbersome rules that people circumvent as soon as they have a chance. What happens then?
/
/
Precedents
/
After negotiations that lack transparency and tricks that were almost legal, the "pseudo" Parliament was built near the Park Léopold in Brussels [and, miraculously, suddenly became the real European Parliament], and above all, cunningly avoided consulting any of its neighbours. The residents of the district where Europe has muscled in with its sincere brutality, had tried to take the matter to court, but this was soon forgotten: it only succeeded in postponing the operation by a few months. The Parliament buildings had already led to latent conflicts between the management of the [illegal] car parks of the EP buildings and the Brussels city administration: it had not authorised this operation, which the EU had probably just failed to notice.
Could we dream and believe that enlightened and sensitive minds might have had the idea of seeking to organise space and architectural images that would venture beyond the expression of the blind [and deaf] public power and that of global [or almost?] wheeling and dealing? A city landscape which is urban-human and not mechanistic-abstract? And which reflects a bottom-up approach and not the usual hierarchy: a landscape of subsidiarity? For example, to avoid the pomposity which led André Jacqmain to adopt an architecture of power and symbolism, the whole building was divided into different fragments, better proportioned and the result of combined efforts of different architects for example; however, the main issue is the following: urban scale and the joy of living.
/
/
Urban biodiversity
/
Can we dream of a multicoloured project? In an age when expression of supranational power is being challenged on such a massive scale, one could imagine a "monument" that would remain virtual: it would be the construction of "popular" opinion by consultation at successive levels of subsidiarity. Districts, professions, informal groups, clients of the institutions, for example: education at various levels, users and providers of public transport, the unemployed, the middle classes, the Cercle Noble, the dustmen, shopkeepers with various sizes of business, public health institutions, and just about anybody. Conferences

would build up urban opinions from grass roots level, gather them into groups on an increasing scale, by successive stages until a very general assembly in national hearings, where a number of main lines of action would be confirmed. But above all, without eliminating the diversities and contradictions, because that is what makes Belgium what it is, and that is what avoids a "prefabricated society".

/

/

Assistants

/

While it is easy to find "social authors", or find "social players" who orchestrate this crowd, and will "really" guarantee them their say, defend them against those who always snatch it away from them, or defend them against themselves when they get tangled up in their collective expression [most arguments are weak and only murmured]. They will move beyond the violent psychodramas that are inevitable at the outset, and hand them back their "plans" interpreted respectively, so that they can amend them and enhance them after reflection, chronicle them scrupulously and enable them to go backwards to take a different path from a crossroads?

/

/

Echoes

/

The Press could help in this, but does it want to, and does it have the ability? Its usual way of playing its role is instinctively to obey shareholders and ratings measurements: they have to sell the news [and the more catastrophic, the better]. It is rather the opposite of this active social role that would be an instrument for progress. But I can still dream …

A staggering example: at the beginning of the year, we organised eight hundred square metres of exhibition devoted to architecture, urban planning and motivations: "free housing". Its organic and ecological "profile" was incompatible with all the usual output of the modern press: despite the usual mailings to press listings, NOTHING was announced. Its audience came as a result of word-of-mouth recommendations, and the event was much the better for that.

Of course, we run the risk of seeing an [unexpected?] project being accepted, which would leave Brussels in obvious chaos and would not be welcomed by the authorities who always take a simplistic view. A genuinely pluralist project, reflecting the post-modern image of this society and whose client does not have to live in constant mistrust of all institutions. The Belgians very patiently constructed a "royal federation" the like of which has never been seen before!

/

/

And then?

/

I am trying to look back on what I have written as if I were a [senior] official who is responsible for the European landscape and who has just landed in Brussels. I cannot see an easy way of conveying this message: the massage is too powerful, as Marshall MacLuhan said. But perhaps, ordinary people would understand: at least, it would make them sad.

/

You must believe me, I am not being at all negative : my natural optimism makes me hope that our "Belgian-ness" will inevitably result in a complex and less brutal form than the result of power-play we have presented so far.

/

/

Lucien Kroll

/

/

/

/

/

/

/

/

/

/

Brussels and the headquarter cities of the European Union

/

«Brussels, Capital of Europe», was the title of a brochure published in 2001.
At the invitation of the President of the Commission of the European Union [EU], Romano Prodi, and the Belgian Prime Minister, Guy Verhofstadt, a group of intellectuals studied the needs and functions of a capital of Europe and how Brussels could fulfil these roles. In spite of the title, which only seems to consider the option of a single capital located in Brussels, the text and the images of the report briefly evoke several headquarters and itinerant functions. However, this issue is not mentioned in the second part of the text, which focuses on how the image of Europe can be developed in Brussels.
To determine an integration policy for the EU in Brussels, it is necessary to carry out an in-depth analysis of the ideas and concepts surrounding the question of the capital of Europe.

/

The terms Europe and capital are cultural, political and geographical phenomena which are still evolving and have long and varied backgrounds. Many efforts have been made to unify the European states with endless discussions about the development and the location of the capital. The conception of the EU and of the institutions that paved the way for it, set up following the Second World War, is the successful result of historic efforts to unify the region. However, in its efforts to create a European identity, the EU is limited by secular history and the geography of its member states. As a result, the EU is a unity with no history and without a specified territory, and exists in a virtual space rather than as a physical reality. The union sees itself as an institutional framework for a new political body which transcends the member states.
Through the ages, it has been the States which have created an identity and symbols and their capitals have played a crucial role in this process. At the same time, the image of a capital city as a political, economic, social and cultural centre has always been an important factor in the construction of nations. The ideal of a prestigious metropolis reflecting a long and valiant history and a glorious future has inspired the architects of many European cities. Europeans often consider Paris as the paradigm of a "real" capital, which combines the functions of a political centre with important economic and religious institutions, while serving at the same time as a cultural pole. This tradition is still alive today. While the member states have conceded important powers to the EU, they continue to invest in their own individual capitals. In the various national capitals, centralised such as Paris, or federal such as The Hague, numerous public works and cultural institutions reflect their particularities.

/

Unlike the member states, the EU does not have territorial authority in the cities where it has set up a seat and the construction of infrastructures and the organisation of events are the responsibility of the individual states or cities in question and are not controlled by the European institutions. For several decades, the design of the European buildings has also been the responsibility of the host state. The member states have difficulties coming to terms with European symbolism. On the other hand, it is difficult and even impossible for the European institutions to become involved in the development of an iconic capital, as is the case for the majority of European cities. Indeed, this may never happen for the simple reason that such an expression of identity would in fact contradict the interests of the member states.

/

Consequently the institutions of the EU generally use the terms "headquarters" or "seat" instead of "capital" and limit the scope of the concept to a handful of office buildings. The use of the term "headquarters" in all official documents is

the result of the particular characteristics of European unification. From one compromise to the next, the EU, after its forerunners, was forced to abandon the idea of a single capital, which had been at the heart of a number of visionary projects since 1945, and subsequently opted for several seats which today constitute a polycentric headquarters focusing on Brussels, Luxembourg and Strasbourg [1].
The fact that the Parliament has several headquarters is often criticised, even by this institution itself, and the precise location of the various institutions is bound to be determined in the future. However, it should be noted that, since the 1990s, the number of EU headquarters has continued to rise as a result of the setting up of numerous decentralised agencies [2]. In addition to the three main headquarters, the EU is also based in about ten other cities. The "polycentralisation" of the EU capital is further highlighted by the existence of itinerant functions such as the Cultural Capital of Europe [fig. 2].
/
These features make it possible to venture beyond the usual group of capitals and to integrate cities of varying sizes that do not necessarily symbolise the nationalism of the 19th century. They also allow many other member states to participate, whose support is essential if European Unification is to make headway. They also complement the more generalised efforts to create urban networks and the European Spatial Development Perspective [ESDP] [3]. While this phenomenon implies the absence of a unique capital, the cities of the host countries do not so much fear the departure of institutions, but rather the stagnation of the number of employees at the location in question.
/
Until now, the intervention of the EU in the construction of these headquarters has been limited to the proposal of guidelines for a balanced and environmentally friendly planning and the encouragement of local projects. The actual locations are encouraged to exploit their geographical position and their infrastructures, to develop their economies and to promote themselves by associating Europe with their name. The integration of European institutions in these headquarter cities is generally the result of a clear political will by the European or national initiatives. In the absence of a clear political will on behalf of the European institutions, European integration is implemented according to the national, regional, local, public and private traditions, methods, strategies and interests of the individual capitals in question. They have taken advantage of this European opportunity to climb up the European hierarchy and strengthen their economy and by ensuring that their "European district" is the expression of their local culture, their urban structures and their typical construction methods.
/
In recent years, the two other main headquarters of the EU - Luxembourg and Strasbourg - have made the most of these opportunities.
Initially reluctant to welcome all the European institutions, the government of Luxembourg was interested in functions which could easily be decentralised and was given the headquarters of the European Court of Justice, the European Investment Bank and other institutions of lesser importance. The Kirchberg Fund, the body responsible for planning the Kirchberg, recently decided to integrate the European institutions in a multifunctional area on this site.
Strasbourg, seat of the European Parliament, welcomes the members of Parliament during its sessions. During the initial decades as a European headquarters, the city of Strasbourg was at the mercy of the French government, which failed to provide adequate support. Only since the city of Strasbourg was regionalised, has it been in a position to take initiatives such as the architectural design competition for the International Court of Justice [Richard Rogers] and the assembly hall of the European Parliament [Architecture Studio]. These projects have reminded European citizens that architecture can play an

essential role in the development of their identity. While Luxembourg and Strasbourg seem to have learnt to live in harmony with the European presence - by focusing on urban integration, architectural quality and the city's quality of life - the Belgian attitude in Brussels has not yet come to grips with these issues. Although Brussels has become the main headquarters of the EU, and despite the various development and planning attempts made by the Brussels-Capital Region, the architectural and urban quality is deplorable. The difficulties involved in creating high level aesthetics and functionality to accommodate the EU in Brussels are partially explained by the large number of EU employees in this city [some 33,000 people in 2003] as well as the emergence of other functions linked to the presence of this institution. However, with nearly one million inhabitants, Brussels is larger than the other host cities. The city of Luxembourg and its urban area for example has a population of 90,000 inhabitants and is home to 6,000 people who work for the EU. In comparison with the local populations, this percentage is much higher than for Brussels [4].

/

The establishment of European institutions in Brussels since the 1950s has been characterised by a close collaboration between the public and private sectors, which set out to transform this small regional centre into a metropolis, while at the same time serving their own interests. The proliferation of players, at national level and at the Brussels-Region level, as a result of the regionalisation process which has taken place during recent decades has not changed much in the way decisions are taken regarding the development of the European quarter. Although the deficiencies of the sites are often associated with the presence of the European institutions, they seem to be inherent to the political, economic and administrative structures of Brussels. Indeed the same problems have arisen for a number of major projects in the Northern district of Brussels and around Midi station.

In the meantime, new European institutions and decentralised agencies have provided other countries with the opportunity to welcome European facilities. Since the 1990s, Germany is home to the European Central Bank [ECB]. The bank's integration in the city of Frankfurt-am-Main is the perfect illustration of the concept of an opportune capital whereby European headquarters are created according to local traditions and interests. The ECB building, to be constructed by the Austrian firm Coop Himmelblau, is the result of an architectural design competition, a procedure which has deep roots in German tradition, and which unfortunately has been neglected for the majority of other construction projects concerning European buildings [5]. Even though the agencies based in Austria, Great Britain, Denmark, Finland, Greece, Ireland, Spain and Portugal only have about a hundred employees at the most, they all contribute to the image of the EU and are part of the system of European headquarters. From Copenhagen to Parma, local authorities are eagerly exploiting the presence of these agencies to promote their local development interests and projects.

/

It is not possible to apply a single architectural policy to all the European headquarters in view of the fact that the European Union itself promotes a policy of local governance. The promotion of a European identity as determined by the Commission, combined with the strengthening of the political character of the EU, could transform Brussels into a hub for the polycentric and itinerant capital. A strategy to create capitals using a "bottom-up" approach may make it possible to develop an image of Europe with the headquarter cities as beacons. If the EU were to consciously promote this approach among the host cities, a financial contribution could be granted to these cities in proportion to the number of officials present in these respective cities and to complement local financing. If this were the case, all construction projects would still have to be seen in a context defined by the respective local governments. This

This kind of resolutely polycentric strategy sounds promising: the intervention of the citizens would increase the legitimacy of the EU and counterbalance what is often considered to be a democratic shortcoming.

/

This means that major investments should be part of long-term concepts at a regional level and that the various actors must be clearly structured and prepared to assume this kind of responsibility [6]. Within the context of the opportune capital, Brussels, instead of trying to become the capital of Europe, should make its mark as figurehead of a network of headquarter cities.

/
/
/

Carola Hein

/
/
/
/
/
/
/
/
/
/
/
/
/
/
/
/
/
/
/
/
/
/
/
/
/
/
/

Notes

/

[1] For an analysis of the visions for a capital of Europe and the reality of the three headquarter cities, see: Carola Hein, The Capital of Europe. Conflicts of Architecture, Urban Planning, Politics and European Union [Westport [CT]: Greenwood/Praeger, 2004].

/

[2] The decentralisation of the capital function and the setting up of decentralised agencies on the outskirts of its territory are realities in the field. This phenomenon is the starting point of the Council and the Commission in their reports on the buildings policy, which not only sets out the situation in Brussels but also that of the other cities concerned, see: Commission of the European Communities, "COM [2003] 755 final. Communication from the Commission on buildings policy and infrastructures in Brussels" [Brussels: Commission of the European Communities, 2003]; Council of the European Union, "From the General Secretariat to the Delegations of the Member States. Subject: Buildings programme for the Council [2004].

/

[3] In French: SDEC or Schéma de Développement de l'Espace Communautaire. On the ESDP and polycentralisation, see for example: Andreas Faludi [ed.], European Spatial Planning [Cambridge, Mass.: Lincoln Institute of Land Policy, 2002].

/

[4] For the number of EU employees in 2003, see: www.europa.eu.int/eur-lex/budget/data/D2003 v1/EN/AP2000182 frm.htm [visited on 13 September 2004]. The city of Luxembourg is home to several institutions. The Commission has guaranteed a presence of 3,400 employees in Luxembourg by 2010. Other institutions include [figures for 2003] the Court of Justice, [862 employees], the Court of Accounts [479 permanent employees and 96 temporary], the Office of Publications [570 employees].
For the figures regarding the presence of the Commission in Luxembourg, see: European Commission, "C[2003]540/2 Text F A sustainable solution for the Luxembourg site. Communication by Mr Kinnock in agreement with the President" [Brussels: European Commission, 2003].

/

[5] For more information on design competitions in Germany, see: Carola Hein, "The culture of design competitions in Germany and Japan", A+, no. 167 [2001]: 96-102. For the ECB design competition and the text of the jury, see: F: www.new-ecb-premises.com/ [read 25 July 2004]. The designs by Coop Himmelblau are presented on www.coop-himmelblau.at/projects/ezb.php [consulted on 25 July 2004].
See also: European Central Bank, "New ECB Premises. Urban planning and architectural design competition. Draft Minutes of the jury meeting on 28/29 August 2003" [Frankfurt: European Central Bank, 2003]; European Central Bank, "New ECB Premises. Urban planning and architectural design competition. Minutes of the jury meeting on 12/13 February 2004" [Frankfurt: European Central Bank, 2004]. On the Internet: www.new-ecb-premises.com/home frame.html

/

[6] This issue has been studied by Carola Hein as part of a research grant from the Brussels-Capital Region. It will be featured in no. 5 of Cahiers, a publication of La Cambre [to be published in 2005].

/
/
/
/
/
/
/
/

fig.2

© Carola Hein

Official Capitals of the EU and the institutions and agencies hosted (date of foundation or location)

Brussels:
- European Commission(ECofEU), 1957-
- European Council of Ministers(ECM), 1957-
- European Investment Bank 1957-1967
- European Economic and Social Committee(EESC), 1957-
- European Parliament(EP), 1977-
- Committee of Regions(CoR), 1992-
- European Communities Personnel Selection Office(EPSO), 2002-

Luxembourg:
- European Commission(ECofEU), 1952-
- Council of Ministers 1952-1967
- European Parliament(EP), 1952-
- European Court of Justice(ECJ), 1953-
- European Investment Bank(EIB), 1967-
- Office for Official Publications of the European Communities (OOPEC),(1952) 1969-
- European Court of Auditors(ECA), 1979-
- Translation Centre for the Bodies of the European Union(CDT),1994-

Strasbourg:
- European Parliament(EP), 1952-
- European Ombudsman(EO), 1992

Decentralized European Bodies and Agencies (date of foundation)

- **Alicante:** Office for Harmonisation in the Internal Market (Trade Marks and Designs) (OHIM), 1993-
- **Angers:** Community Plant Variety Office (CPVO), 1996-
- **Bilbao:** European Agency for Safety and Health at Work (EU-OSHA), 1994-
- **Cologne:** European Aviation Safety Agency (EASA), 2002-
- **Dublin:** European Foundation for the Improvement of Living and Working Conditions (EUROFOUND), 1975-
- **Copenhagen:** European Environment Agency (EEA), 1990-
- **Florence:** Historical Archives of the European Union (HAEC), 1986-
  European University Institute (EUI), 1972-
- **Frankfurt:** European Central Bank (ECB), 1998-
- **Lisbon:** European Monitoring Centre for Drugs and Drug Addiction (EMCDDA), 1993-
  European Maritime Safety Agency (EMSA), 2002-
- **London:** Agency for the Evaluation of Medicinal Products (EMEA), 1993-
- **Paris:** Institute for Security Studies (ISS), 2002-
- **Parma:** European Food Safety Authority (EFSA), 2002-
- **The Hague:** Europol: European Police Office, 1999
  Eurojust: EU body co-ordinating police and judicial co-operation, 2002-
- **Thessaloniki:** European Centre for the Development of Vocational Training (Cedefop), 1975-
  European Agency for Reconstruction (EAR), 1999/2000-
- **Torrejón de Ardoz:** European Union Satellite Centre (EUSC), 2002-
- **Turin:** European Training Foundation (ETF), 1990-
- **Vienna:** European Monitoring Centre on Racism & Xenophobia (EUMC), 1997-

Sources and Useful links

/

/

www.europa.eu.int

/

www.monarchie.be - The Belgian Monarchy

www.kbs-frb.be - Roi Baudouin Foundation

/

www.belgium.be - Belgian Federal Government

www.statbel.fgov.be - National Institute for Statistics [INS]

www.iristat.be - Statistics on Brussels

www.bruxelles.irisnet.be

Official website of the Brussels-Capital Region

/

www.prd.irisnet.be - Regional Development Plan

www.pras.irisnet.be - Regional Land Use Plan

www.ibgebim.be

The Brussels Institute for Management of the Environment

www.monument.irisnet.be

Monuments and sites in Brussels

/

www.ccib.be - www.500.be

Chamber of Commerce and Industry for Brussels and the Brussels Association of Companies.

/

www.portdebruxelles.be - Port of Brussels

/

www.brusselsairport.be - Brussels Airport

www.b-rail.be - Belgian Railways

www.stib.be - Brussels Public Transport Company

/

www.ulb.ac.be - Université Libre de Bruxelles

www.ucl.ac.be - Université Catholique de Louvain

www.vub.ac.be - Vrije Universiteit Brussel

www4.fusl.ac.be

Facultés Universitaires Saint Louis

/

/

/

/

/

www.hospitals.be

Belgian Association of Hospitals

/

www.brussels-congress.be - Let's meet in Brussels

www.trabel.com - Belgium Travel Network

/

www.xpats.com

Expats - Belgium on-line in English

/

www.ephemeride.com

general-interest website with practical information and atlas

/

/

/

/

/

/

/

/

/

/

/

/

/

/

/

/

/

/

/

/

/

/

/

/

/

/

/

/

/

Evolving towards urbanity?

/

/

Did you say "Brusselisation"? The term refers to fragmentation, the lack of a comprehensive vision, a landscape of compromise and a multitude of façade styles. And where does contemporary design come into play?
For example, the Rue de Laeken with its vernacular and neoclassical style that now serves as a model. We could call it the Prince Charles effect. This "chocolate-box" street inspired the town of Poundbury in England which was designed by Leon Krier…

/

Of course the time had come to take action. To stop the destruction of the city and the fleeing of its population. Today, the city centre is still suffering from depreciation and about 15 % of homes are vacant.
Brussels is famous for its disrespect for scale. A simple house adjacent to a high-rise tower: brutality. "It's the scale and the absence of scale that is scandalous about Brussels", deplores Benoît Peeters. After all, we are not living in a comic book… The landscape speaks for itself: the fabric is suffering. The time has come to turn this situation around.

/

Of course, we could content ourselves with these isolated, soulless towers and these impersonal districts, but we would be giving in to a depressing complacency.
On the other hand, we are stuck with the current landscape. It is a fact that has to be worked around. It is reminiscent of Daniel Libeskind who rethought the Alexander Platz in Berlin, refusing to demolish some of the more unrewarding objects and redesigning the site using these hostile elements. The future will call for this kind of balancing act and for new urban concepts. For example, Edouard François, who designed a façade in Paris using live bamboo plants, has also thought of erecting a 70 m vegetable tower in the heart of Brussels.

/

The city of Horta, formerly the city of art nouveau and art deco, has begun its battle to win back its public space. Within the confines of its Ring, Brussels continues its fight against anonymity. It still has to be seen whether the Place de l'Europe with its imposing golden circle, the icing on the cake of the Alain Sarfati project on Boulevard de l'Impératrice, will be the turning point for a different kind of urban policy. Is it an isolated case, or the beginning of a new approach that has brought Lyons and Barcelona, for example, to the forefront?

/

Let us reflect on this idea of a contemporary scene and emphasise two new designs. Not far from the famous Métropole Hotel, stands the national theatre, a building constructed completely in glass, which bears a triple signature [SCA - L'escaut - Atelier Gigogne] and which differs in many ways from the post-modern box of Michael Graves... Next, some 300 m further, another theatre, the Beursschouwburg, is a fine example of a subtle renovation of a building dating back to the beginning of the previous century - by B-architecten and DHP.
As the capital of three entities - Flanders, Belgium and Europe - Brussels was also the cultural capital of Europe for a year. It should be noted that the city did not build any emblematic buildings, unlike Bruges, which dared - and that is the right word for it - to infiltrate modern ideas into the heart of this world heritage city in the form of a small pavilion by Toyo Ito and the concert hall by Robbrecht and Daem; or like Graz, which at various locations was radically creative with work by Vito Acconci, Cook and Fournier. On the contrary, in 2000, Brussels preferred to focus on sustainability and created CIVA, the centre for architecture. Promote and encourage analysis, expand the scope: this was already a sign of change.
Since then, change seems to be in the air. On

the Place Flagey, one of the most questionable urban developments is being reassessed thanks to the efforts of local residents' committees. The time is now ripe for new projects that have been well thought out and designed accordingly. However, we must wait to see the results of this contra-project strategy because it does pose a fundamental question: is successful architecture the result of a social consensus?

/

Social is the key word. It is in Schaerbeek, one of the suburbs of Brussels with its old XIX century bourgeois houses, where the highest residential high-rise tower of the city mushroomed one day, at the heart of the multi-faceted juxtaposition of architectural styles and nationalities, that two buildings can be found that carry the promise of a bright future. First, the angular building in Corten steel designed by Mario Garzaniti. This is a small project which is extremely visual and has an enhancing effect on the area. The building plays the role of go-between on a very difficult square, a geometrical shape which is disproportionately long.
Nearby, "the house of the citizen" can be found: it resembles a long dining table which has been laid for al fresco eating. It is a building with a fifth façade designed by Pierre Hebbelinck. Following his work at the industrial site of Grand Hornu, which can be considered as a modern masterpiece in its own right, the architect has left the XIX century behind and confronts us with the realities of the XX century. A sign that Brussels is finally evolving towards urbanity?

/

/

Francis Rambert

/

/

/

Francis Rambert is an architecture critic.
A journalist and former editor in chief of the magazine "d'Architectures", between 1990 and 2004 Francis Rambert wrote about architecture for the Culture section of Le Figaro newspaper. He has written several works on architecture (including a monograph on Massimiliano Fuksas) and has also been commissioned for several exhibitions. He is currently director of the IFA (French Institute of Architecture) in Paris.

PROJE

/

CTS

DISSEM MEDITA

/

Casagrande & Rintala

/

/

/

/

/

INATE/
TE

Casagrande & Rintala
/
/
/
/
/

Human layer Brussels
/

Brussels is introducing a new layer to the city based on traditional humanistic values inherent in European culture. An organic matrix of democratic spaces is installed over the existing city structure into carefully studied crosspoints. European culture is also a culture of slowness, communicativity, conversation, contemplation. It has to clearly distance itself from over productivity, self-inflicted stress, dominance of invented powers not based on real reality which are about to destroy the global ecological balance and mental health of modern man.

/

Human layer spaces are democratic offerings of the city of Brussels as an example of a modern European community.

/

Small-scale encounters prepare for the coming together of cities and nations.

/
/
/
/
/
/
/
/
/
/
/
/
/
/
/
/
/
/
/
/
/
/

Human Layer elements in Brussels:

/

1. Lighthouse

- Series of spaces for reading in silence
- Each tower will be thematically specified for drama, justice, sports, humanism, antiquity, media, mysticism etc.
- Ascending over the rooftop level passing by shelves filled with mysteries and knowledge.

/

2. Bathouse

- Archaic spaces containing one method of bathing.
- Hot baths, sauna, swimming pool, cold bath etc.

/

3. Firehouse

- Open air structure containing a fireplace, benches and firewood.
- Possibility of discussing around the fire. Smell of smoke in the clothes.

/

4. Greenhouse

- Open air walled garden space introducing nature.
- Terrarios designed with biologist to house complex ecosystems of flora and fauna.

/

Real Reality

/

The hacking rhythm of life with no space to see the horizon, no supporting values to look for the horizon.
Consuming without questioning and destroying nature which cannot be seen around and so making all this easier. Nature being a loser in economical speculation.

/

Globalization is concrete in the means of pollution. Economic expectations, speculations are fictive. Streams of material are close to reality. Pollution is reality. The responsibility of environmental design is lost to fictive economic speculations with no connection to real reality. Surroundings shaped by no real values will destroy us. Design has replaced reality.

/

/

A bear has hair because it is hairy and not because somebody has decided so.

/

Architecture is turning into the designing of objects, city planning inhuman. A modern metropolis brings a new perspective to urban development. Responding to the new urbanism with its chaotic, unpredictable energies and orders with structures constructed to house financial functions has left the architects powerless or prostituted. Sensing, not to mention planning, for real reality has become underground.

/

The city cannot be treated as a camp for a fixed number of legionaries. Instead of design we need psychoanalysis. The hectic rhythm of life and dominance of economics is reflected in the cityscape, causing bad environments, ecological problems and the illusion of stress. The illusion of stress is the atmosphere in which pollution and prostitution is created. This atmosphere is closed and paranoiac as in malaria. The atmosphere of temporariness provides an excuse not to consider the future. Horizon is of no social value.

/

A city is organic and the human layers are everywhere in small scale. To save the city this must be scaled up and the structure of human layer must be introduced. It will be easy. People know, what is good, the real reality.

/

All human existence should be in connection with to eternity, nature.

/

Thinking of the real reality, looking at the horizon is mysticism - being in contact with the realities that are behind the reality that we see. Mysticism also applies to modern man.
Old people are not shot as they should be according to laws of economics. People sense that isn't kind to kill the old people and kindness is real reality. Kindness is kindness, concrete. Real reality cannot be financially speculated, or otherwise - it is concrete.

© 2004 Image Détrois sa

/
/
/
/
/
/
/
/

/
/
/
/
/
/
/
/

We should not be blindfolded by stress, the realm of economics, the online access to entertainment and information. What is real, is valuable. Urban planning must find a way to be connected to real things, not destructive things or design as entertainment. What is not real is not valuable.
/
Horizon needs space to be seen, time is not money. One has to have the possibility of being taken from this place and time 1000 years back to see, things are the same. Forcing oneself out of this time and place and going medieval let us go from the illusion of today. It is the social responsibility of artists and architects to look for the future, to be sensitive enough to see the reality and to show horizon. The power of environmental design, such as city planning, has to be taken away from material powers. Nowadays architecture is traumatised by the building industry and other external influences.
Ethical awakening in connection with nature should be religious. A city can find its inner peace by admitting her mortality. We must find a strong sense of layers of reality other than material. If so, death is a beautiful end to begin a new life. But if we are stressed by running after money and material, stress for stress' sake, death is a defeat, bankruptcy.
/
/

Economic surroundings do not lend themselves to kindness. Without kindness there will be no positive results.
/
Urban design has become the economic designing of dead cities with temporary masses. Thinking cities as microchips, replacing components with more effective ones. Human layers are not valued, the connection between modern man and nature does not fit into the context of urban planning.
/
We must find new methods to understand the organic city and for organic design. The reality is to bring nature to the city, with its rhythm, mental space and values. Nature's flexibility and capacity to adapt to new situations or to die and by dying fertilizing ground for better solutions. Nature works on all scales from mega structure to one cell as one. Man is a part of nature.
/
/
/

Real reality, values and ethics are always finding a way to push back. They are like the air around us, we notice it when we are running out of it. New air always comes in - the corners are windy. Today's void in a valueless society will be filled with ethics. People are good deep down in the end - that reality is now depressed by material nonsense.

/

The thinking of Real Reality is partly inspired by the comments of professor Jaakko Hämeen-Anttila, who translates medieval Arabic literature and especially Arabic poems and comments on modern society and lifestyle. The blue lines are his.

/
/
/
/
/
/
/
/
/
/
/
/
/
/
/
/
/
/
/
/
/
/
/
/
/
/
/
/
/
/
/
/

/
/

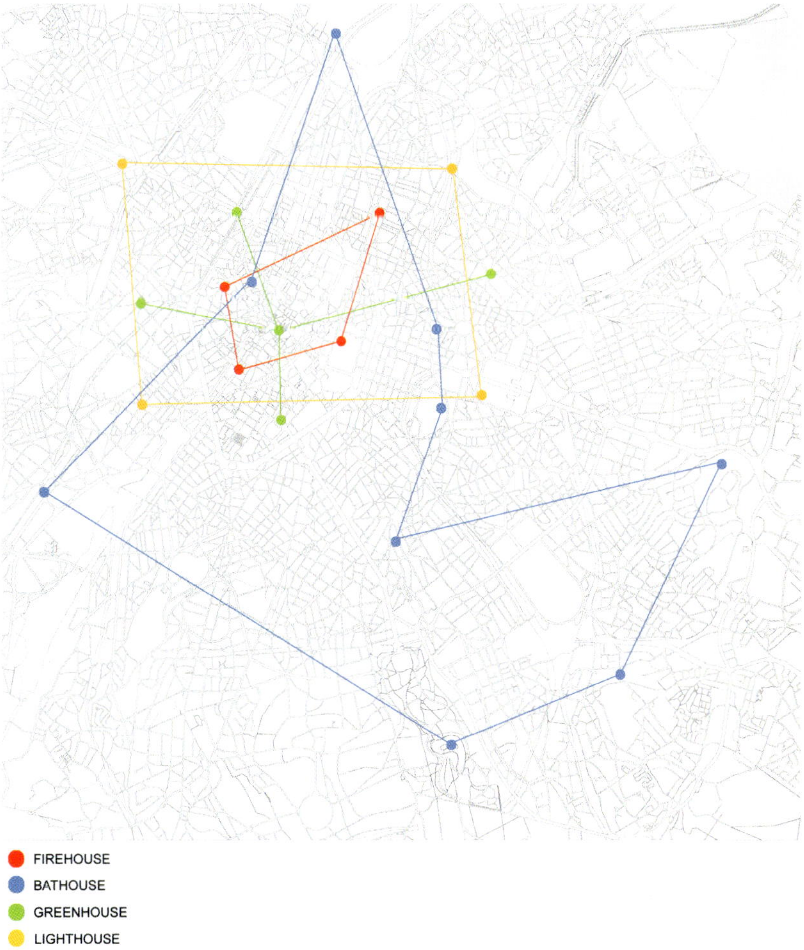

/
/

CROSS/
PROLON
REVITA

/

ACTAR Arquitectura/Joël Claisse
Architecten/WEST 8/Odile Decq B.

G/
LISE

'XDGA Xaveer De Geyter
noît Cornette /MVRDV/

ACTAR Arquitectura

/

/

/

/

/

/

/

/

/

/

/

/

/

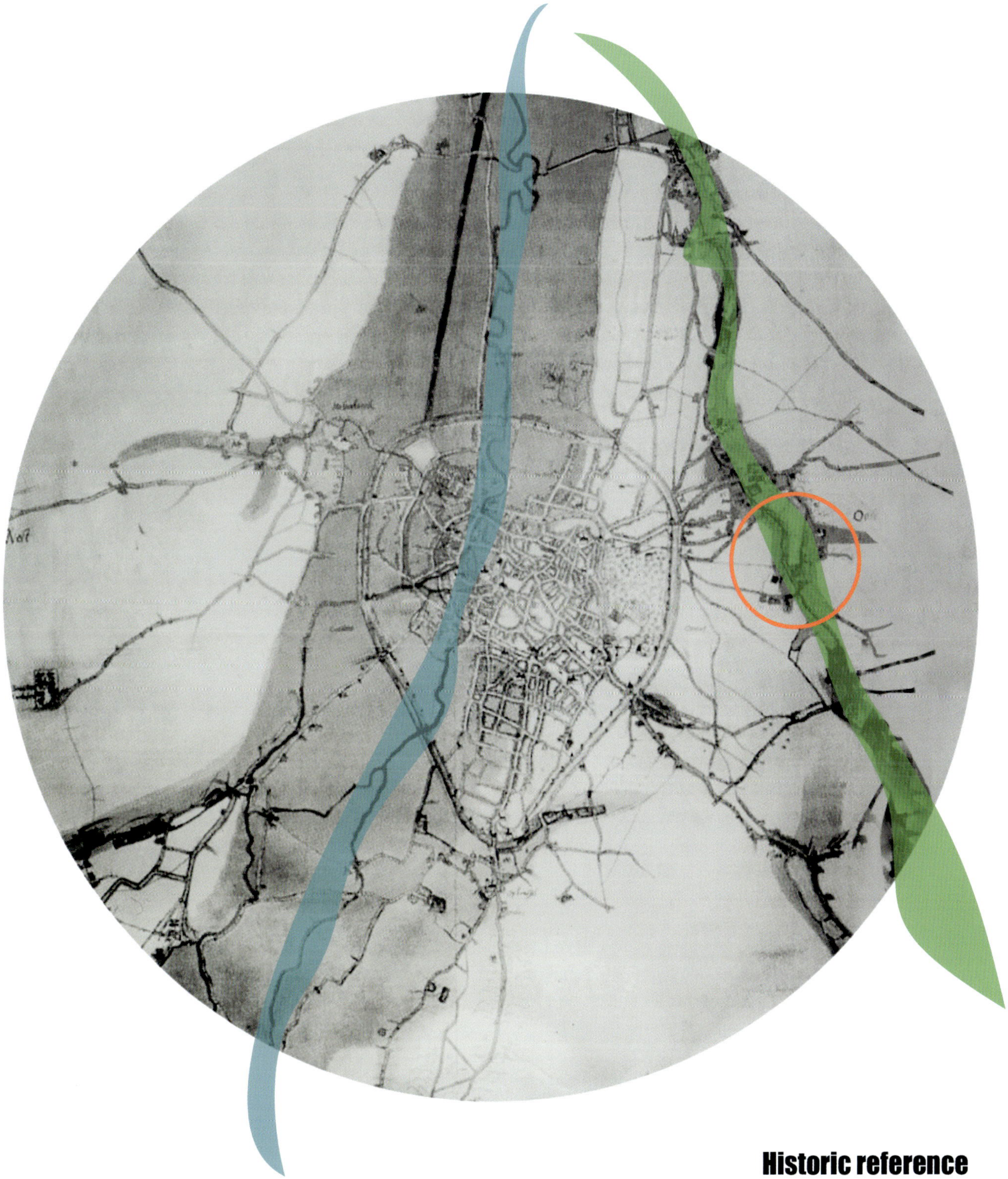

Historic reference

Plan de Bruxelles
(1550 -1554)

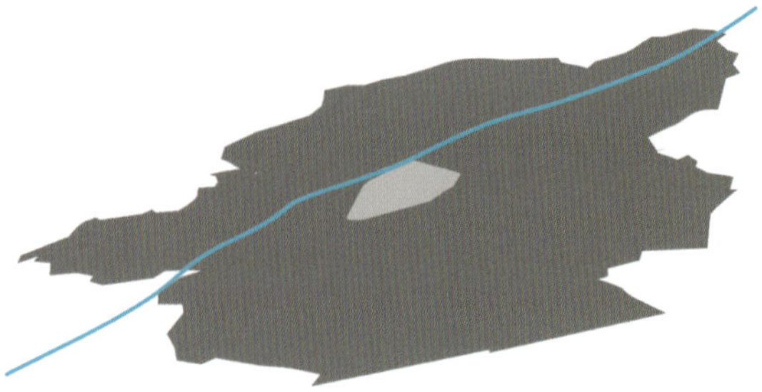

The river as a green highway

Vacant plots are available along the canal that could be used for water-based activities. This would make it possible to not only revitalise the canal itself but also to use it to breathe life into a part of Brussels' green infrastructure.

/
/
/
/

Central Attractors

The city centre should be conserved as the main green area. It would work in the same way as New York's Central Park.

/
/
/
/
/
/

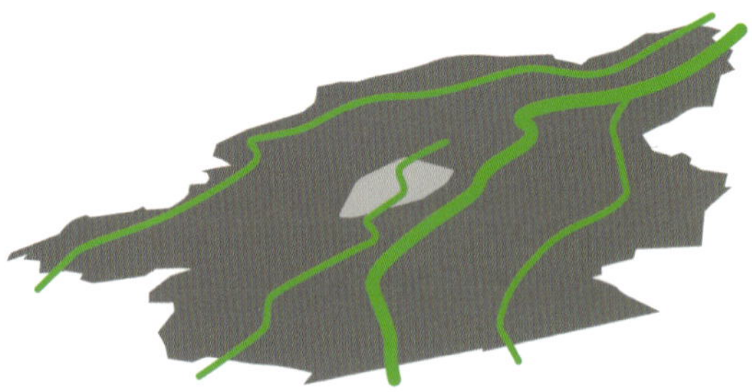

Vertical Corridors

The Vertical Corridors serve as the main linear corridor within the city. As some parts of the land are already built-up, the updating of the corridor would be adapted to each situation.

/
/
/
/
/

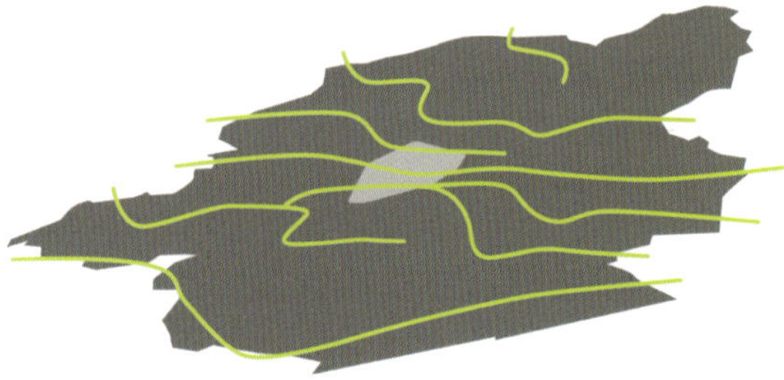

Horizontal Corridors

The Horizontal Corridors serve as the substructure connecting the Vertical Corridors.

/
/
/
/
/

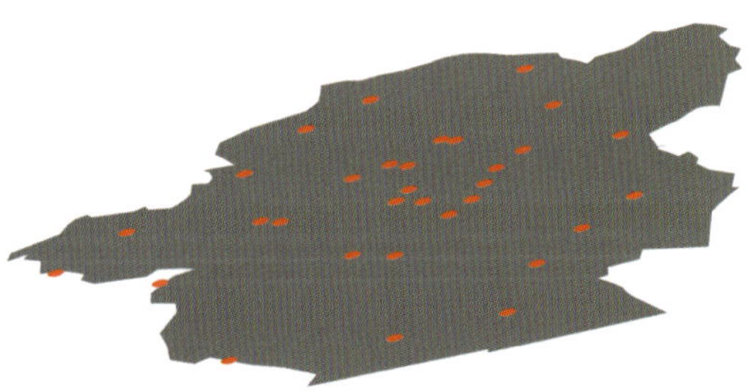

Hot Points

"Hot Points" as nodal elements of the system. They focus the activity and flows that intensify urban relations.

/
/

Définition d'origine
Plan d'espaces verts

Le concept de maillage vert introduit en 1999 dans le PRD, constitue une réponse au déséquilibre spatial mais aussi un outil de planification visant à rencontrer les demandes des habitants. Ses objectifs principaux sont de:

1. favoriser l'aménagement d'un espace public convivial et "verdurisé";
2. favoriser la mobilité des piétons et des cyclistes;
3. améliorer les qualités paysagères da la ville;
4. préserver le patrimoine naturel et accroître la biodiversité.

(www.prd.irisnet.be)

Réinterprétation diagrammatique
Rayons et franges

- Points attracteurs
- Vert (surface)
- Vert (linéaire)
- Fleuve

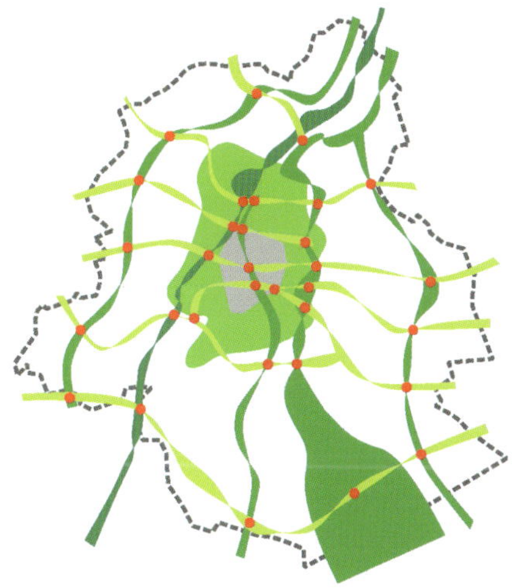

Redéfinition stratégique
Landsflows verts

- Hot Points
- Couloirs verticaux N-S
- Connecteurs transversaux E-O
- Attracteurs Centraux
- Fleuve comme axe vert

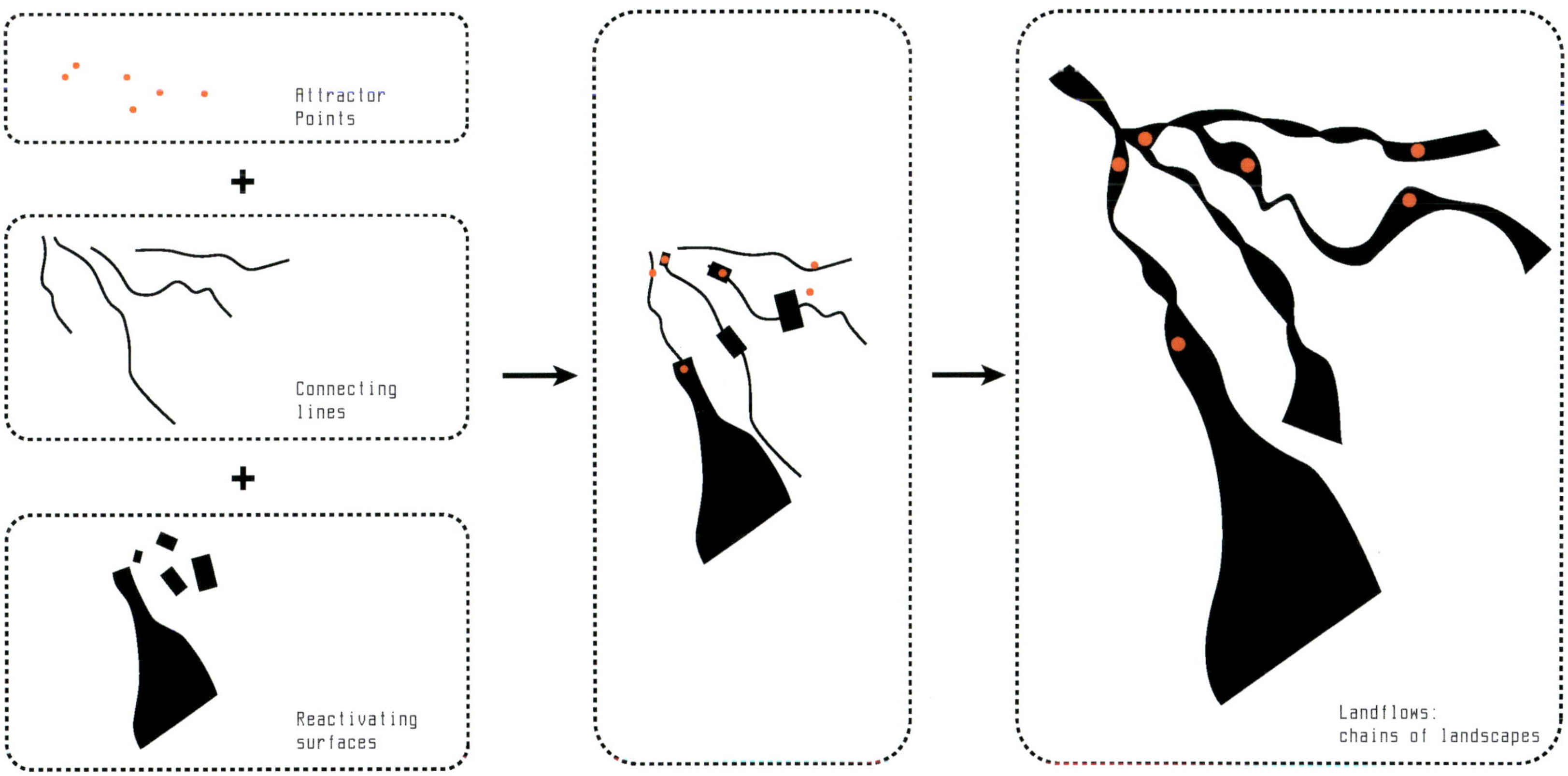

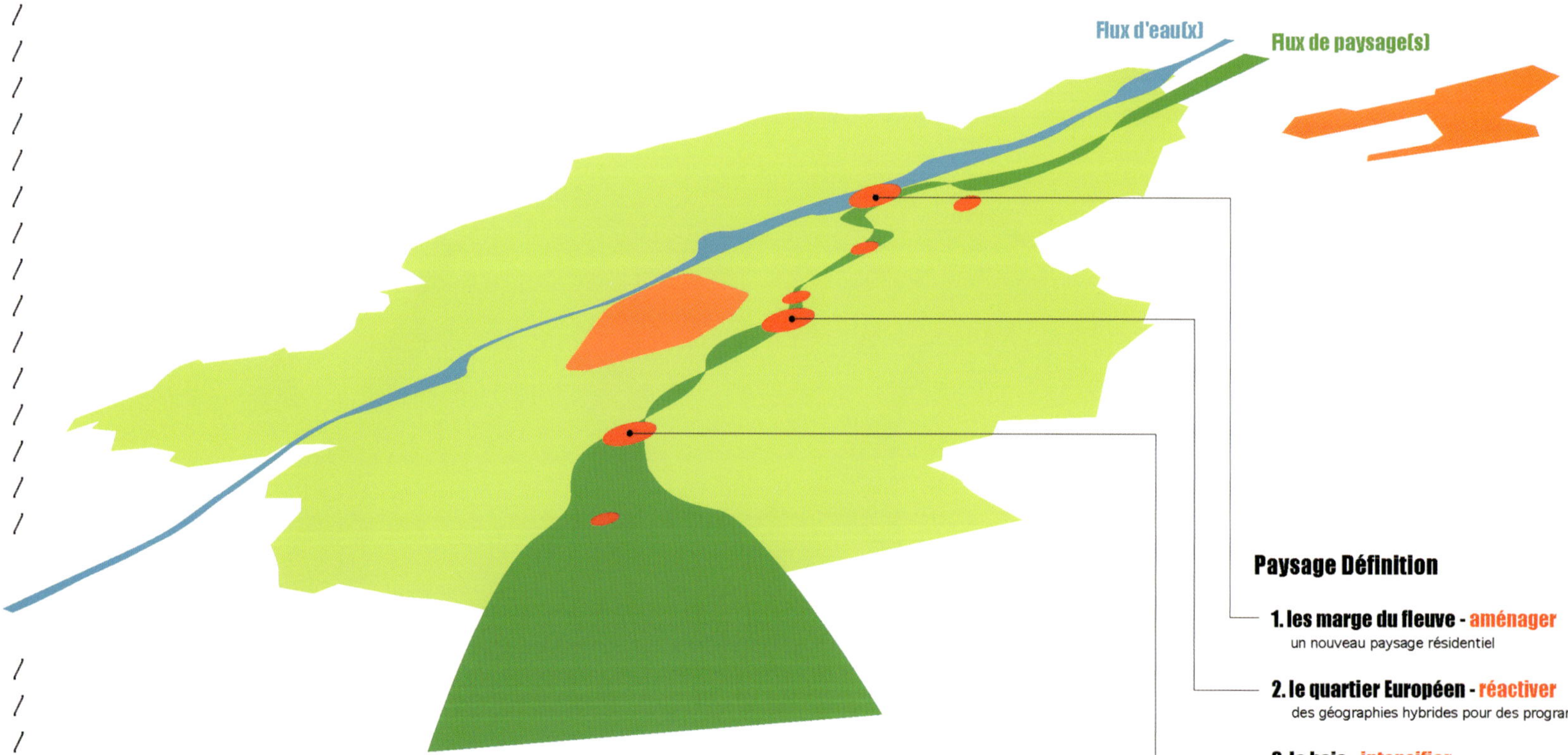

Paysage Définition

1. les marge du fleuve - aménager
un nouveau paysage résidentiel

2. le quartier Européen - réactiver
des géographies hybrides pour des programmes actifs

3. le bois - intensifier
un parc natural et des "sous espaces" associés

3
Airprint

Bruxelles Landsflow - Base
0 200 400 600 800 1000 2000m
Échelle - 1:20000

/
/
/
/
/
/
/
/
/
/
/
/
/
/
/
/
/
/
/
/
/
/
/
/
/
/
/
/
/

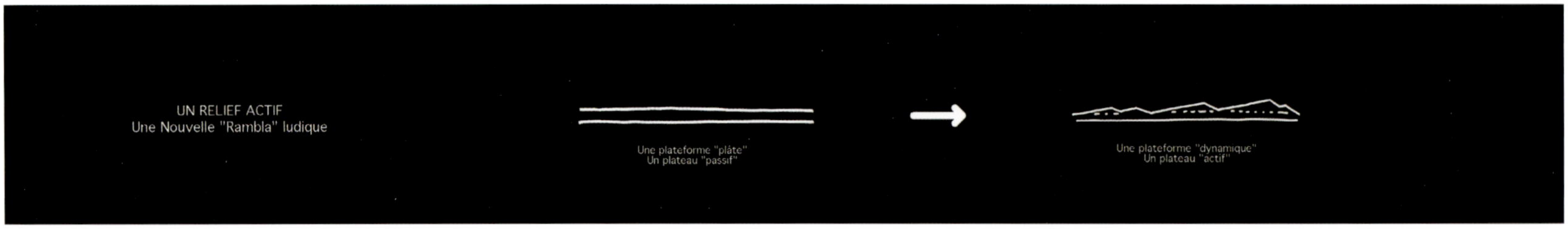

1. La Rambla

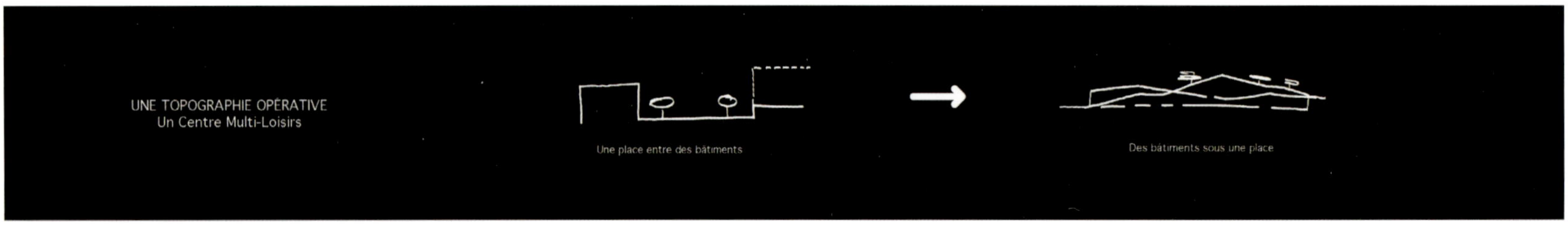

2. Place Jean Rey

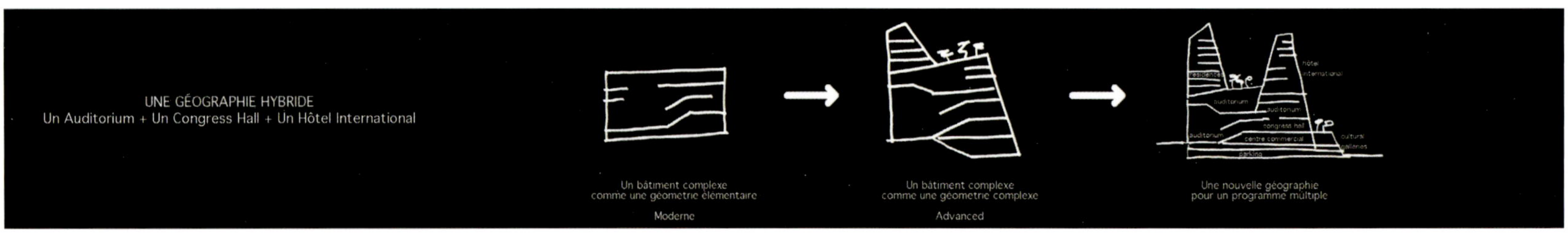

3. Juste Lipse

/

/

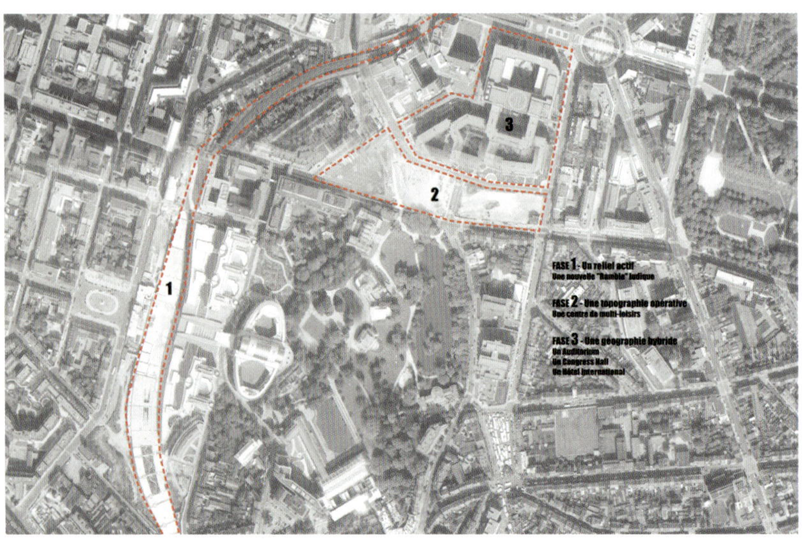

/

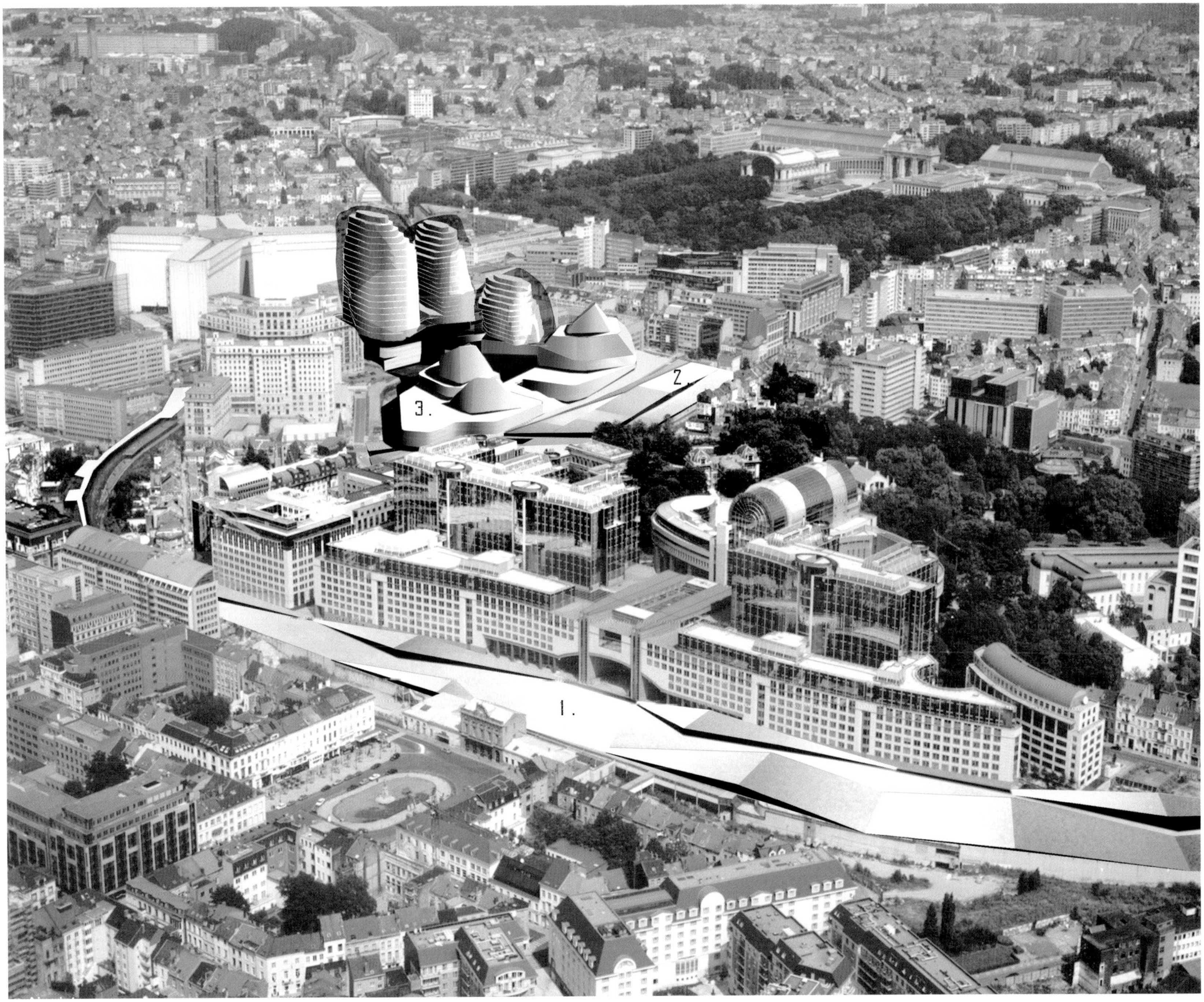
3.
2.
1.

/
/
/
/
/
/
/
/

1. A new ludic rambla
/
/

1 bar-terrasses
2 boutiques
3 restaurant
4 café
5 kiosques
6 petit commerce
7 tapas-bar
8 little station mall
9 jardins plateaux
10 entrée parlement
11 entrée gare nord
12 entrée gare sud

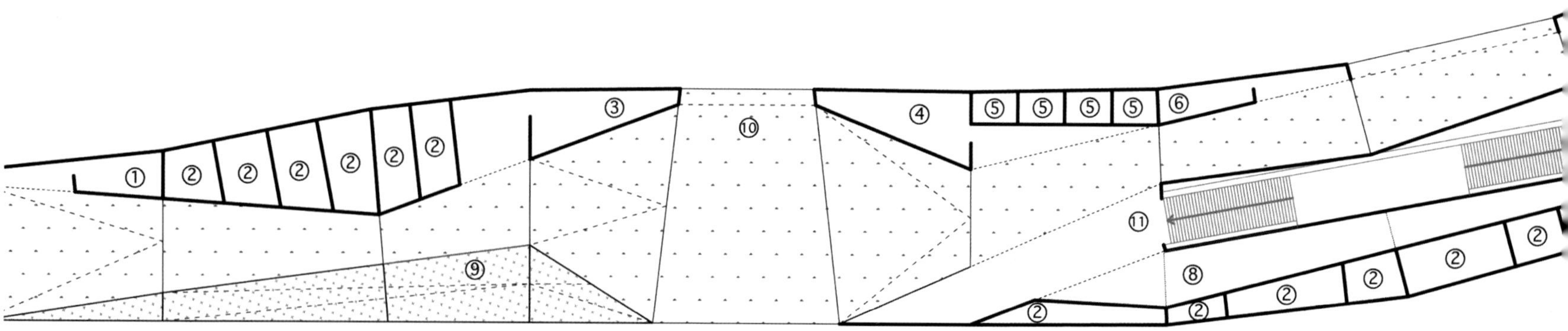

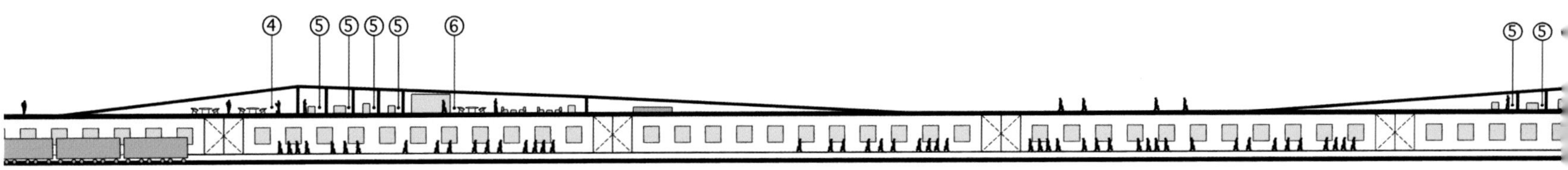

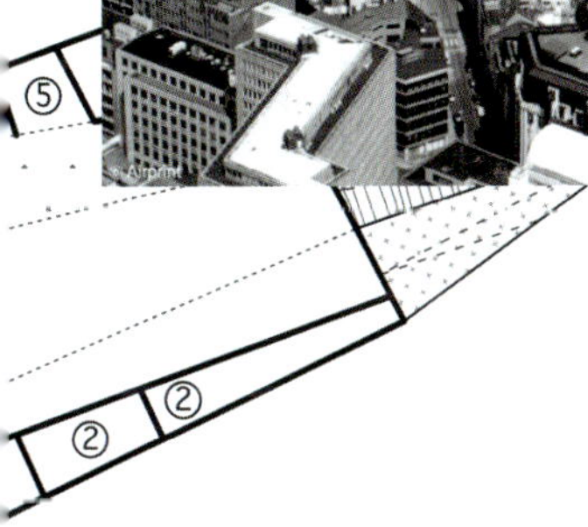
⑤
②
②

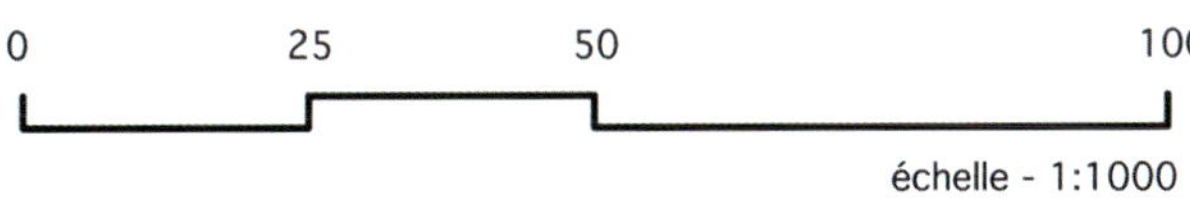
0
25
50
100
échelle - 1:1000

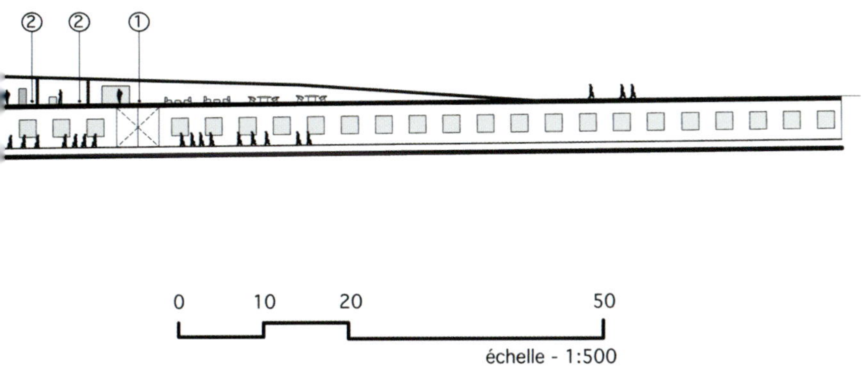
②
②
①
0
10
20
50
échelle - 1:500

/
/

/
/
/
/
/
/
/

2. An operative topography…
/
/

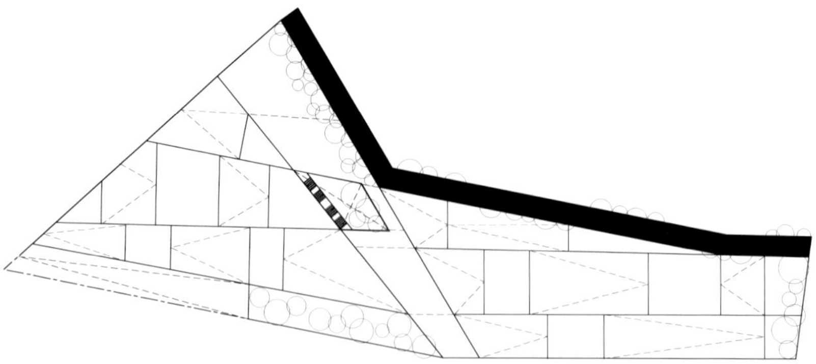

plan toiture

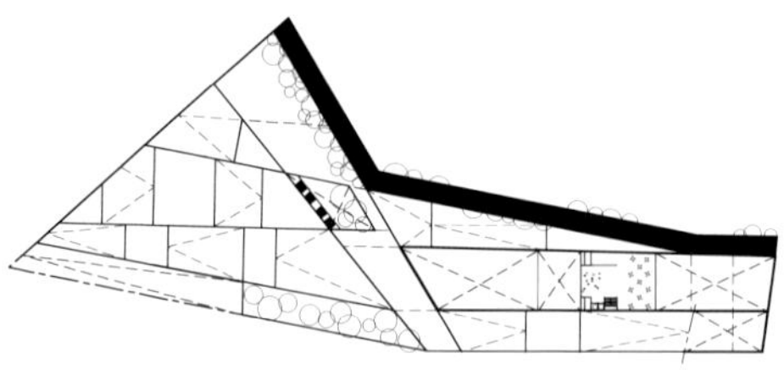

niveau +54

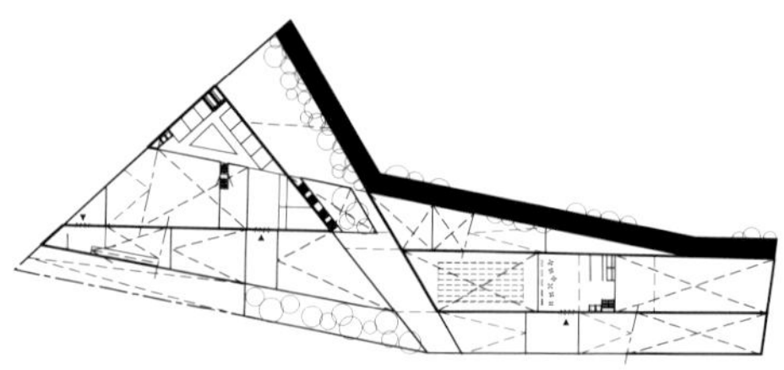

niveau +51

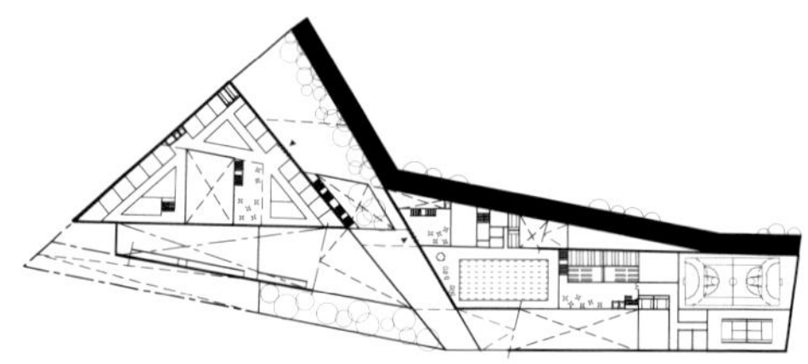

niveau +48

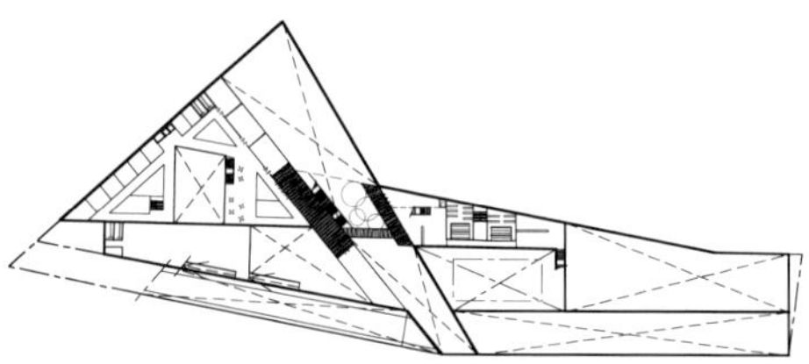

niveau +44

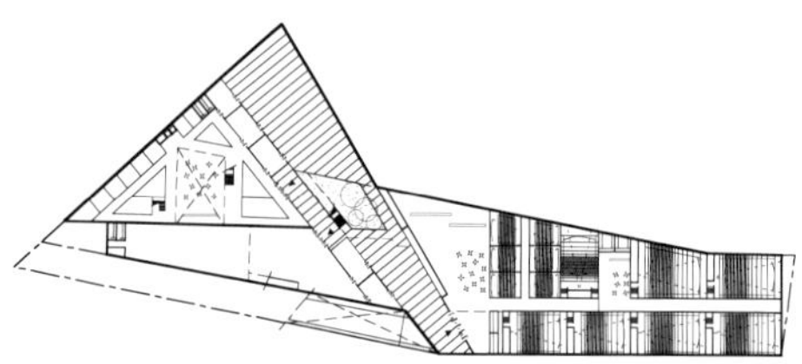

niveau +40

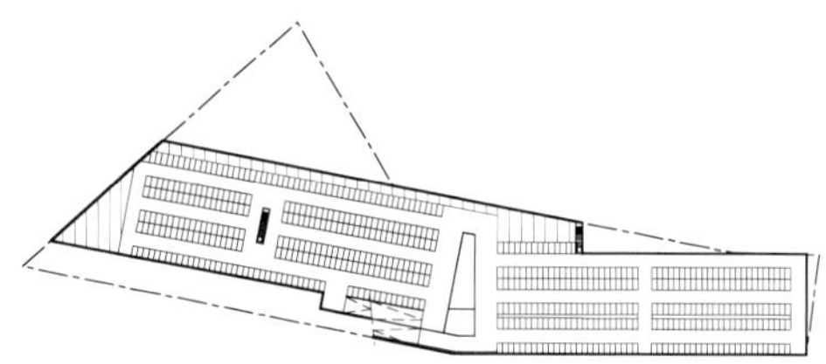

niveau +37, 34

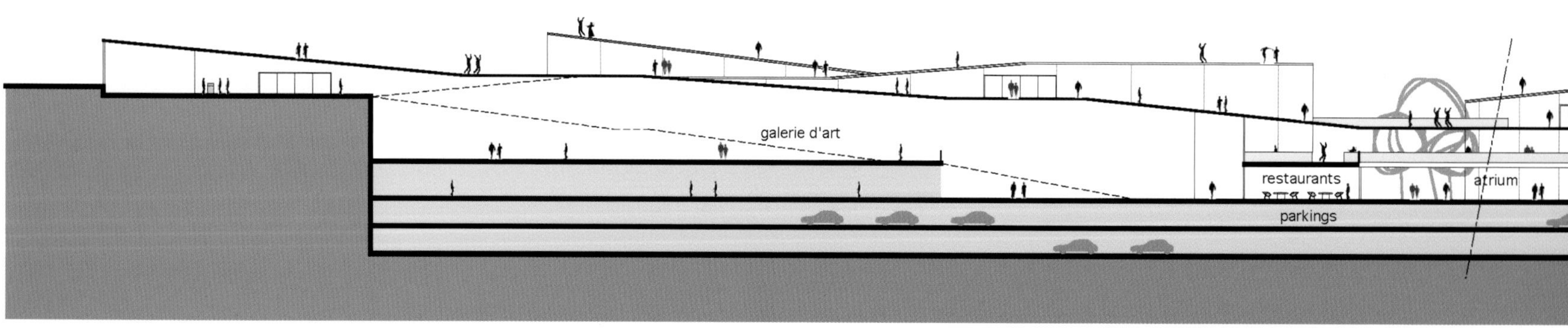

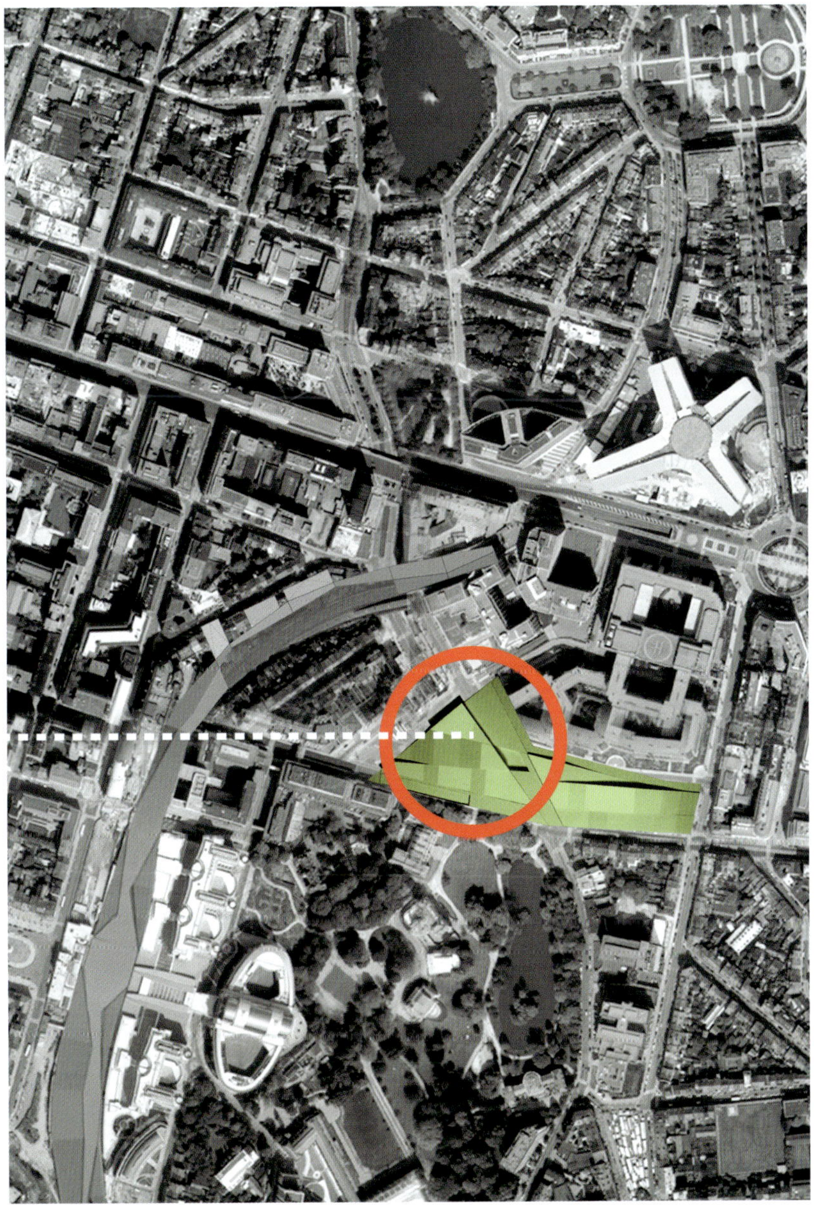

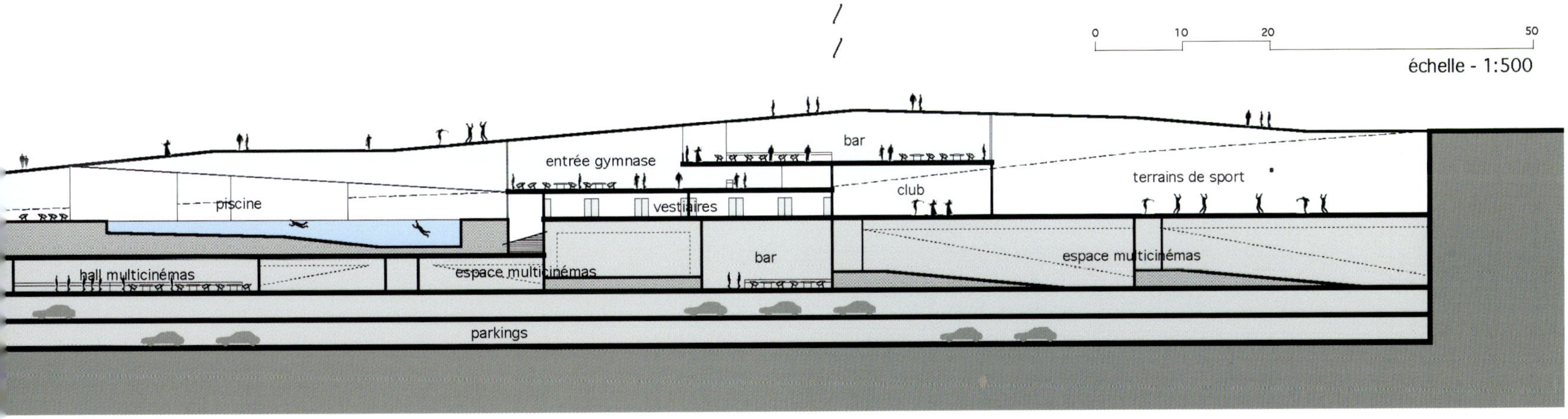
0
10
20
50
échelle - 1:500
bar
entrée gymnase
club
terrains de sport
piscine
vestiaires
bar
hall multicinémas
espace multicinémas
espace multicinémas
parkings

/
/
/
/
/
/
/
/
/
/
/
/
/
/
/
/
/
/
/
/
/
/
/
/
/

CROWNE PLAZA

3.A hybrid geography
Auditorium, Congress Hall, International Hotel

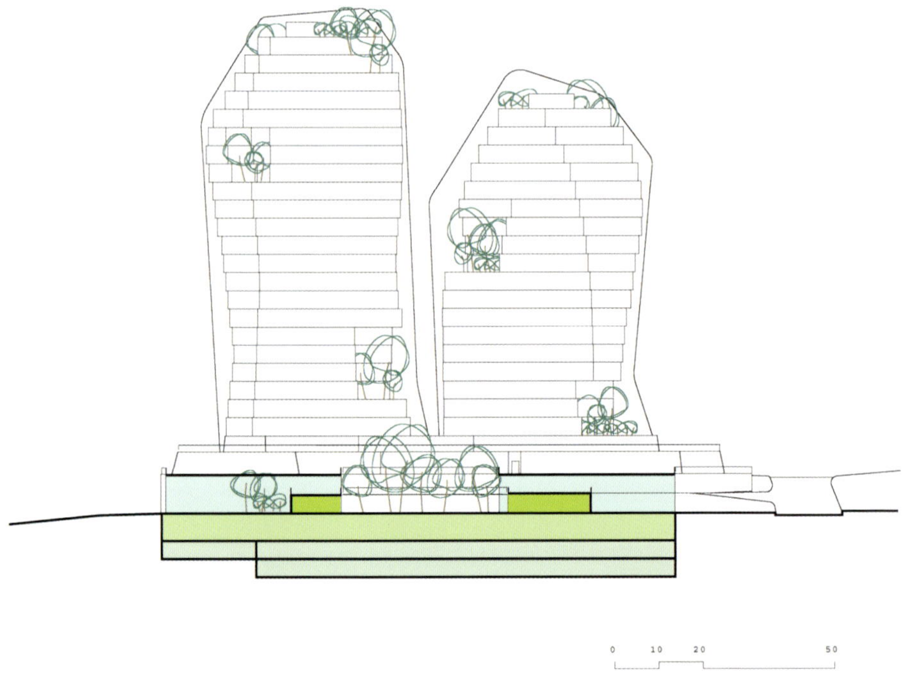

coupe BB

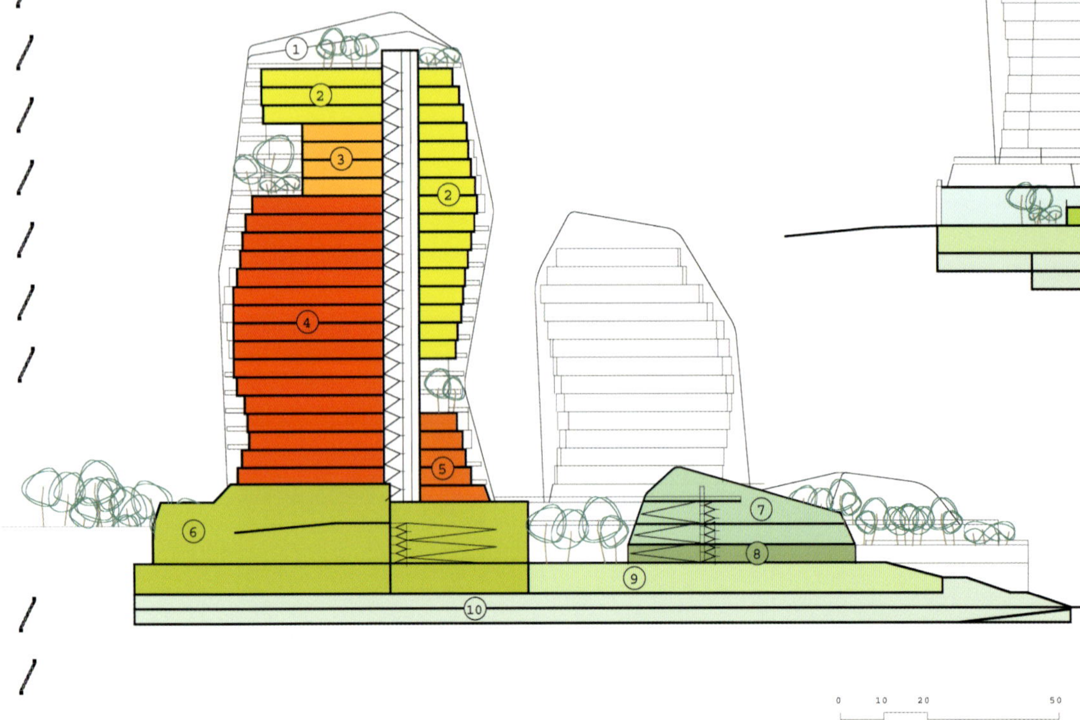

coupe AA

1 terrasse
2 logements
3 appartements
4 hôtel
5 appart-hôtel
6 auditorium
7 galleries
8 centre de congrès
9 centre commercial
10 parking

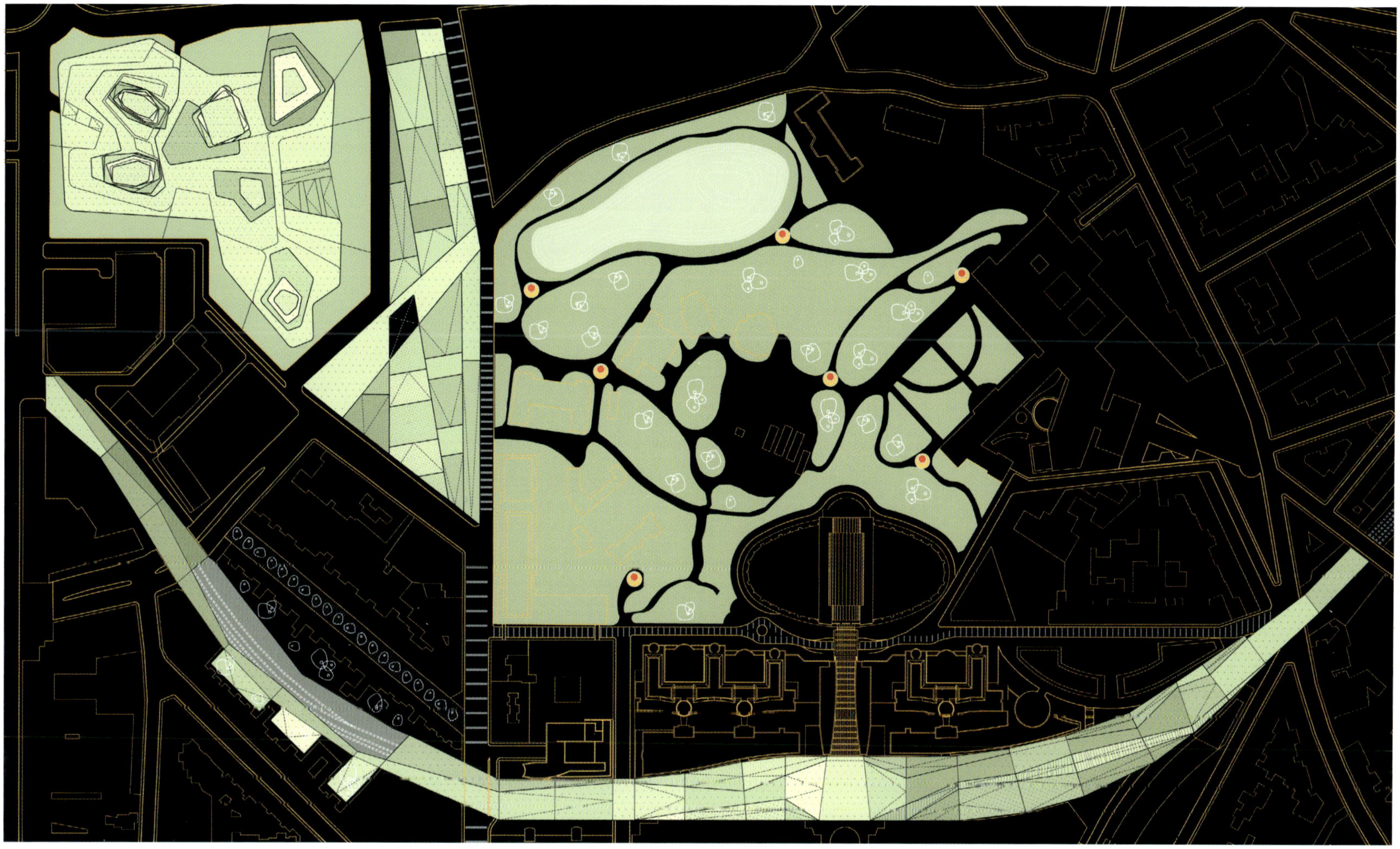

0 10 20 50
toitures

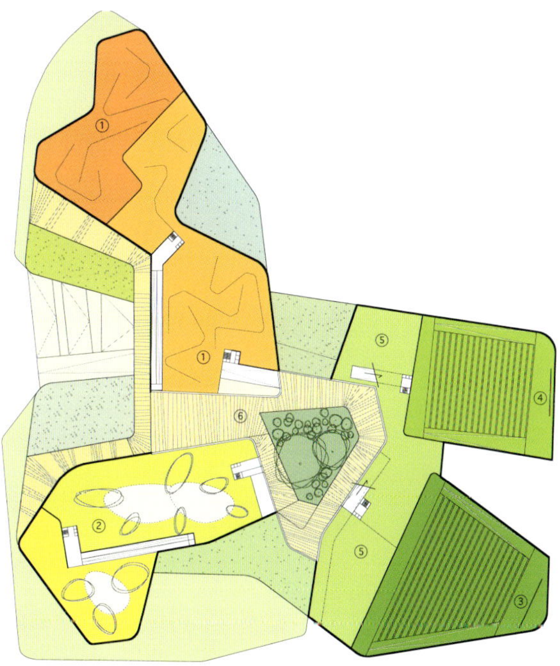
1
1
2
3
4
5
5
6
1 espace d'exposition (art)
2 hall d'exposition (congrès)
3 auditorium (1200 places)
4 auditorium (800 places)
5 foyers
6 plateforme / hall d'accés
0 10 20 50
nivel 50.00

CROWNE PLAZA

/
/
/
/
/
/
/

Joël Claisse Architectures

/
/
/
/
/
/
/
/
/
/
/
/

Widening of the Canal

/

Brussels is a major hub of communication for international traffic, by road and by rail, as well as by inland waterways. It would be simplistic to reduce its role only to the unloading of cargoes from Antwerp and the loading of goods bound for Wallonia and France: the exchange of goods takes place in both directions, both with the north [Antwerp, the Netherlands, Germany and Central Europe via inland waterways, the rest of Europe by sea transport] and with the south [Wallonia and France by inland waterways].

/

/

/

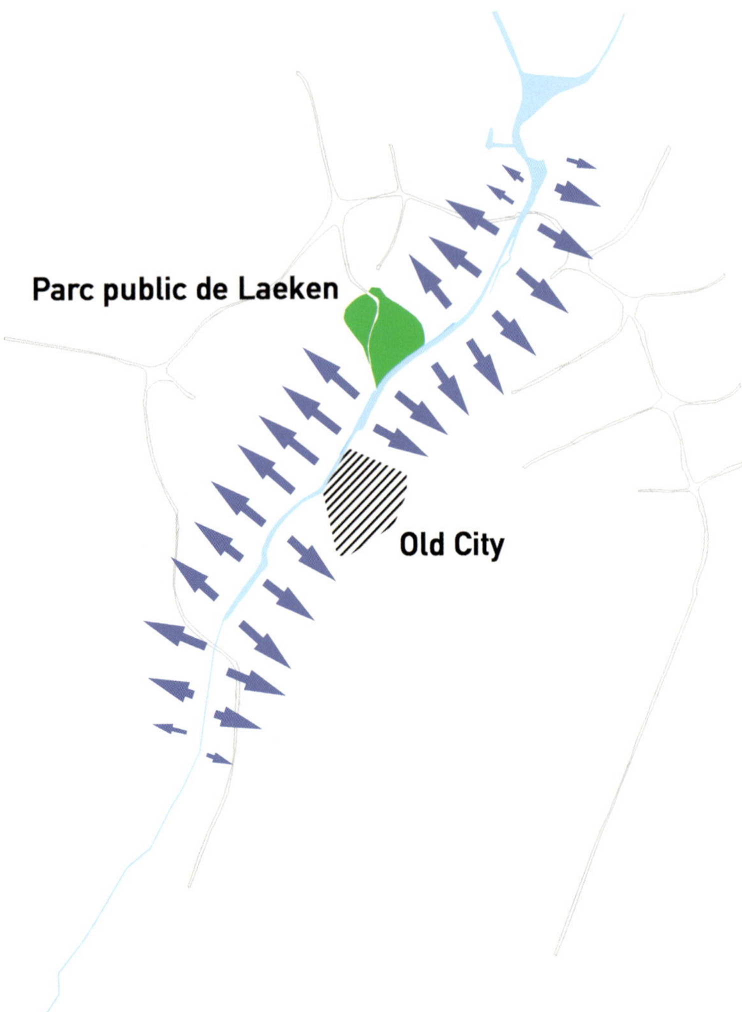

The capital of Europe needs to be a precursor in applying European directives. One of the prerogatives resulting from the "White Paper: European transport policy for 2010: Time to decide" requires promotion of inland waterway transport within the European Union. The current vision of inland waterway transport [ecologically sound, viable, safe, economical, and helping to reduce traffic on the roads] makes it the means of transport of the future.

/

At present, Brussels is considered as a bottleneck in the waterways system. The canal is only 10.5 metres wide at the point where the barges pass under two bridges: that of the Porte de Ninove and that of the Anderlecht lock. The width of the navigable channel between Cureghem and Sainctelette is an average of 20 metres. That has not prevented traffic so far, since all of the Brussels waterway is effectively accessible to RHK barges. This is proven by the growth in traffic over recent years [see table below, in which the growth in domestic traffic concerns, in particular, the waterways to the south of Brussels - the Biestebroek basin - while transit traffic has to pass through the southern part of the canal].

/

/

/

In million of tons

	1998	2003	Change
Domestic traffic	3.4	3.8	+13%
Transit traffic	1.5	2.7	+76%
Total	5.0	6.6	+32%

/

On the same stretch of a few kilometres, the radius of curvature of the path of the canal in the scattered urban fabric of Brussels poses a problem. Even if it is possible to pass through, the high number of tricky manoeuvres necessary to cross Brussels makes it a traffic black spot.

/

Without additional investment, the waterway in Brussels is capable of attracting goods traffic of up to three times the current level. The long term problem of the waterways in Brussels is actually the height of the bridges: container traffic along waterways is growing constantly, and the European standard for this form of transport is 7 metres of headroom, to allow the passage of barges with two tiers of containers. In the long term, it will be essential to adapt the bridges on the southern crossing of Brussels (and the Walloon region is demanding this vigorously), but it will require architectural creativity to connect the bridges to the adjacent roads.

/

Comments about the table of polluting emissions

/

When we compare the costs of modes of transport, we usually refer to external costs (i.e. those taken into account by society, and which also include the cost of noise, accidents, etc.). The figures for external costs per mode of transport used by the European Commission in the White Paper are as follows:

/
/
/

Relative external costs per mode of transport

/
/

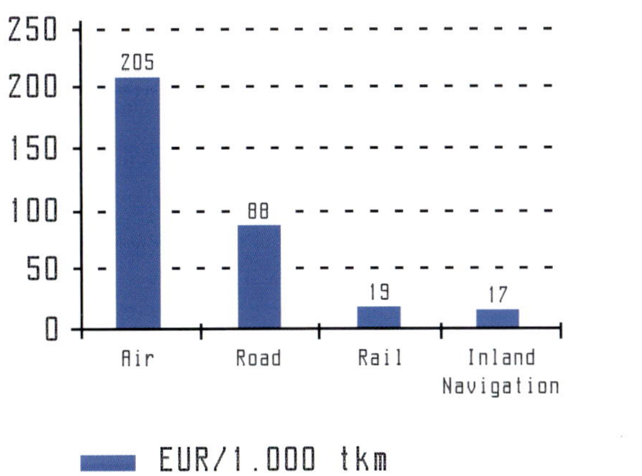

source: « External Costs of Transport », INFRAS/IWW, March 2000

/
/
/

The possible widening of the canal (and/or the building of a second canal) would enable the expectations described above to be met. This proposal also offers an opportunity for the ribbon development of a city which, until now, has grown concentrically.

The canal and the corridors that it generates can serve as a driving force for a new urban enterprise working according to a different logic: new prospects for a city regenerated by a waterway redevelopment project. It is dotted with high-potential sites such as the Royal Park of Laeken which would become open to the public, the future high-speed train station in Schaerbeek, the Tour et Taxis site, the Pentagon and its preserved memories, the Petite-Ile site in the middle of the tracks at the Gare du Midi and many others. Like a backbone to the new city, along which all the city functions could be established (leisure, culture, urban agriculture, housing, offices), the canal would become a place for living, enjoyment, nature, density, movement. A widening would inevitably generate a reduction in the number of crossings between the banks, a phenomenon which would increase the importance and the density of the crossings that are retained, and future crossings would be envisaged with multifunctional habitable bridges.

/

In addition, this new layout should allow a new artery of mobility with vaporetti and taxi boats. Greenery would also have a place with entire islets whose decaying buildings have no further use in the 21st century being converted into public parks with beaches of fine sand. One of the basic conditions for the viability of our future cities.

/

Through this project, Brussels will finally become aware of the water which crosses it and exploit its potential to create a city looking resolutely towards the future.

/
/
/
/
/
/
/

Extract taken from the map of
Europe's waterways

København
Kaliningrad
Vilnius
Minsk
Wolgast
Peene
Anklam
Szczecin
Oder
Odra
Velten
Rathenow
Berlin
Brandenburg
Königs Wusterhausen
Frankfurt a/d Oder
Eisenhüttenstadt
Noteć
Warta
Poznań
Wisla
Warszawa
Pripyat
Desna
Kijev
Bug
Dessau
Elbe
Halle
Riesa
Dresden
Wroclaw
Lovosice
Děčín-Loubí
Usti nad Labem
Mělník
Praha
Labe
Kolín
Gliwice
Dnestr
Erlangen
Fürth
Nürnberg
Regensburg
Straubing
Passau
Donau
Linz
Krems
Wien
Enns/ Ennsdorf
Bratislava
Váh
Komárno
Gyor Gonyü
Duna
Budapest
Tisza
Dunaújváros
Körös
Baja
Kišin'ov
Prut
Galati
Brăila
Tulcea
Dunărea
Carnavoda
Constanza
Ljubljana
Zagreb
Drava
Osijek
Dunav
Dunav-Tisza Kan.
Novi Sad
Begej
Vukovar
Sava
Pancevo
Beograd
Smederevo
Orsova
Drobeta-Turnu-Severin
Calafat
Vidin
Lom
Corabia
Dunava
Giurgiu
Rousse
Zimnicea
Oltenita
Călărasi
București
Venezia
Mantova
Sarajevo
Sofija
Skopje
Tiranë
Roma

Polluting Emissions Comparisons

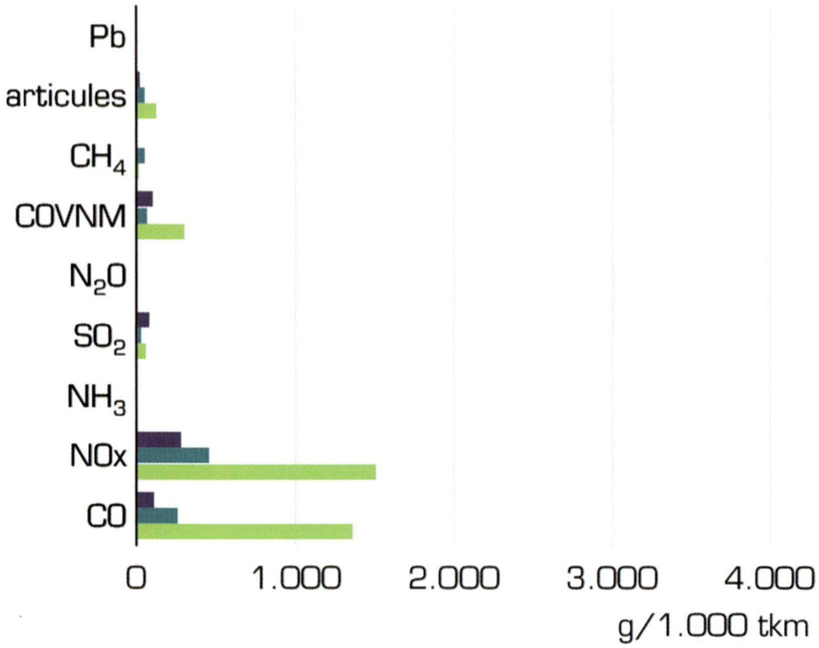

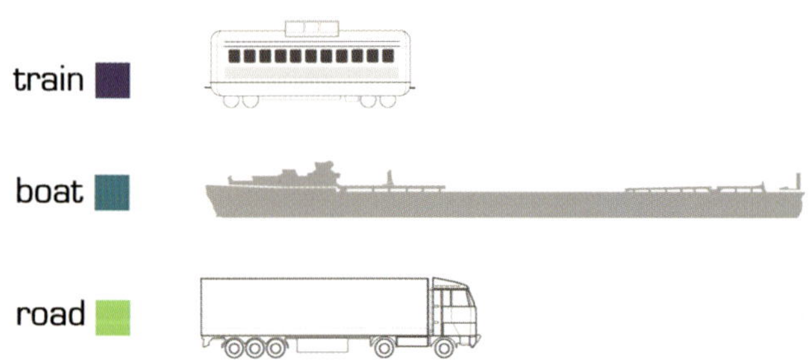

Energy Efficiency Comparisons

5 litres of fuel are necessary to move
1 tonne of goods over a distance of

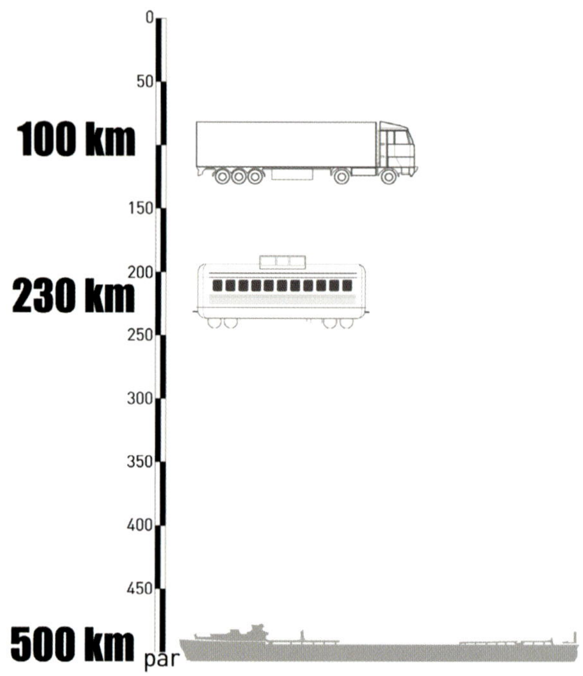

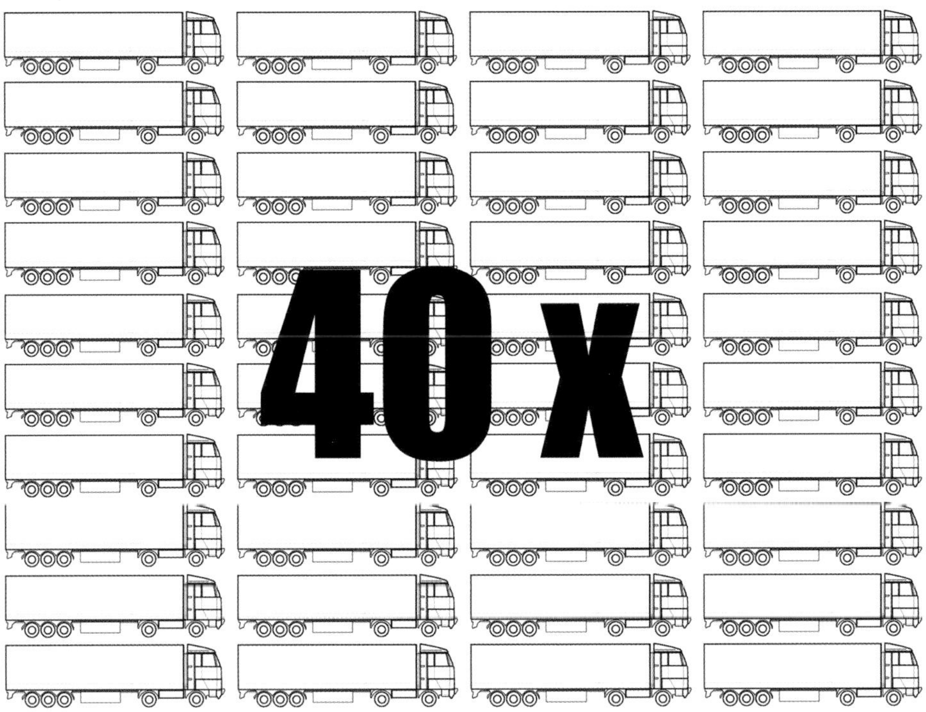

Poids lourds 34 Tonnes
de 18,75 m x 2,5 m

/
/
/
/
/
/
/
/

=

Peniche Automoteur 1409 Tonnes
(jauge moyenne)
type Rhein-Herne-Kanal [RHK]
de 80 m x 9,5 m

/
/

Sources : Port of Brussels

Petit Château

/
/
/

2000
/
/
/
/

2020
extend

2040
add greenery

Pont de Cureghem

/
/
/

2000
/
/
/
/
/

2020
split

2040
add greenery

/
/
/
/

2060
cross

2080
expand

2200
transform

/
/
/
/
/
/
/
/

2060
make denser

2080
enjoy

2200
come to life again

/
/
/

Aerial views: Port of Brussels - Airprint
Architects and graphic designers: Laurent Troost, Vehap Shehi

Porte de Ninove

/
/
2000
/
/
/
/
/
/
/
/
/
/
/
/
/
/
/
/
/
2020
/
/
/
/
/
/
/
/
/
/
/
/
/
/
/
/
/
/
/
/
/

2040
/
/
/
/
/
/
/
/
/
/
/
/
/
/
/
/
/
/
/
/
/
/
/

2050
/
/
/
/
/
/
/
/
/
/
/
/
/
/
/
/
/
/
/
/
/
/
/

XDGA
Xaveer De Geyter Architecten
/

Contributors: Xaveer De Geyter, Jeroen Beerten, El Hadi Jazairy
Mock-up photos: Hans Werlemann
Client: EuroStation
/
/
/
/
/
/
/
/
/
/
/
/
/
/

The scope of the study in its broader context: Brussels, Antwerp, Ghent.

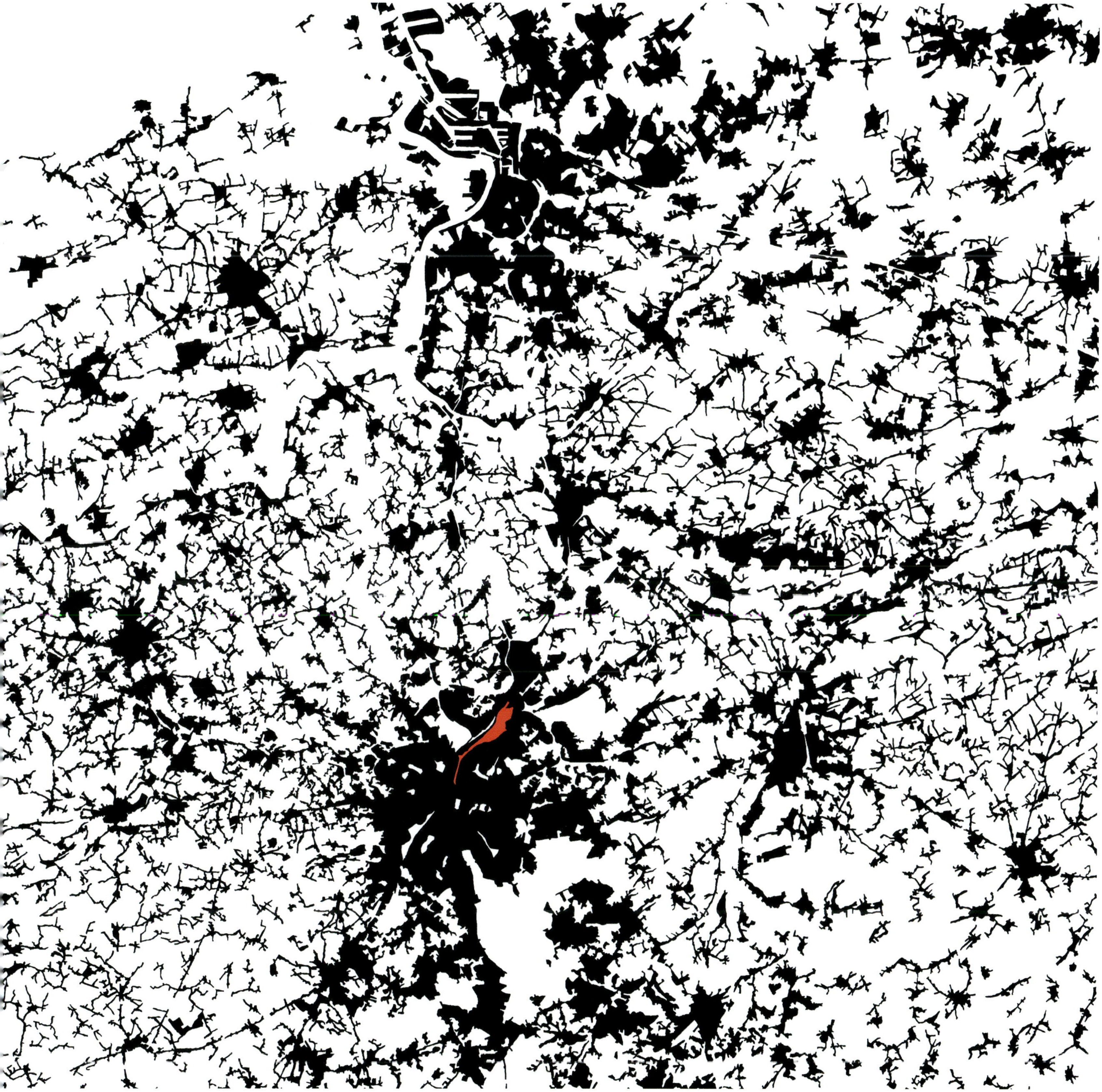

Brussels: redevelopment model for the canal zone - north zone

/
/
/
/
/
/
/
/

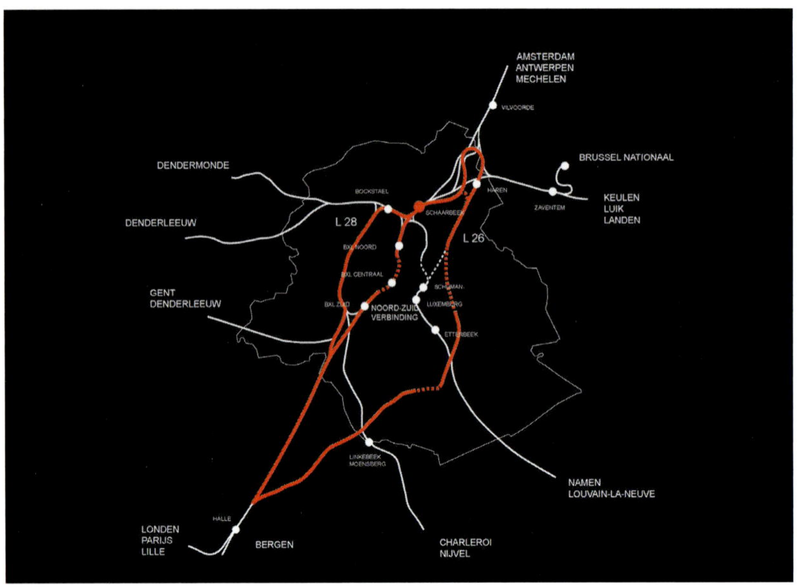

Location of the 2nd HST terminal in Schaarbeek:
Central junction of the North-South links in Brussels.

/
/
/
/
/
/
/
/
/
/
/
/
/

Evolution of Brussels:
Expansion of the urban fabric through the ages in relation with the green spaces in the city.

1. 1357: First city walls.
2. 1777: Second city walls.
3. 1858
4. 1880
5. 1930
6. 1975
7. 1990
8. 2002

/
/
/
/

Belgian railways came up with the idea of building a second HST terminal to the north of Brussels on a site, at a site where the three existing north-south tracks that cross Brussels can come together. This reflection looks into how this idea would fit into the broader.
/
The focal point is the current local station of Schaarbeek and the expansive area that extends to the north which is used as a shunting and train assembly infrastructure. This area will gradually become vacant and is obviously part of this study.
/
The first step in this exercise consists of demarcating the scope. Besides the shunting station and the site for the new station, the entire zone between the canal and the maze of tracks that lead to the Nord station has been identified as a site with a certain amount of coherence: it coincides topographically with the valley of the river Senne and is dominated by transportation infrastructures and related facilities. However, from a development point of view, the area is still in a period of transition, isolated from the surrounding city and many features are in dire need of urbanistic redirecting. The proposal therefore covers the entire transitional zone between the inner-city and city outskirts, over a distance of some ten kilometres, including the unfinished and mono-functional Northern district.
/
Most of the area is vacant and undeveloped: railway tracks, asphalt, warehouses, decorative green areas between high-rise flats and fragments of nature reserve form a potential void which could be used to structure the entire northern zone of Brussels. The proposal consists of exploiting this prime quality: the open spots are to be merged gradually into a continuous space using a contemporary green concept and this area can then be sharply demarcated by a series of dense areas that each link to the surrounding suburban fragments outside the zone. The new park landscape, on the scale of the entire agglomeration of Brussels, can function as a magnet for new developments.

The green area consists of 'wild' nature on the side of the inner-city which gradually transforms into a refined park along the suburbs.
The soil of large parts of the open space is to be decontaminated with particular plants. The rolling green landscape mingles with the transportation infrastructure and the large-scale facilities: the Van Praet bridge, the new HST station, remaining railway tracks and a new Olympic stadium. In the long term, existing green zones will be annexed: the Jardin Botanique in the centre, the Drie Fonteinen Park in Vilvoorde. The scale and impact of the project are similar to those of the Terkamerenbos/Bois de la Cambre on the south side of Brussels.
/
The large open space is the main element of the proposal, however, the new building development on the various 'islands' is also quite substantial: in total, 6,000,000 m^2 of new buildings. Building on these islands will be as dense as possible with a minimum of open space and a maximum of mixed programme. For example, the North quarter will be mainly built up with high-rise housing, including the green area of the central Avenue Albert II; the bases of the existing office buildings are to be reused for shops and restaurants while the sides facing the park are to be sealed off.
/
The metamorphosis shall occur gradually. The islands between the different railway tracks in the shunting station will become available one by one. Changes which are currently in progress, such as the moving of industrial activity, are to be co-ordinated by means of a long-term planning process.
/
/
/
/
/
/
/
/
/
/

/
The canal and the Northern district
/
/

/
The morning market
/
/
/
/
/
/
/
/
/
/
/
/
/
/
/
/
/
/
/

/
Schaarbeek Station
/
/

/
Haren
/
/
/
/
/
/
/
/
/
/
/
/
/
/
/
/
/
/
/

/
Overview of project from inner city
/
/
/
/
/
/
/
/
/
/
/
/
/
/
/
/
/
/

/
/
/
/
/
/
/
/
/
/
/
/
/
/
/
/
/
/
/
/
/
/
/
/
/
/
/
/
/
/
/
/
/
/
/
/
/
/
/
/
/
/
/
/
/
/
/
/
/

The Nord station.
Existing spatial fragments, large infrastructures.
/
- NATO
- Canal
- Railway infrastructure
- Industry
- Open space
- Park
- Structure of allotments
- Suburban tissue
- Urban tissue

Possible development scenario.
To achieve the aim, the proposal does not require a radical tabula rasa approach but a gradual process that directs the changes which are currently in progress. The vacancy of buildings and plots, the moving of old industry, the delocalisation of companies and industrial activities near the ring road and the possible implantation of a HST station make it possible to organise a new process.
The zone between the canal and the railway embankment from the pentagon to the outer ring road can be transformed gradually and in a relatively short period of time into a metropolitan park that will attract many new developments.

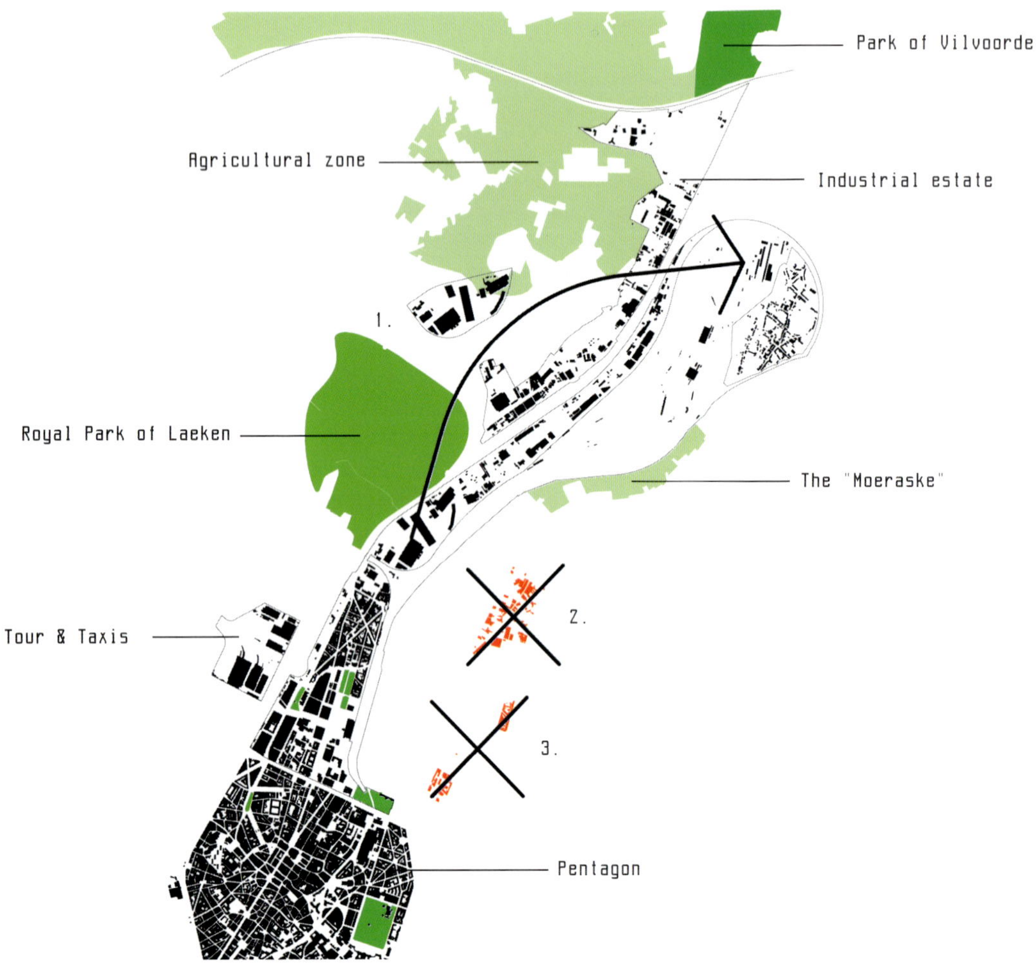

Actions to be taken:
2002: Existing situation.

1. Morning market: delocalisation to "Schaerbeek Formation"
2. Centre of Brussels: phase out industrial activities.
3. Northern district: demolition run-down buildings.

2010: Planned date for opening of 2nd HST station.

4. Schaerbeek Station: move port activities further north.
5. New HST station on site of Schaerbeek Station:
Link to major infrastructures is partially underground: metro network, ring roads, E-19 motorway, Avenue Lambermont.
6. Premises of Morning market: Construction of first part of metropolitan park.
7. HST station: initial developments.
8. Northern district, Old Schaerbeek: densifying existing islands:
9. Turn & Taxis: redevelopment of the site.

/
/
/
/
/
/
/
/
/
/
/
/

/
2025: Intermediate phase

10. "Schaerbeek Formation": Optimisation of railway activities generates extra space:
11. Industrial estate to be redeveloped as green campus.
12, 13, 14, 15, 16, 17. Further relocation, densification and new developments.
18. Entire site: A continuous park from the outer ring road towards the Pentagon
/
/
/
/

/
/
/
/
/
/
/
/
/
/
/
/

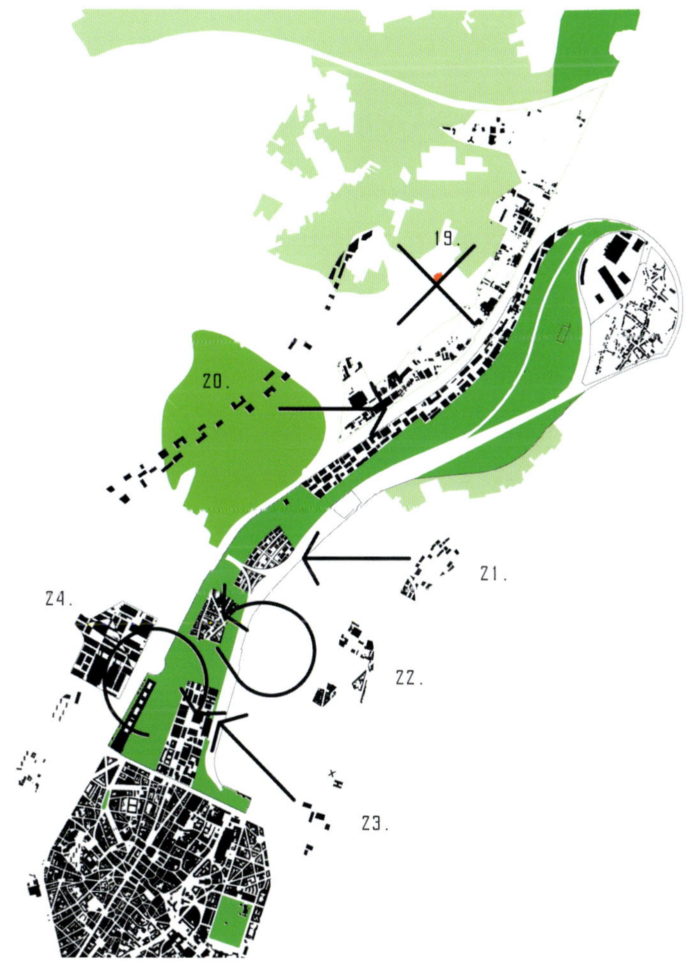

/
2050: Completion of the project:

19. Delocalisation of incinerator at end of life.
20, 21, 22, 23, and 24. Further densification inside the demarcated zones.
/
/
/
/
/
/
/
/
/

Programme :

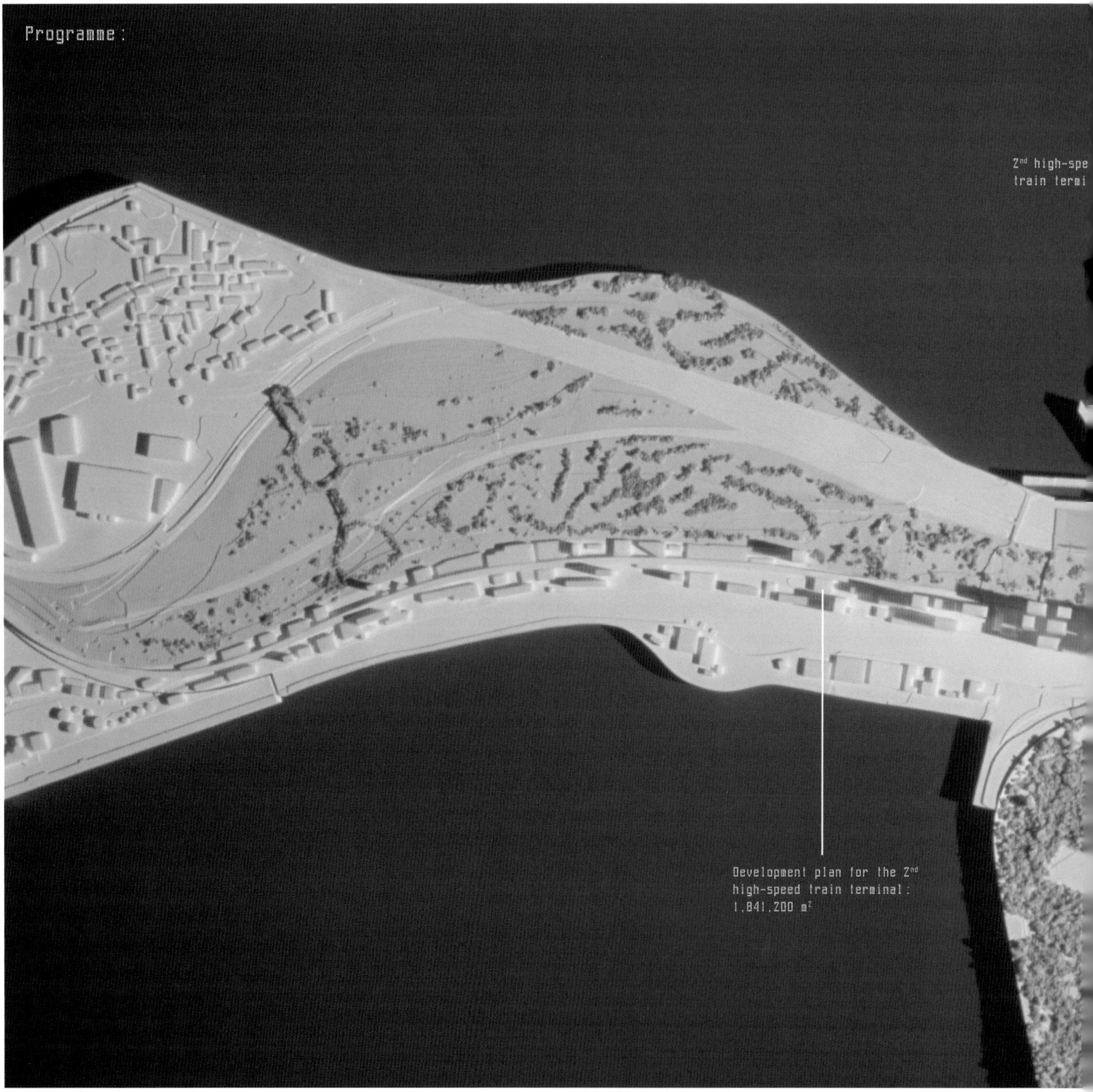
2nd high-spe
train termi
Development plan for the 2nd
high-speed train terminal:
1,841,200 m²

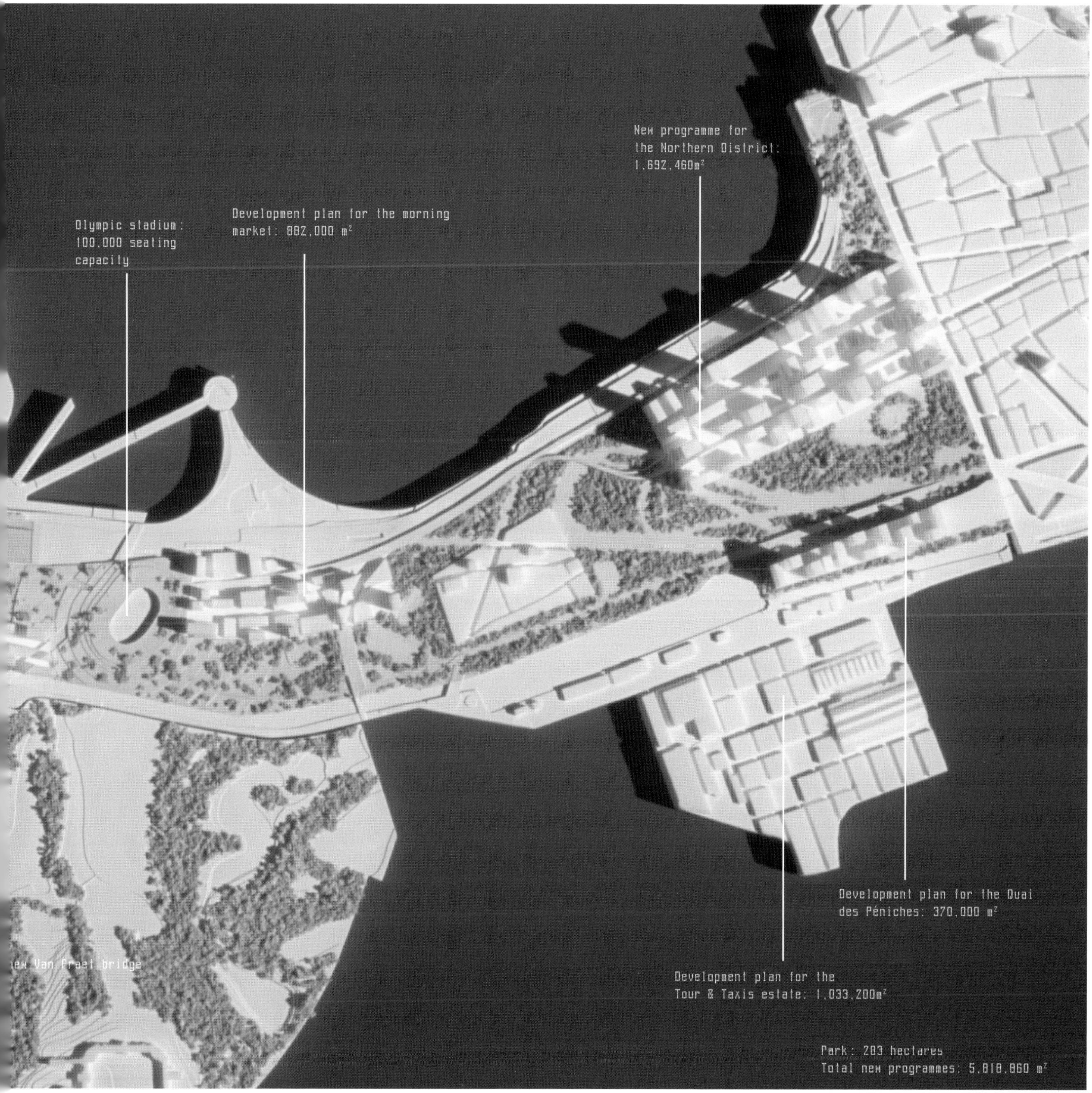
New programme for
the Northern District:
1,692,460m²
Development plan for the morning
market: 882,000 m²
Olympic stadium:
100,000 seating
capacity
Development plan for the Quai
des Péniches: 370,000 m²
new Van Praet bridge
Development plan for the
Tour & Taxis estate: 1,033,200m²
Park: 283 hectares
Total new programmes: 5,818,860 m²

/
/
/
/

Northern District: existing situation
/
/

Northern District: higher density versus 'wild' nature
/
/

Northern District: densification, reduction of public space, demarcation by park
/
/
/

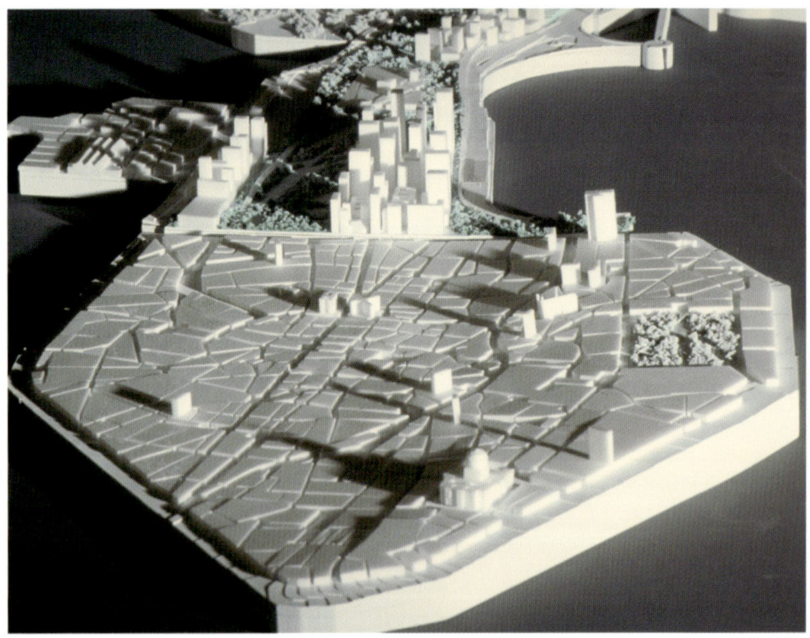

Northern District: link to the inner-city
/
/
/
/

/
/
/
/
/
/
/
/

Old Schaarbeek: perspective in the park as an extension of the existing streets
/

Old Schaarbeek: new context
/
/
/
/
/
/
/

/
/
/
/
/
/
/
/

Surroundings of HST station: artificial landscape above new infrastructure
/
/

Surroundings of HST station: protecting the perspective from Royal Palace
/
/
/
/
/
/
/

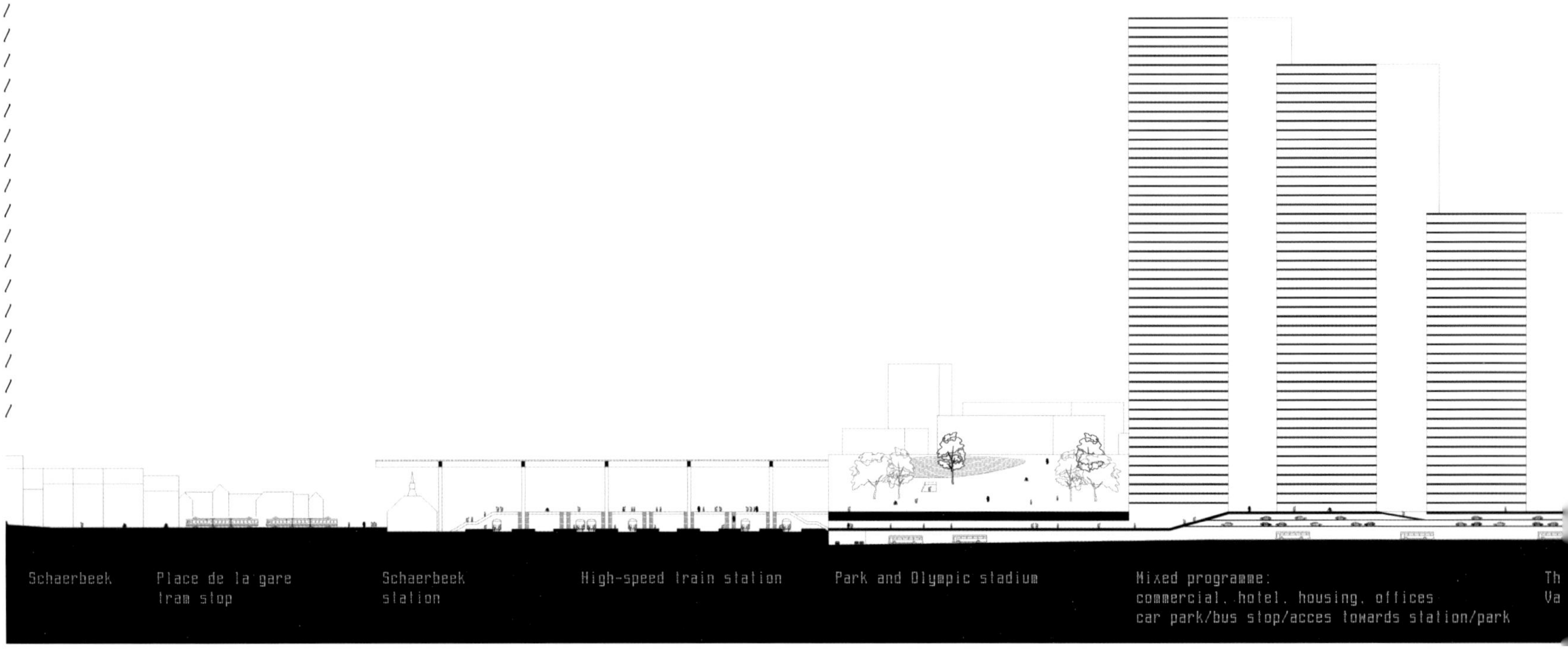

Section through HST station

The project in no way involves the SNCB, which, furthermore,
does not have any plans at present to develop these premises.

/
/
/
/
/
/
/
/
/

/
/
/
/
/
/
/
/
/
/
/
/
/
/
/
/
/
/

"Schaerbeek Formation": French garden links islands across railway tracks

/
/
/
/
/
/
/
/
/
/
/

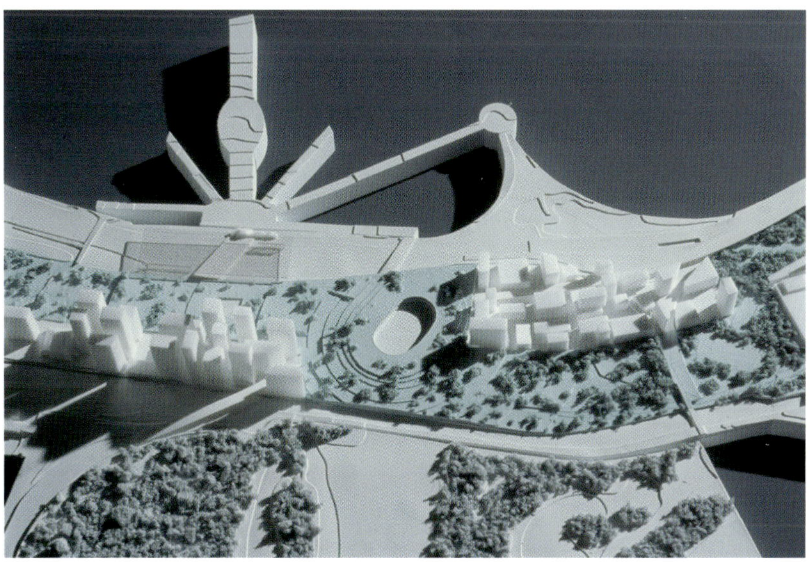

Surroundings of HST station: submerged Olympic stadium

/
/

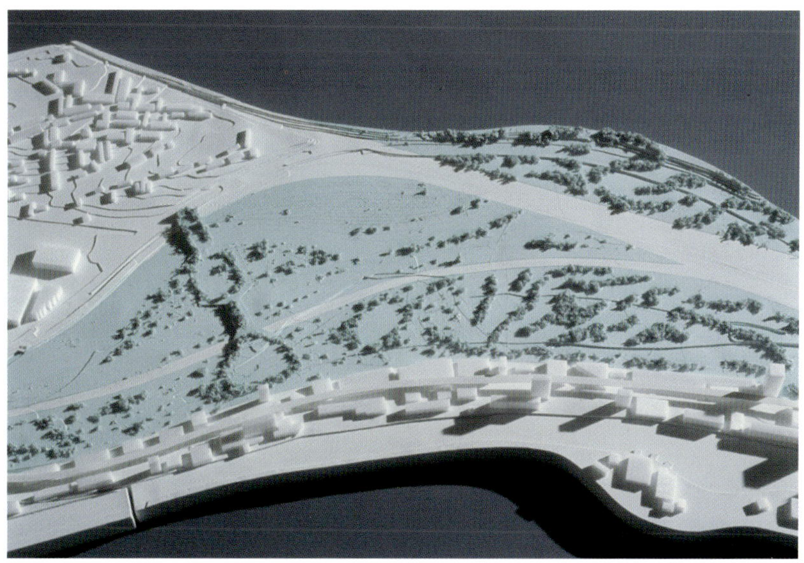

"Schaerbeek Formation": French garden links islands across railway tracks

/
/

WEST 8

/

Architects:
Adriaan Geuze, Edzo Bindels, Maarten van de Voorde
Designers:
Lennart van Dijk, Marco van der Pluym, Riëtte Bosch
Client: EuroStation

/
/
/
/
/
/
/
/
/
/
/

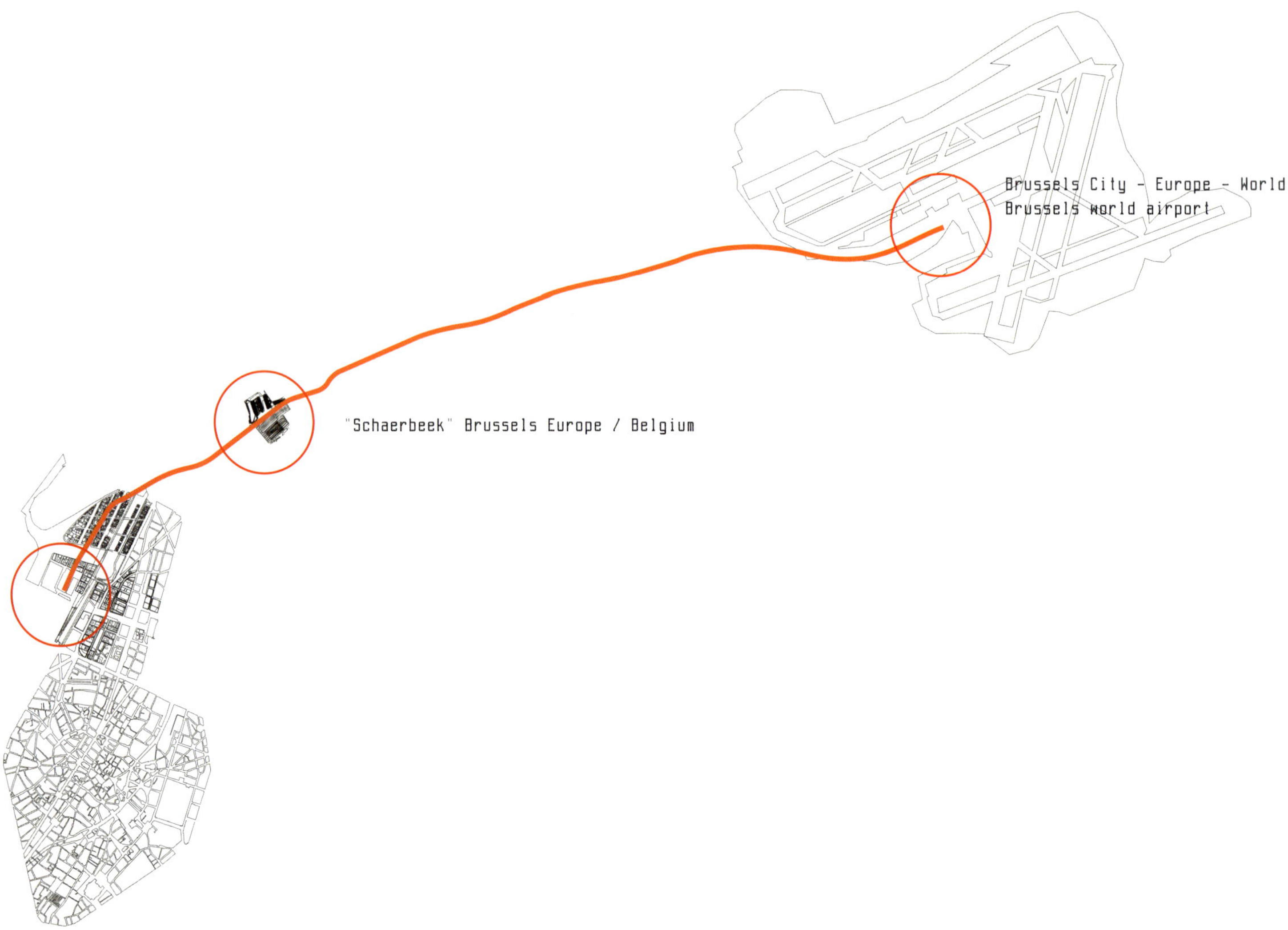

High-speed train station Brussels-Schaerbeek Town-planning vision

/

/

West 8 urban designers and landscape architects put forward their project within the specific framework of the overall problems of the Brussels-Capital Region. Their thinking is based on the fact that Brussels is perceived as a fragmented city in which there is little relationship between business zones and residential zones. The buildings are inward-looking. West 8 poses the fundamental question "is large-scale development around the Terminal desirable?" The demand from the Region for new urban developments is limited. The time needed for the construction of the Northern district proves that an urban region with a million inhabitants cannot undertake development works of such magnitude without encountering some difficulties. Because of this, new large-scale developments will not only repeat the fragmentation phenomenon but also accentuate the problem of unoccupied buildings in other parts of Brussels and in other regional towns in Belgium. This is why the designers have opted for urban development around existing stations and decided to bolster existing districts.

/

Two stations are under consideration in this project: Tour et Taxis and Schaerbeek Station. They are considered to be "bi-polar" in the urban structure. Schaerbeek Station must function above all as a logistics centre. The new Terminal would provide a transfer between the different traffic flows and be linked directly to the regional road system without extra access roads to the city centre. The project does not envisage particular changes to the existing road system but the railway links are seriously affected. Tour et Taxis Station must firstly be linked efficiently to the railway network. To achieve this, there

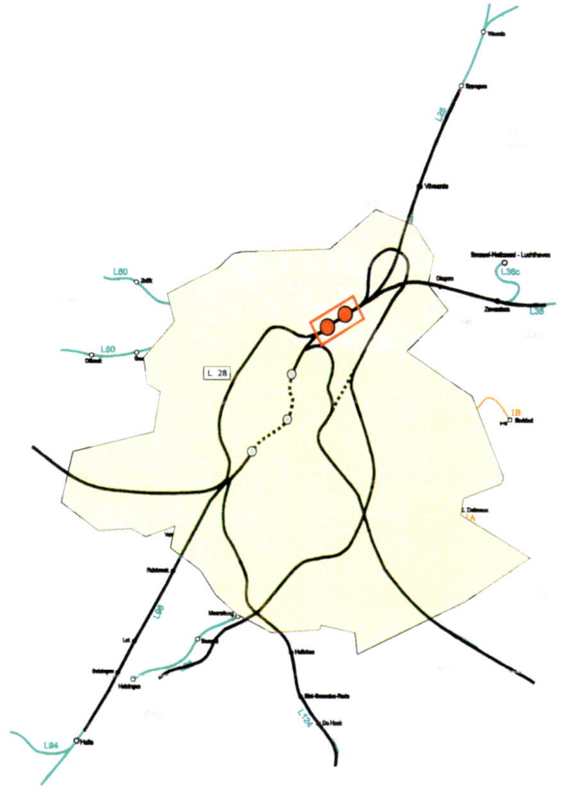

The aorta of the Belgian railways forms the basis for location of new station

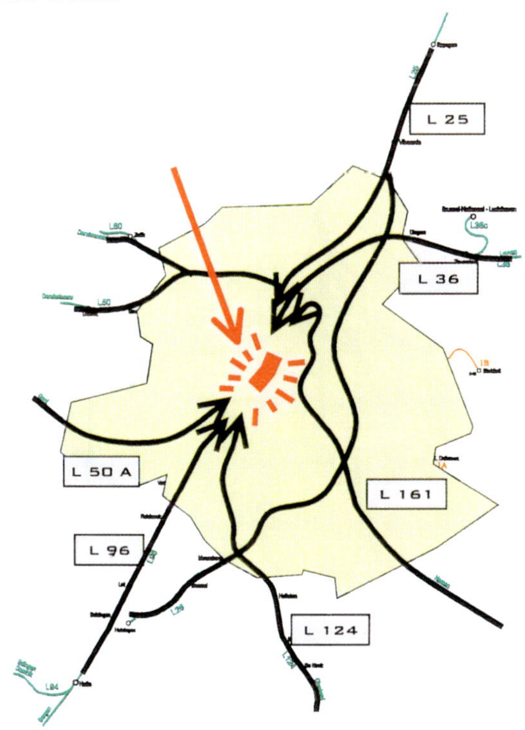

Capacity problems at Midi station and underground north-south junction

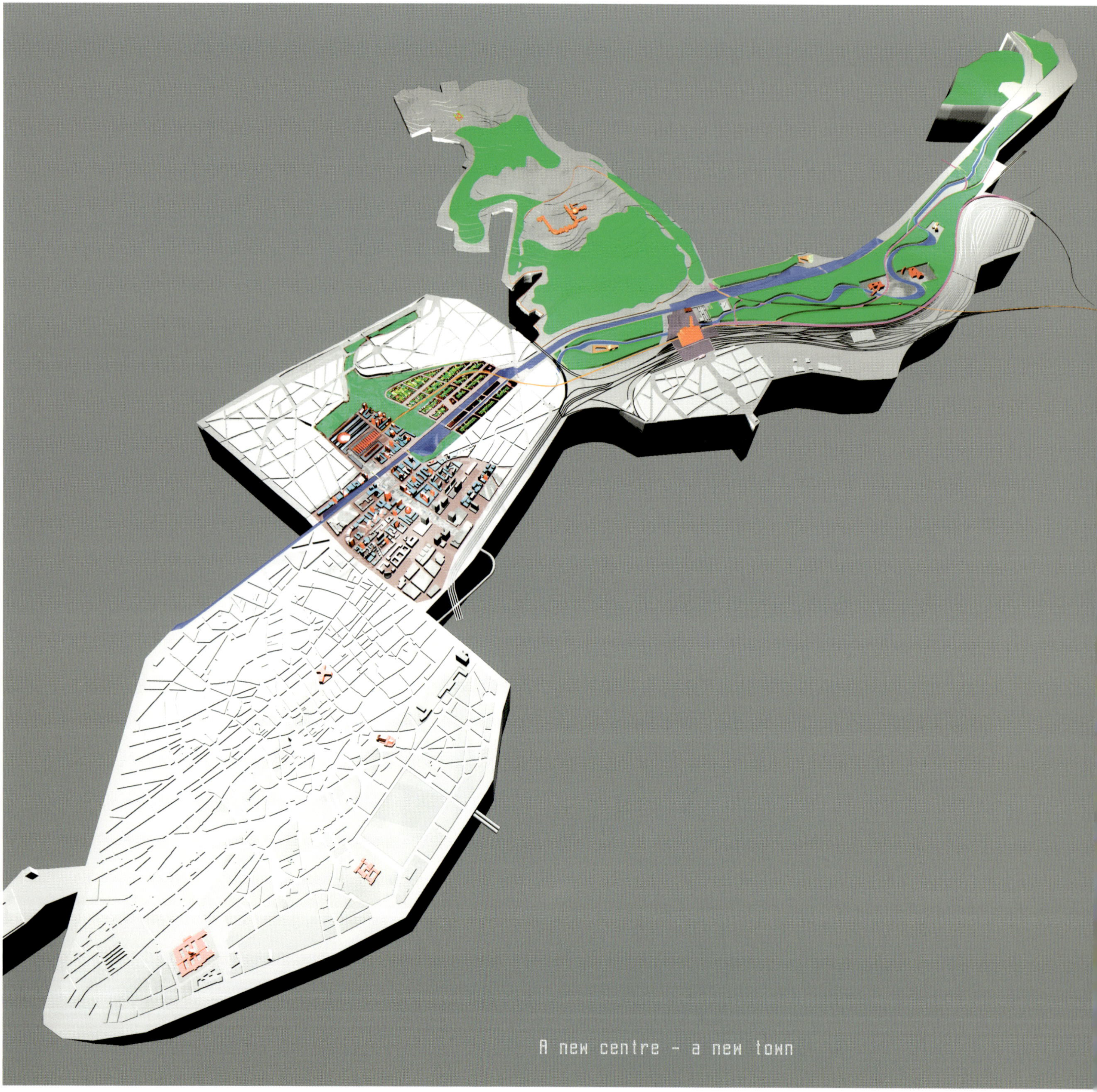

A new centre - a new town

are two alternative solutions: either developing the existing link [line 28] - the station then becomes "end-of-line" causing loss of time for connections - or building a new direct line from Midi Station. These railway links are not included in the proposal. The choice of Schaerbeek Station is based on the question of the capacity of the North-South link. From a logistical point of view, Schaerbeek-Station is the best place to link international, national and regional transport systems. From a planning viewpoint, West 8 proposes three options to link Tour et Taxis to the railway system. This disused area in the city centre could become the starting point for future development of the Northern district as a business district. To link the new epicentre of development and the Schaerbeek-Station terminal, the planners propose three "light-rail" routes: along line 28, through the Gaucheret district or along the Laeken bridge district. The last option has been accepted for this study. The Tour et Taxis site occupies a key position in the project and offers the possibility of ancillary developments. The main customs hall would become the main concourse of the Terminal. The zone currently vacant to the north of the existing building would be filled with high-rise buildings for activities linked to the Terminal. At the end of the zone, the planners envisage establishing a park with the aforementioned symbolic European titles. To the north, the existing district will be replaced by a residential zone as far as rue Marie-Christine and the Laeken bridge. Schaerbeek-Station will offer only facilities and services for travellers. The rail lines will be doubled because of international traffic. The "people mover" linking Tour et Taxis to the airport would be flanked by a separate building for travellers. Some services for travellers such as shops and an information stand are planned near public transport. An interchange fed by a new road connection from the Ring and the E19 is planned for the HST terminal. The "people mover" and existing public transport routes will ensure transit of travellers to centres of employment or health care facilities.

This project is in line with the objectives of the Brussels-Capital Region as defined in the last Regional Development Plan. It is interesting to note that the development programme for the area near the HST terminal remains open. This goes hand-in-hand with the linking of the project to existing facilities on the Tour et Taxis - North Station - city centre route.

/

/

Text extracted from the book Eurostations by Evert Lagrou and Marc Dubois

/
/
/
/
/
/
/
/
/
/
/
/
/
/

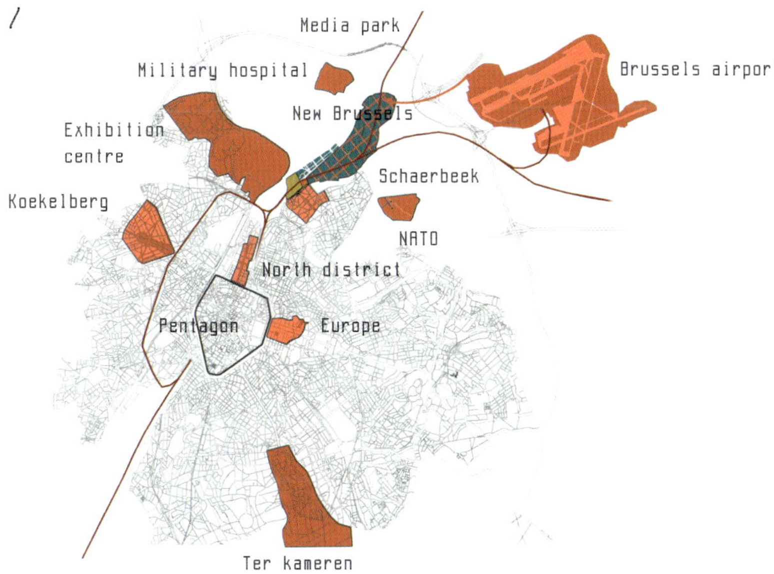

/
/
/

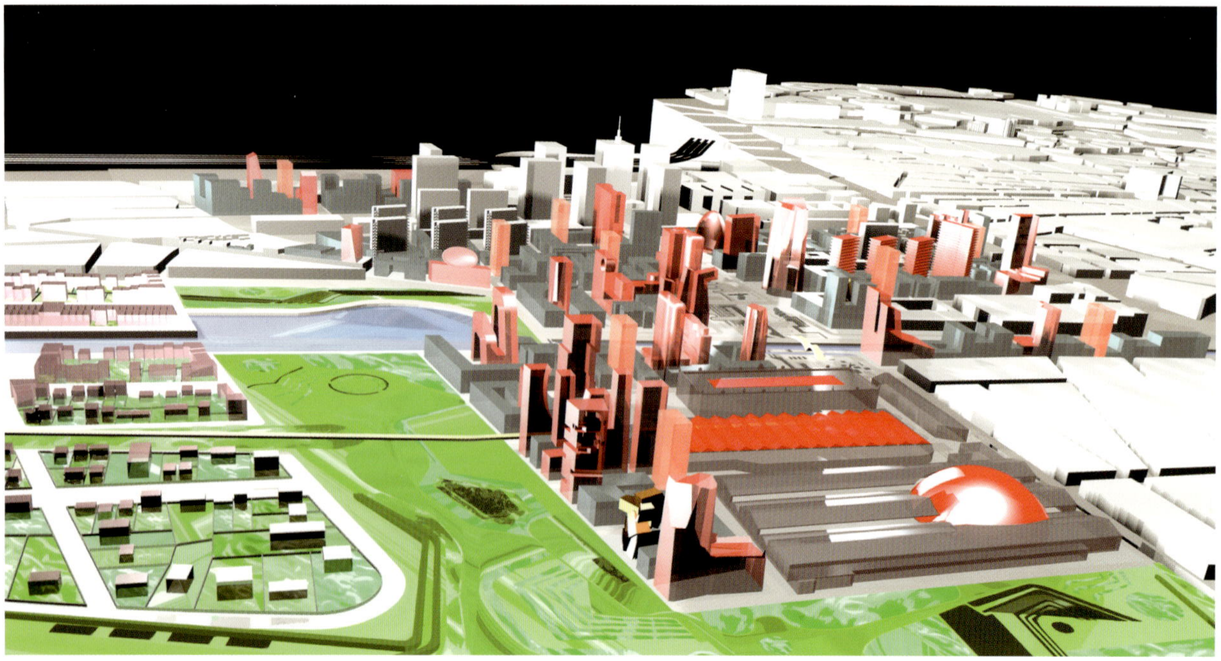

/
/
/
/
/
/
/
/
/
/
/
/
/
/
/
/
/
/
/
/
/
/
/
/
/
The project in no way involves the SNCB, which, furthermore, does not have any plans at present to develop these premises.

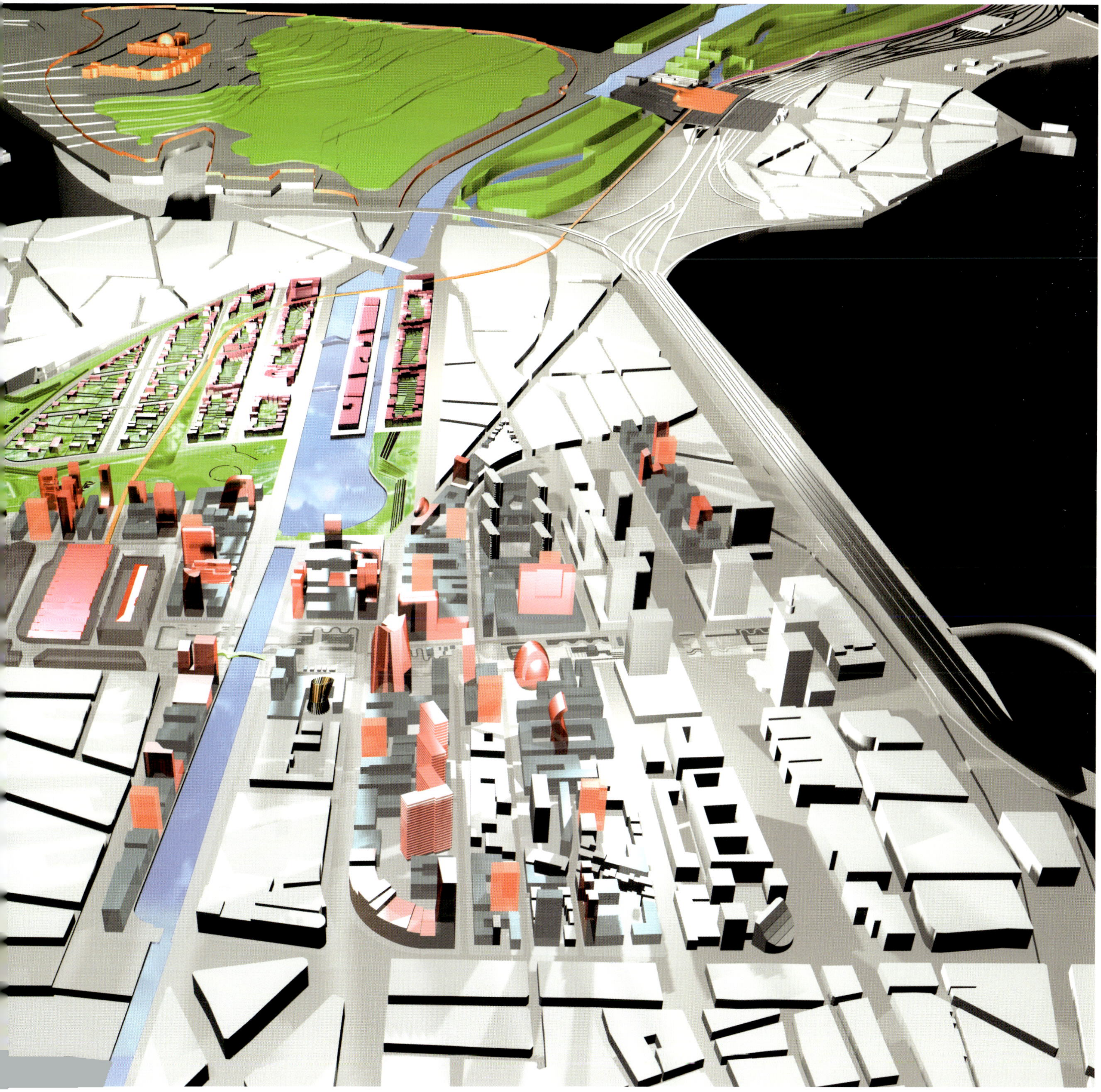

Odile Decq Benoît Cornette

/

/

/

/

/

/

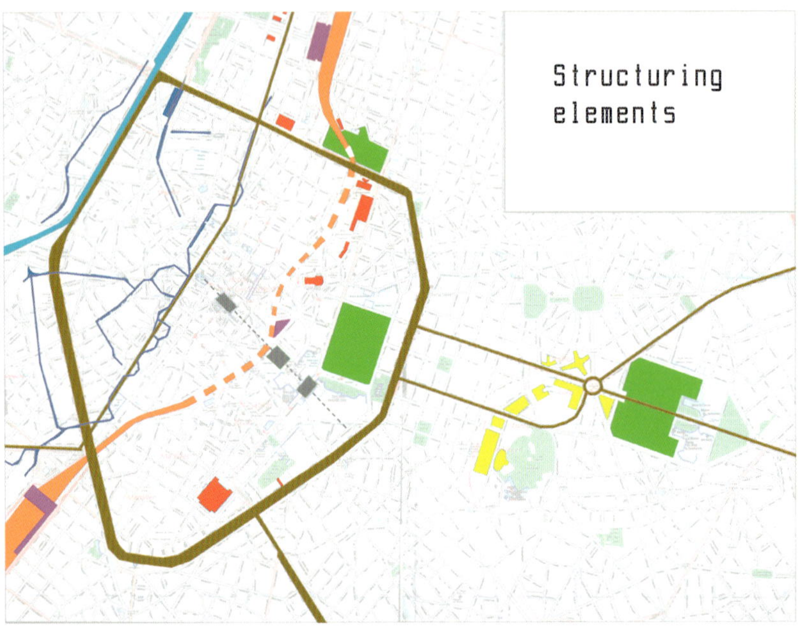

Stations
Railways
Ring and main thoroughfares
Landmarks
European district
Canal
Former layout of the «petite Senne»
Parks
Emblematic sites

Through the looking glass
/
/

What does the future hold in store for the city of Brussels, situated at the crossroads of European cultural and economic exchanges, due to its position at the heart of the interconnections between the other European capitals: 2 hours 20 minutes by train from London, 1 hour 20 minutes from Paris, 2 hours from The Hague and 2 hours 30 minutes from Cologne.
Europeans in transit between these cities pass through, stop and spend time in Brussels.
Of course Brussels is the capital of Belgium, but the regional division of the country has made the city a region in its own right.
At present, Brussels' city centre seems to have been scattered in every direction following the numerous decisions, alterations and restructuring schemes carried out all over the city for more than fifty years; the centre is no longer a point, a place, it is dispersed all over the city.
The interior of the historic Pentagon fills every morning and empties every evening to the rhythm of the journey of commuters living in the outskirts and working in the city centre.
The location of the European institutions is another of the phenomena which has accentuated this process of de-structuring of the historic centre of the city.
/
/
/
/
/
/
/
/
/
/
/
/
/

Instead of attempting desperately to reconstruct a historic image of the city centre it seems possible to us to think of Brussels in another way, and to construct a different identity for the city.
The development of high-speed train lines linking the large cities in Northern Europe has made Brussels its intersection.
Of course that is due to the geographical position of the city but also to the link between the Nord and Midi stations which was built through the city centre in the 20th century, thus avoiding breaking bulk during the crossing of the city, as is the case in other cities.
The passage of the railway line through the centre has left marks which are still visible today in certain places like scars which have not completely healed.
/
The North-South link both reveals the successive historic layers of the city and is the location for a potential return of the city to its centre.
Today, station concourses are increasingly being filled in with many associated businesses, hotels, shops, restaurants, services, etc. ranging from services for transit passengers to the opening of shopping centres in their own right, and even the construction of giant hotel/shopping mall/business centre complexes, a sort of vertical city above the station.
/
Stations are becoming virtually autonomous urban centres which could even lead us to believe that they are the city.
In response to the specific situation of Brussels - autonomous city at the heart of European rail connections but with an unstructured centre - we propose to make a true city centre out of the north-south rail link.
A first stage, which would be temporary, could consist of installing a series of mirrors on the railway line in which the city would be able to gaze at itself or be depicted.
/
In order to "re-construct the centre in the centre", instead of the mirrors, a line of blade

like buildings would be constructed, linked together but discontinuous, connected to the three railway stations onto which they would be grafted: the effect of their intersection becomes the vertical city.
The transition from the city in 2D to the city in 3D will provide the density of relationships and exchanges usually connected with the city centre, on the scale of the city.
The fluctuating structures, a superimposition of tiers and networks instead of the rail network itself, would give the urban development its density without having to suffer the constraints of convergence connected with the development of the city on the surface.
Here, the centre in 3D, connected to the network, will ultimately transform the identity of the city of Brussels and reveal its hub-like dimension in the centre of Europe.
/
/
/

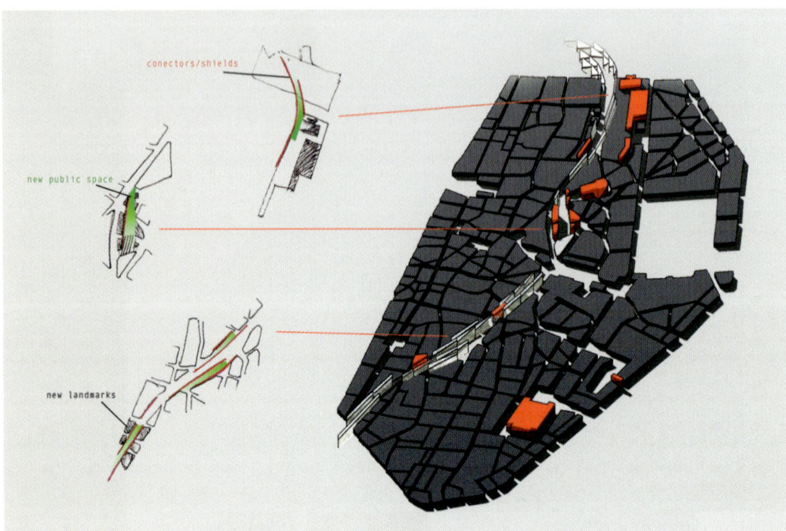

/
/
/
/
/
/
/
/

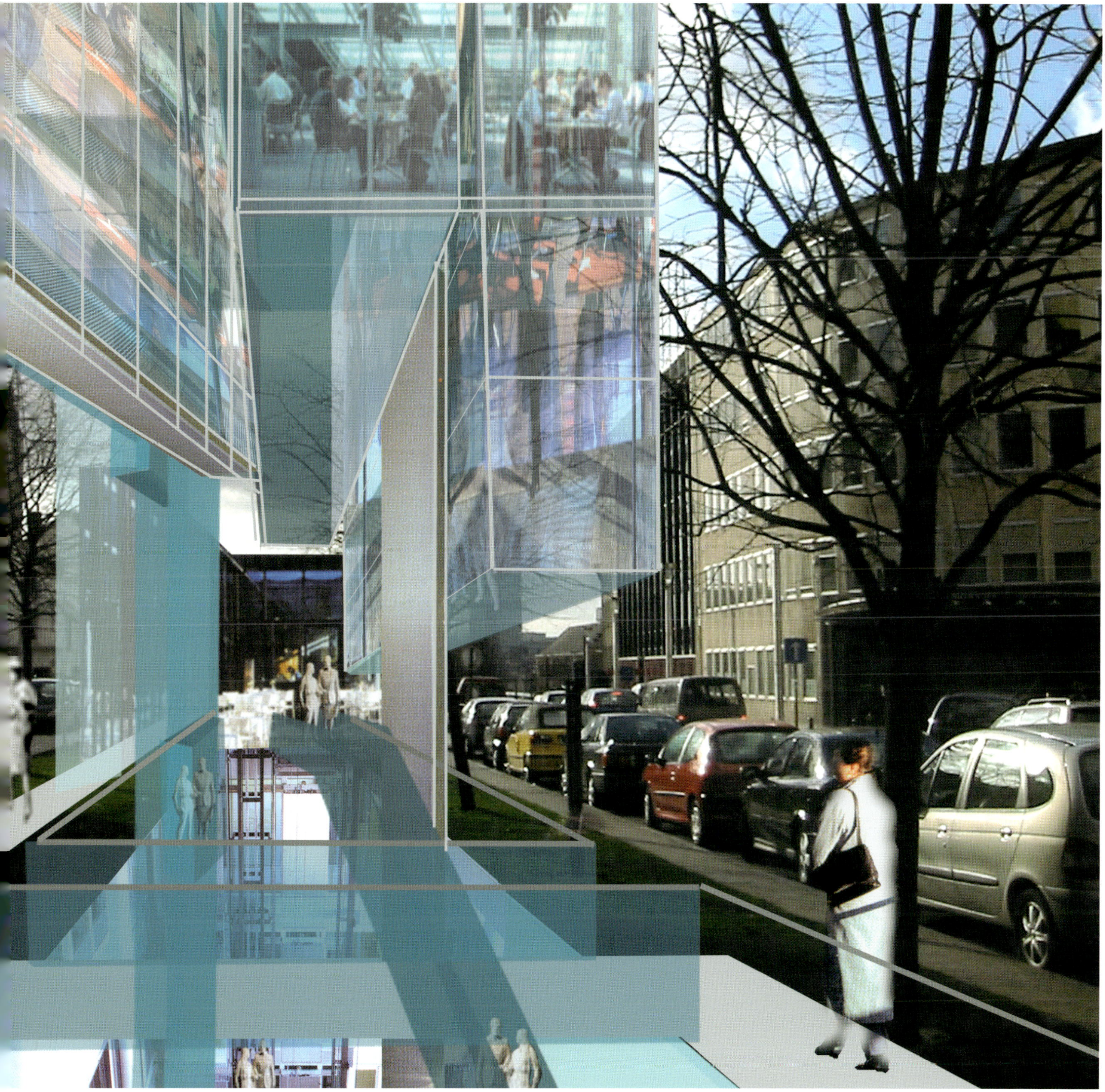

Jones

MVRDV

/

Winy Maas
Jacob van Rijs
Nathalie de Vries

/

With René Marey,
Bart Hollanders, Marnix Vink,
Arthur de Roover, Kersten
Nabielek, Thijs Ultee
and Andreas Pedersen.

/

Client:
EuroStation

/
/
/
/
/
/
/
/
/
/
/

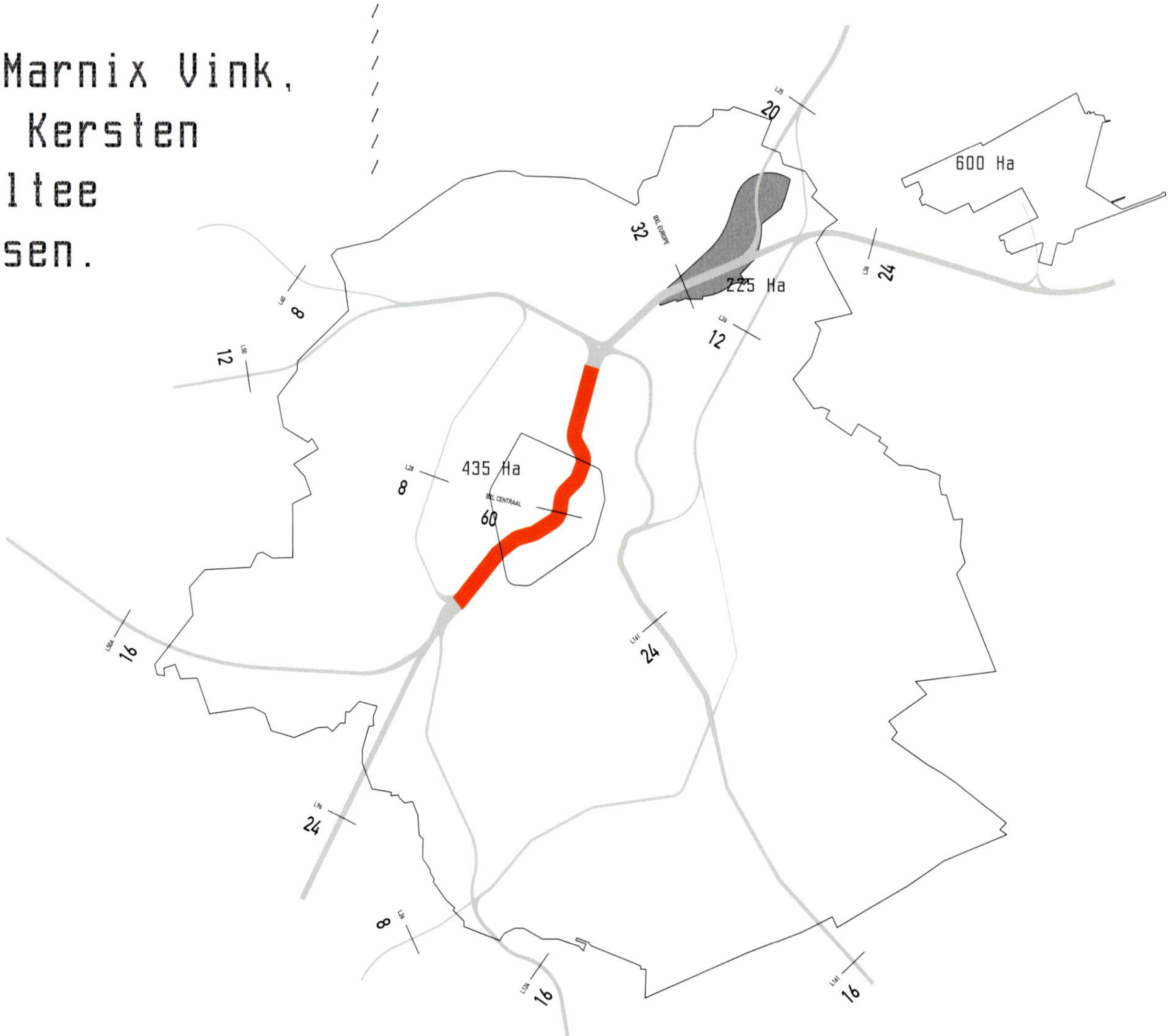

Forecast for 2010 - 2020
Capacity problem along north-south junction

Two stations or just one?

/

In the long term, the arrival of the Thalys and Eurostar train services and the improvement of the link to Zaventem airport will require extensive work on the transport network of Brussels and the city outskirts.
The North-South junction, a six-track link beneath the centre of Brussels plays a leading role. In the near future, its capacity will be insufficient to accommodate high-speed trains as well as national and regional train services plus the underground, underground trams and commuter trains.
By-pass solutions are being proposed to serve all the lines of the two main railway stations in Brussels [Nord and Midi], giving them an unequal capacity. In that case, the problem of tensions between the communities would come into play.

/

Due to the complicated route of these by-pass lines, Brussels North would receive fewer passengers and a new hub would develop around the Schaerbeek-Passengers marshalling yards and station - located in a part of Brussels where urban development and utilisation is not intensive. That station could improve the area. What are the conditions for such an initiative? What should this hub look like?

/

This dynamic could raise questions about whether it makes sense to double the number of stations for the Brussels agglomeration [two separate hubs]. In the run-up to such a decision, the question needs to be asked whether a central station is not preferable to two peripheral stations.

/
/
/
/
/
/
/
/
/

Scenario 1 - 41 km of extra tracks

Scenario 2 - 38 km of extra tracks + tunnels

Starfish

/

First of all, this solution would upgrade the Schaerbeek-Passengers station at the expense of Brussels Nord station, in order to be able to build the by-pass routes to the east and west of the city centre.
To make the new station and its environs a success, and to encourage the use of public transport [including for passengers heading for Zaventem airport], the station would be served by all means of transport, so a multimodal hub would develop. Not only would high-speed trains [to Amsterdam, Paris, London, Cologne] stop there, but also IC [inter city] and IR [inter-regional] services, the commuter trains, the airport link, the underground and overground trams and trams, motorways, local roads, pedestrian and cycle paths.

/

Connections will need to be built with the Brussels Ring motorway as well as with the main service roads. The area will develop into a spaghetti-like junction, which will have a positive impact. With these new transport links, not just for the new station, but also serving the new amenities, this area will become an attractive business zone, which would co-finance the operations required. This part of Brussels would be transformed into an attractive area.

/

At the station, by combining these transport links with functions, amenities will be served directly. These include streets with conference centres, shops, car parks, a university, European facilities and government offices, each connection having its own character.

/

The station could probably be the embodiment of this concentration. A branching and divergent infrastructure which generates such amenities and incorporates them into a robust built-up complex. The result is like a star-shaped "network building" above the railway lines, connecting the platforms and the islands between the tracks, allowing the roof to function as a public space. This would create an urban space that could be used as an event location, the place de l'Etoile of Brussels. A podium for Europe, offering panoramic views over Brussels. The tentacles would link the site to the surrounding area and set the building and the public space in context.

/

The building of the roof, the floor and the walls in steel grid forming a tubular construction, would allow large suspended spans, avoiding columns between the tracks, and simplifying the building. Where the tubes are wider, patios would be laid out, contributing like "suspended loops" to the rigidity of the construction system. Like a giant starfish, the building would hover over the valley holding the tracks and platforms. The steel spider's web would make any configuration possible, and by changing the shape of this tissue, the skin of the star, infinite variations would be possible. Passages would alternate with domes, giant cave areas, sheltered valleys and narrow passages. Deformations of the floor would create impressive domes above the platforms, creating a station concourse. The patios would allow sufficient light to penetrate the station.

/

The curved roof would introduce a new hill to Brussels, from which panoramic views of Brussels would be possible.

/
/
/
/
/
/
/
/
/
/
/
/

Building the star using a combination of stainless steel and glass will give it a shiny appearance, and at night, illumination will make it a fabulous sight, creating a new icon for Brussels: the crossroads of Europe. The tentacles of the star would be built on sites that may already be developed, but which are currently isolated. They would serve these islands where a choice of amenities could be established. An archipelago of villages would form there. They are the prototype for the transformation of the Senne valley between Nord station and Vilvoorde into a new "Silicon Valley" in Brussels: the Eurovalley.
/
/
/
/

/
/

Total = 634.000 m²
/
Car parks = 125,000 m²
Shopping = 100,000 m²
Kiss and ride short-term parking = 67,000 m²
Services = 35,000 m²
University = 40,000 m²
Conference centre = 30,000 m²
Sports centre = 30,000 m²
Bus station = 28,000 m²
Museum = 10,000 m²
People mover [service] = 11,000 m²
Taxis = 15,000 m²
Exchange platform = 30,000 m²
Interface = 23 000 m²
Intermediate platform = 12 000 m²
/
/
/
/
/
/
/
/
/
/
/
/
/
/
/
/
/
/
/
/
/
/
/
/
/
/
/
/
/
/
/
/

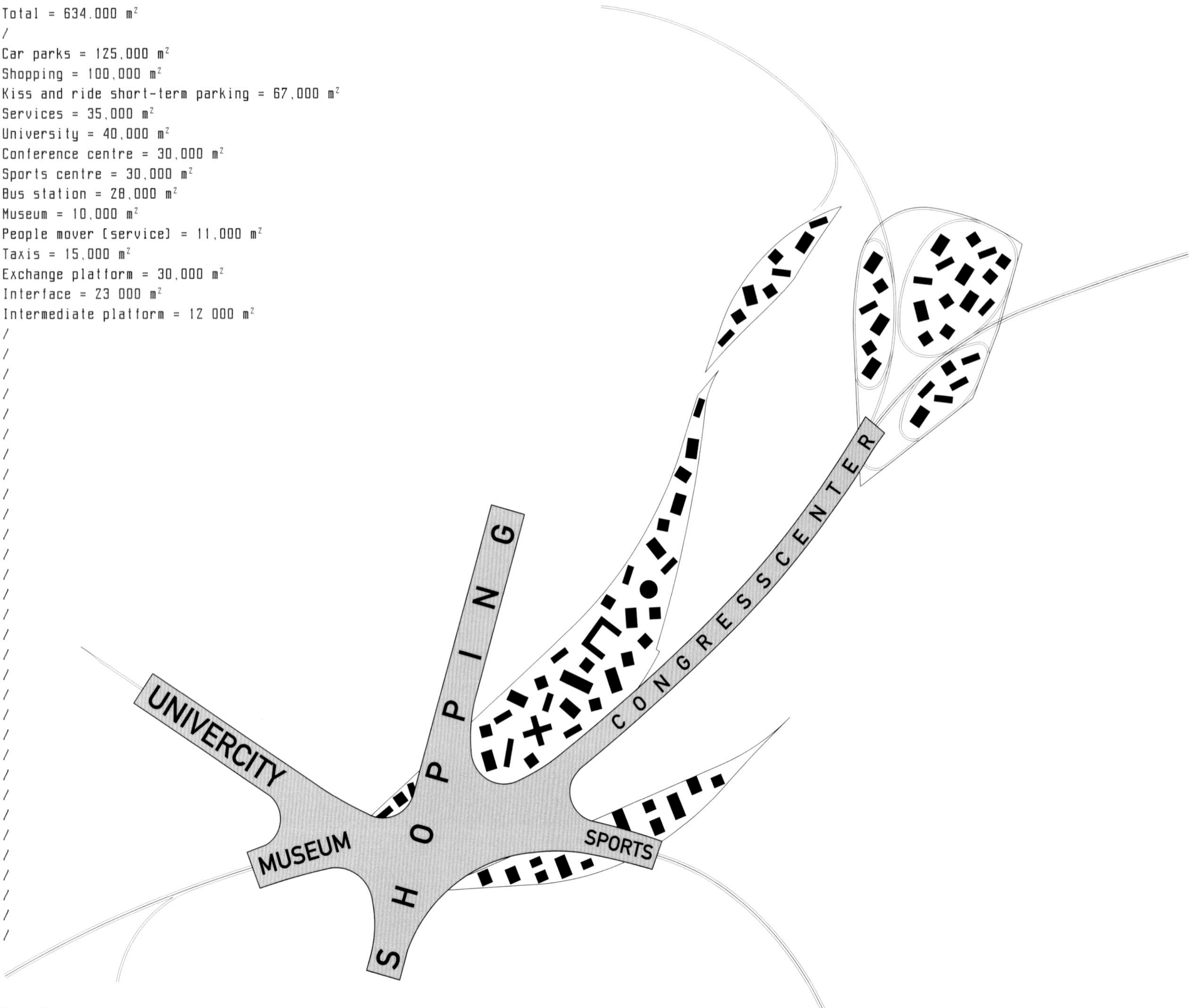

Thematic connections
/
/
/
/
/
/
/
/
/
/

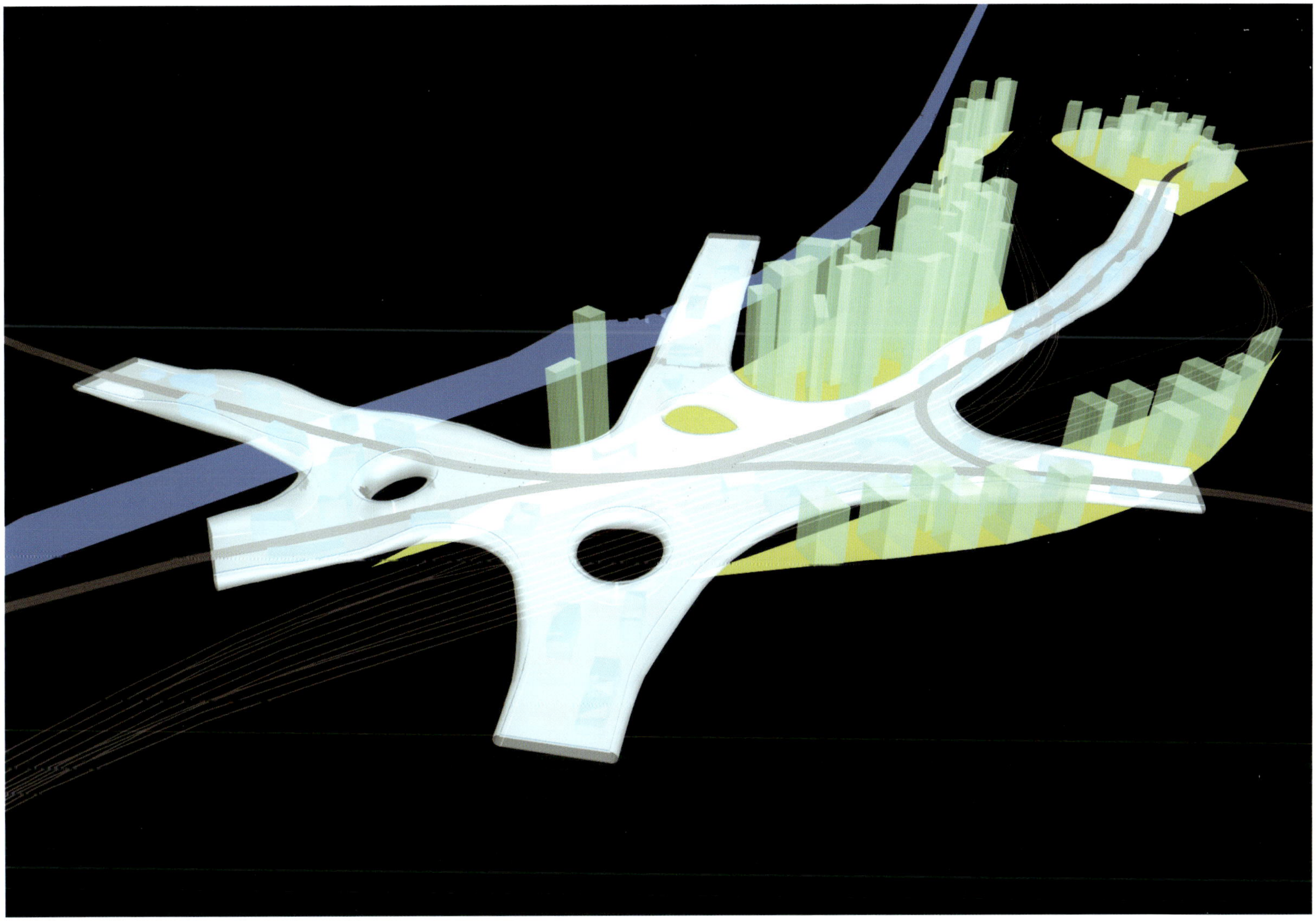

/
/
/
/
/
/
/
/
/
/
/
/
/
/
/
/
/
/
/
/
/

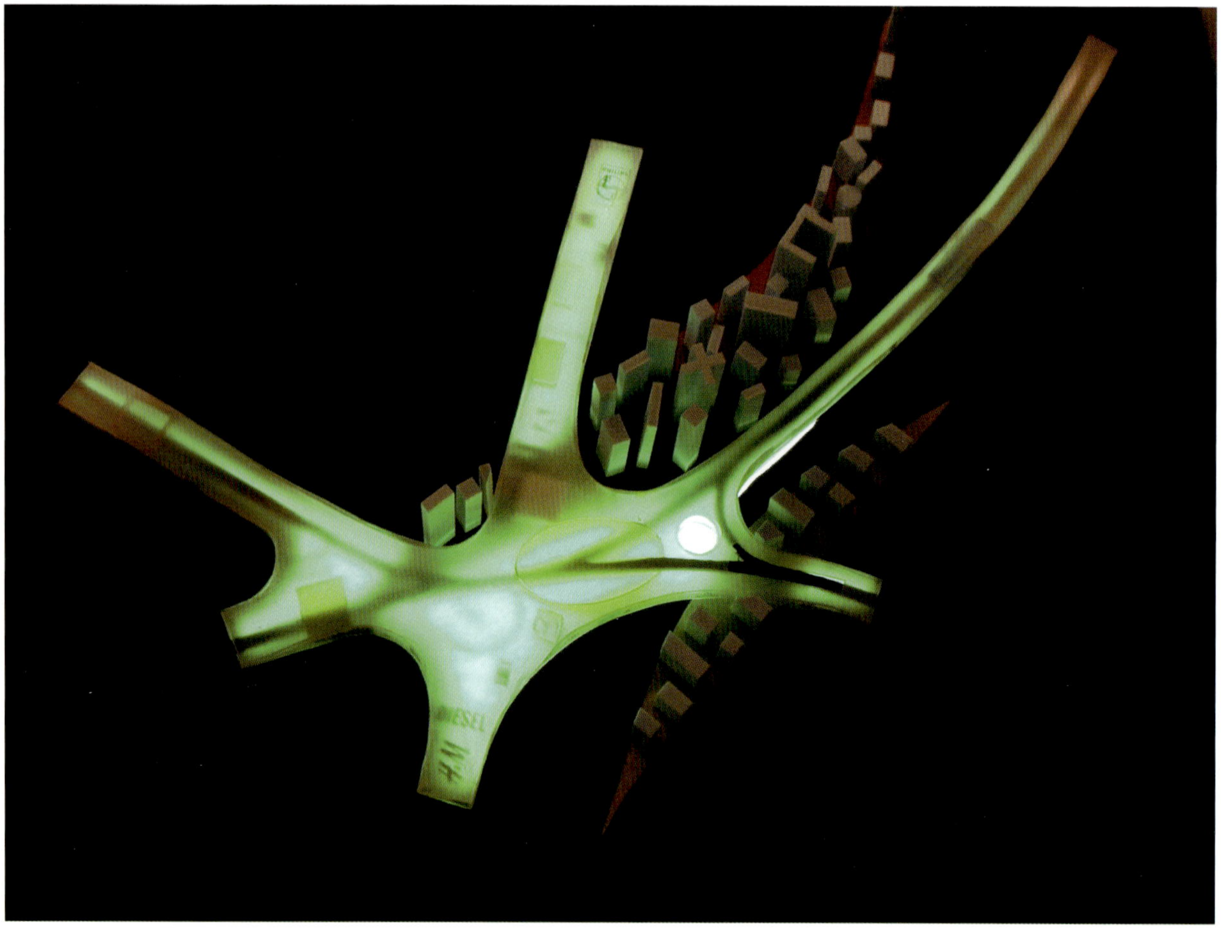

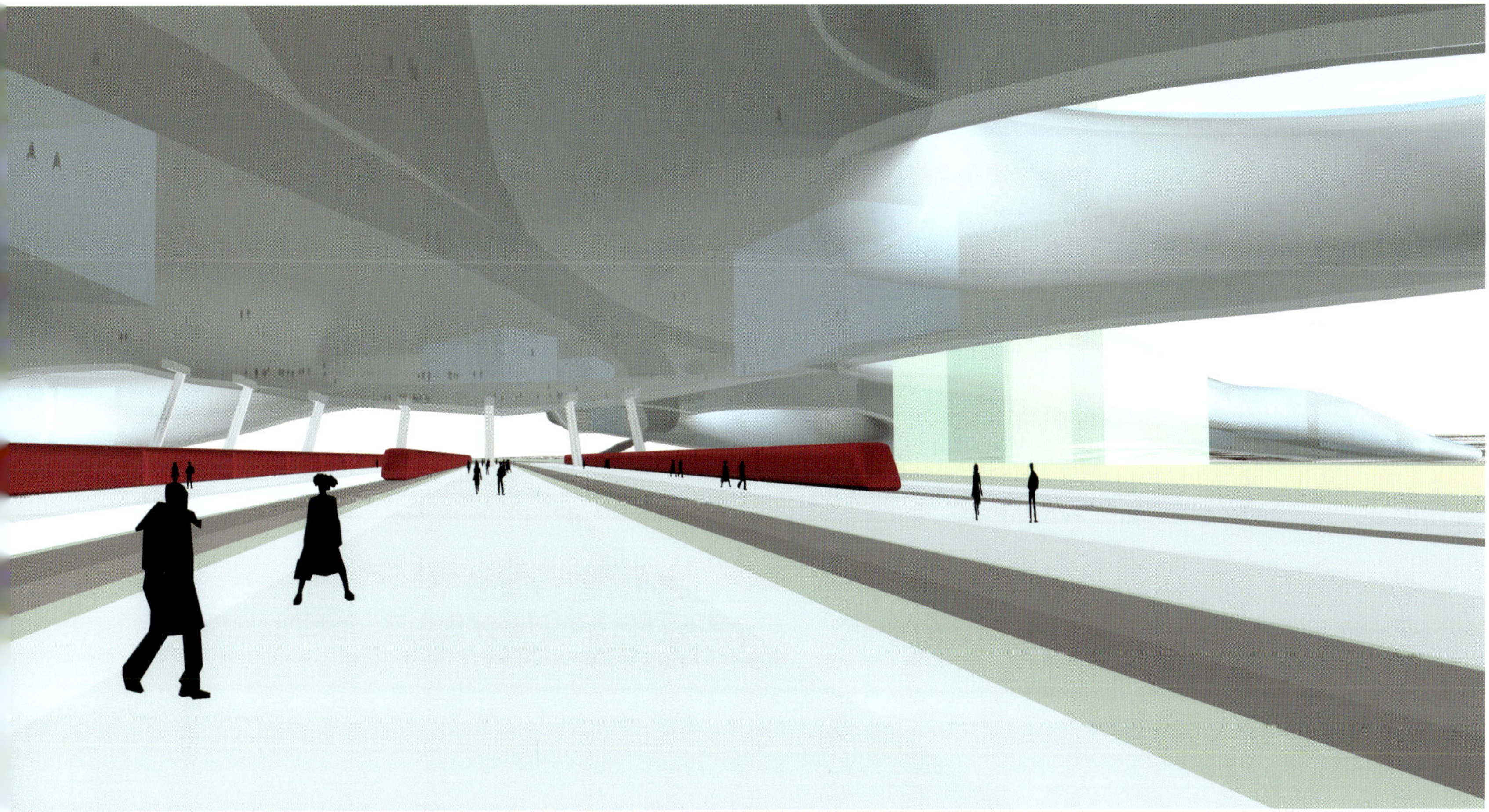

The dome

/

The possibility of improving the existing central station is both exciting and unexpected. It would give Brussels a truly European dimension.

/

It would be preferable for the high-speed trains to stop in the city centre so as to compete with short-haul flights. Using the latest geotechnics, the city centre would not be greatly disrupted by the building work. So it makes sense to come up with a second solution and compare it. What would such an initiative look like? What are the prerequisites? What would be the pros and cons of this alternative in comparison with the station at Schaerbeek-Passengers?

/

A calculation shows that four additional tracks would suffice to make the North-South junction operational in 2020, and by enlarging this additional tube, making it both wider and higher, a space would be created that is just right for a station.

/

By locating part of the tracks underneath boulevard Stalingrad / Rue du Midi, a larger hub is created, capable of serving the Bourse district directly. The tunnel of the East-West metro line functions in this way, as a link turning this tube into a dome space, creating a central area that connects all the routes. A giant urban dome, an underground cathedral, from which appendages would lead to the major amenities in the centre: the Sablon, la Monnaie, Mont des Arts, Palais de Justice, Manneken Pis and the Grand Place. These tentacles would illuminate the excavated area, and an underground Sputnik would appear, while, at the same time making the existing underground areas accessible: car parks, metro and underground tram stations, underground shopping arcades and museums. A second city would be created beneath Brussels: Brussels -1.

/

/

By creating a few tunnel links to the "petite ceinture" [inner ring road], car traffic would also be connected. Car parks would complete the station development.

/
/
/
/
/
/
/
/
/
/
/
/
/
/
/
/
/
/
/
/
/
/

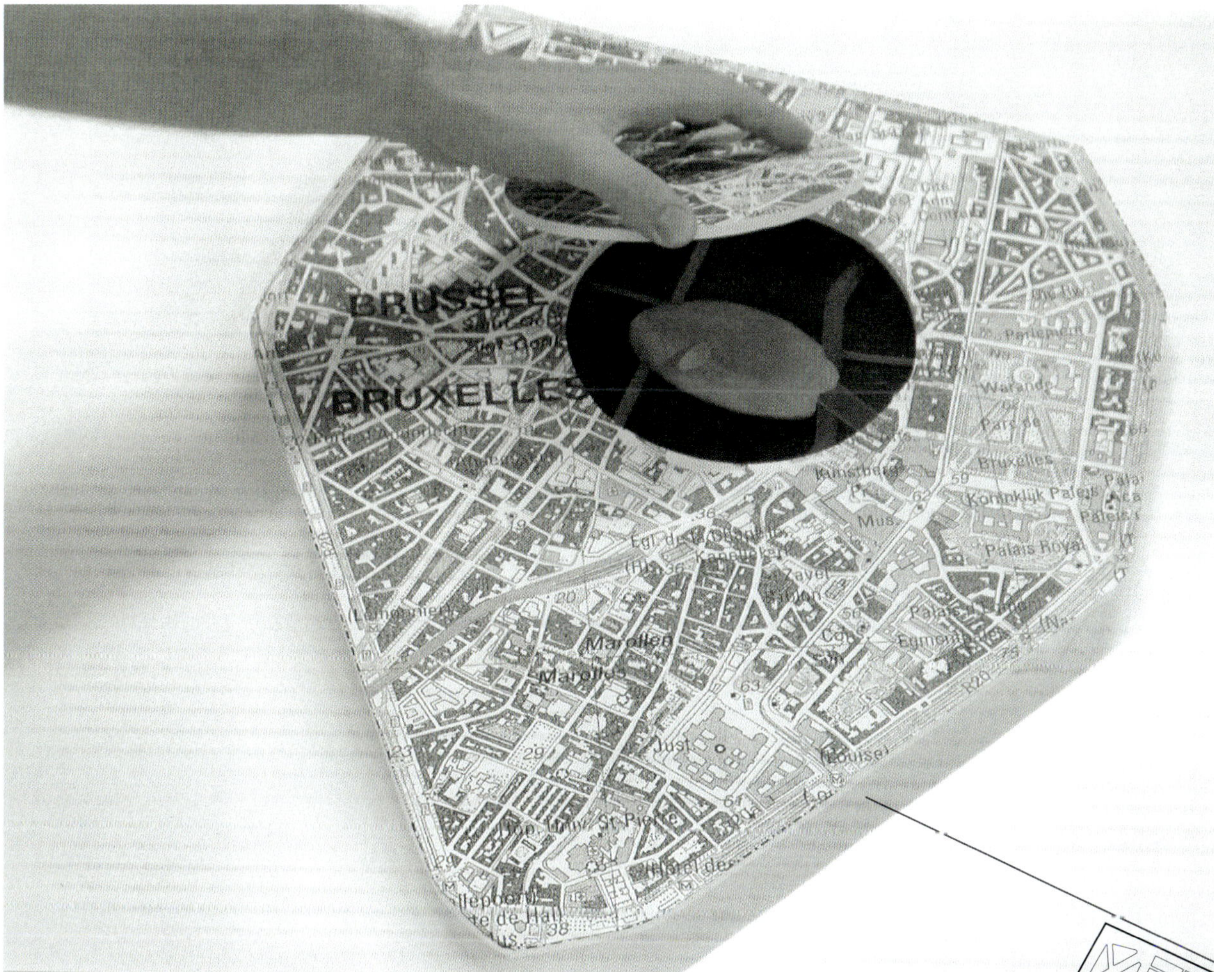

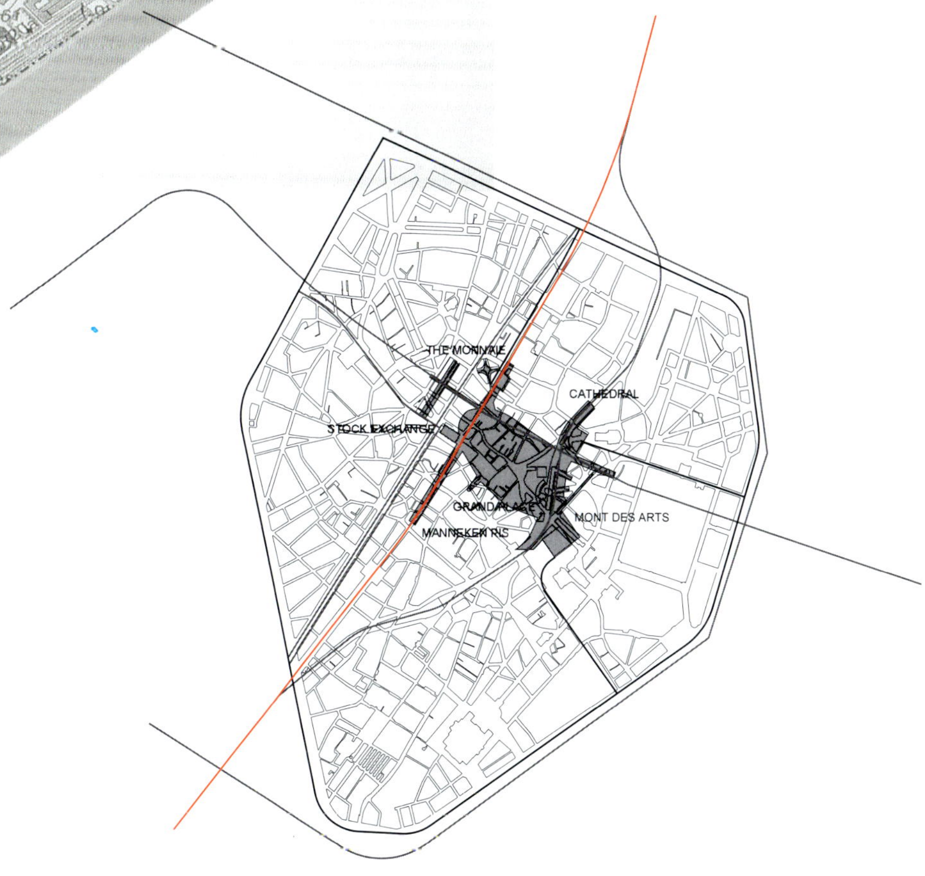

/
/
Connections / exits
/
/
/
/
/
/
/
/
/
/
/
/
/
/
/
/
/
/
/
/
/
/

/
/

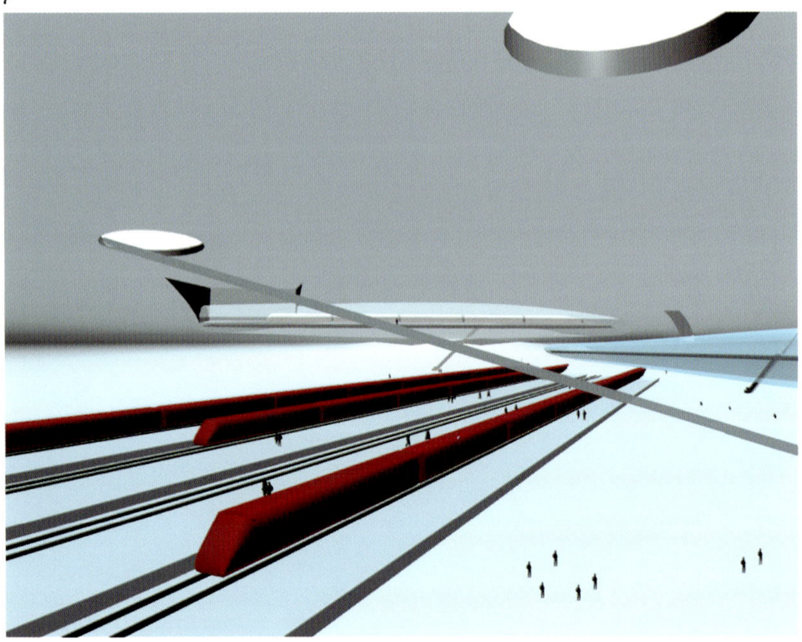

/
/
/
/
/
/
/
/
/
/
The project in no way involves the SNCB, which, furthermore, does not have any plans at present to develop these premises.

ACUPUNC

/

ARIES/MSA (Moritz & Simon archi

CERAU

/

/

/

/

/

/

/

TURE

ectes]/IDOM

ARIES
MSA [Moritz & Simon architectes]
IDOM

/
/
/
/
/
/
/

OmbudsPlanMédiateur

/

/

Commissioned by: Chancellery of the Prime Minister and Cabinet of the Minister-President of the Brussels-Capital Region
Design firms: ARIES / MSA [Moritz & Simon Architectes] / IDOM
Website: www.ombudsplanmediateur.be
Graphics: SPECULOOS

/

/

The result of a public tender published in 2003, the following proposal attempts to define a new identity for the district of Brussels that houses the European Institutions.
It is an answer to the wish of the contracting authorities to develop a new balance between the different activities that currently exist: "The objective of the study is to come up with a global concept which will be able to create a balance between the different functions and the various actors that can be found in the zone. The mixed character of the district and the diversity of activities must be stimulated in order to be able to make the European district a more integrated part of the city of Brussels and the surrounding communes."

/

In order to do this and to change the general perception of the site in a positive manner, the study proposes that in 2007-2008, to mark the 50th anniversaries of the Treaty of Rome, the presence of the European Institutions in Brussels, and the Universal Exhibition of 1958, a major cultural event be organised with as central theme the urban revival of the European district. On this occasion, European facilities which would be open to the citizens, reflecting the universal ambitions of the sites, would be created on Place Jean Rey, on the crossroads of the institutional axis [Schuman-Luxembourg] and the citizens' axis of the Valley of Maelbeek. The project also sets out to launch an extensive programme of housing projects and facilities, to create and develop public spaces and transportation infrastructures and to refresh the green spaces.
Although the period 2007-2008 constitutes the first major deadline, the entire proposal is scheduled for completion by the year 2020 to coincide with the ultimate enlargement of the Union.

To summarise, in the short and medium term [2007-2008], the project sets out to:
- provide accommodation for 2600 new inhabitants
- create 27,000 m^2 of shops and facilities
- create a European civic and cultural pole
- build a new tram line along the Valley of Maelbeek
- design a new multi-functional station on the site of the current Schuman station
- renovate 28 ha of parks [Parc du Cinquantenaire]
- renovate 13.8 ha of existing public space, including the Schuman roundabout, Avenue de Cortenbergh, Rue Belliard, Chaussée d'Etterbeek, Boulevard Charlemagne, ...
- define a new traffic plan
- set up of a co-ordinating body which will be responsible for implementing the project

/

In the long term [2020], the project sets out to:
- build a metro line between Schuman, the Luxembourg railway station and the Midi railway station
- extend the main seats of the 5 European Institutions
- create 2.3 ha of new public spaces which will enhance the transitions between the European district and the bordering districts.

/

/

/

/

PS: At the current time, the project is still being studied.

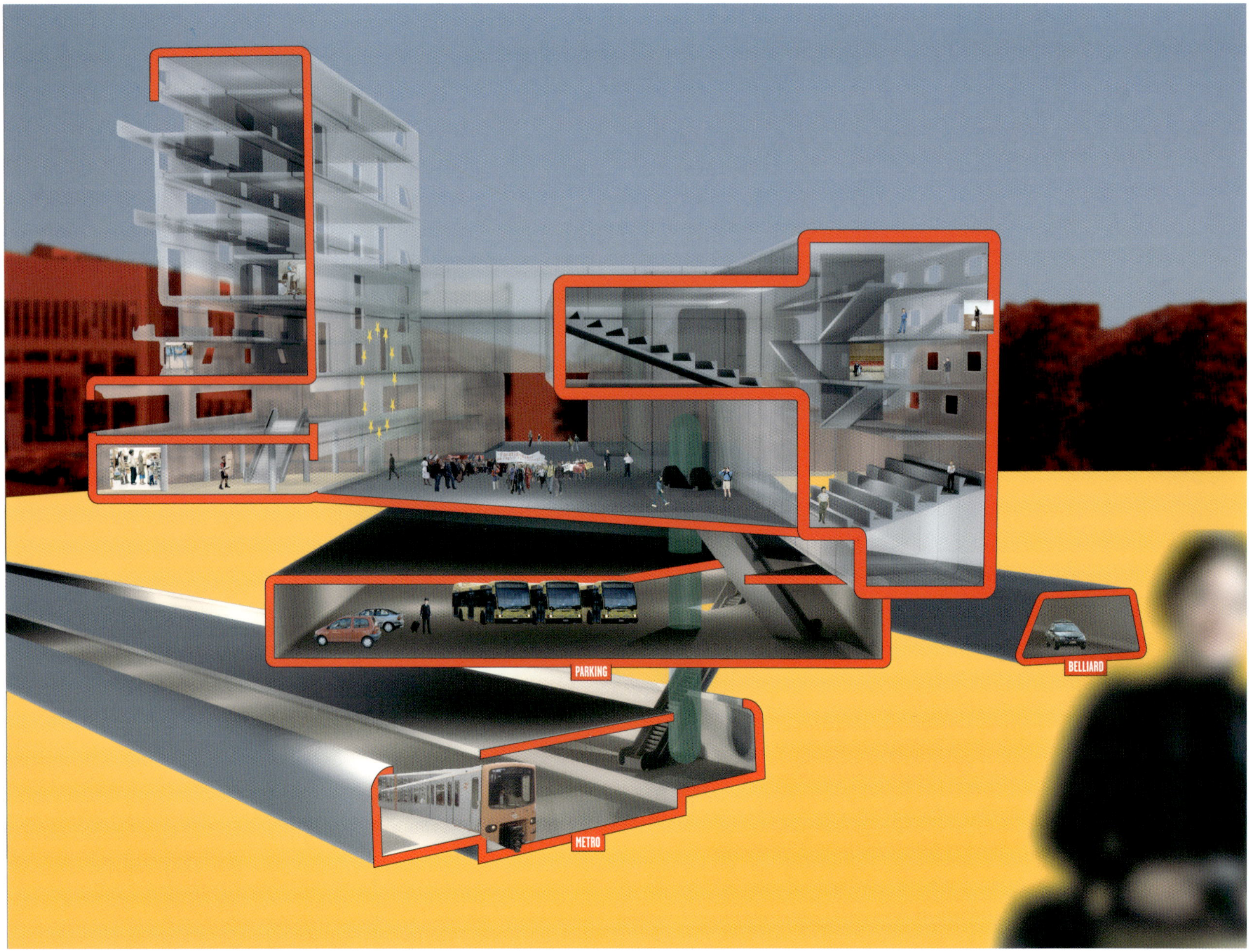

Creation of a cultural pole

/

The new centre is designed to act as an urban catalyst. It will be a multifunctional complex which is geared towards culture and which creates a sense of unity among the different levels of interest that can be found in the district.

/

The urbanity of the centre will be expressed through the mixity of its functions and uses:

- Temporary and permanent exhibition areas
- Performance areas: concerts, plays, dance, film projection, etc.
- Working and meeting rooms
- Bookshop and media centre
- A centre devoted to civil society [NGOs]
- Hotel, restaurant and catering areas/
- A supermarket with European food products
- Administrative offices
- 8,000 m² of housing [in conformity with the PPAS]
- A bus station with parking for 25 buses and a 150 -space car park.

/

The European centre will represent civil society and the European Institutions in all their diversity. At European level, this facility is a new dimension of the institutions and, at local level, a motor for a new cultural network. At the intersection of the different European Institutions, the open centre will be a new platform for debate on the European question and the urban question. In parallel with the quality of the architecture, the symbolic dimension can be expressed by incorporating the spirit and the letter of the new convention.

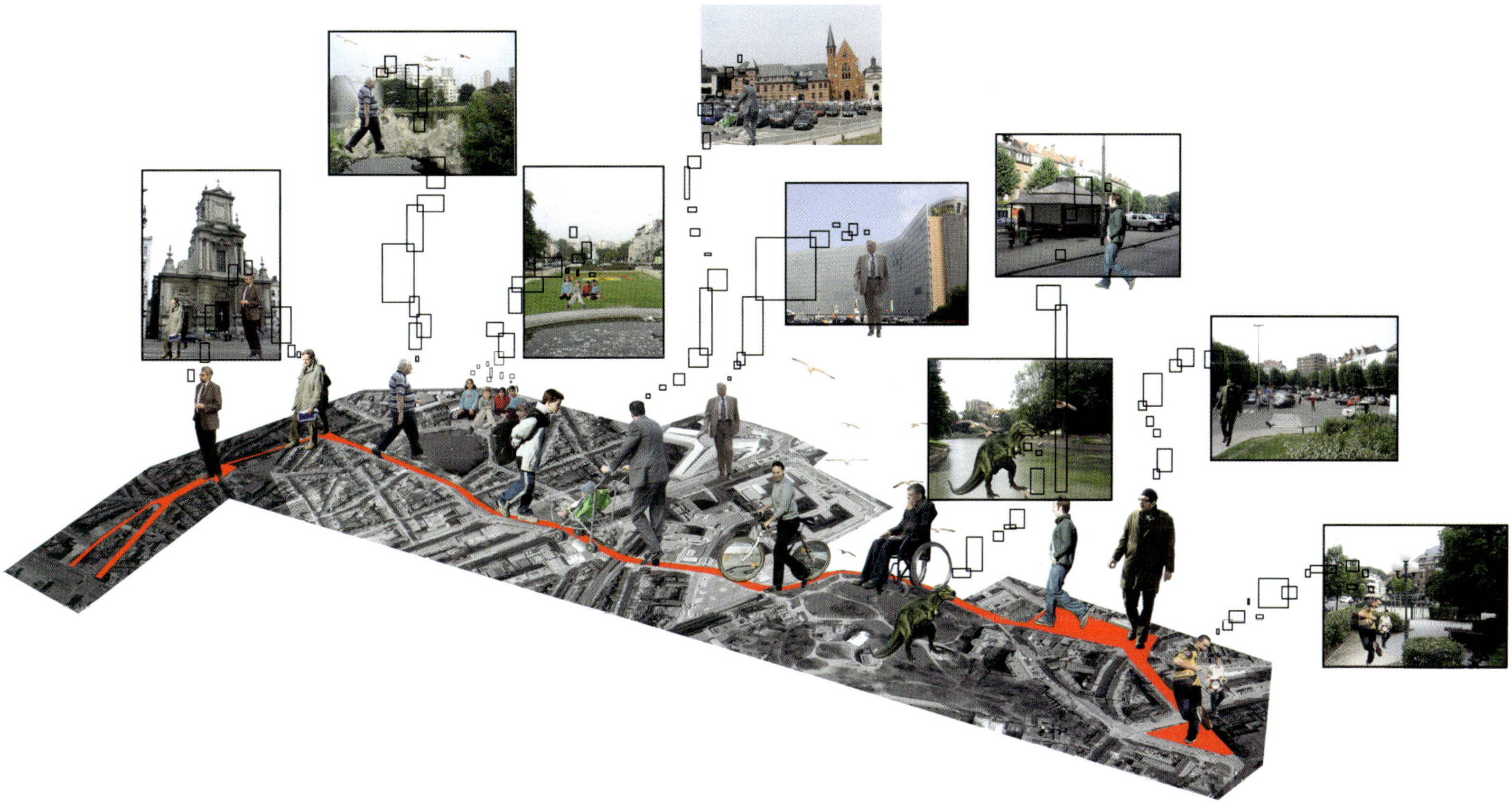

FORMALISATION OF A POSITIVE IDENTITY

Like Paris, Washington and Vienna, which have forged their identity as national capitals by adapting the typology of public buildings and urban spaces [variations on the theme of the Boulevard in Paris, the Mall in Washington and the Ring in Vienna], we propose that the European District should also have a feature that clearly identifies its position within a contemporary urban perspective. Furthermore, unlike the great capitals of the nineteenth century, Brussels is not the capital of an empire but rather the capital of a decentralised political entity. Without resorting to classical monumentality, the organisation of this 'decentralised capital' should afford an opportunity to create a new model of the capital city: the 'networked' capital. Within this framework, we propose to develop a unifying feature for the territory which is home to the most emblematic European Institutions, that is, the Valley. The urban feature made up of unified fragments is an element that reflects the global scale embodied by the reconfiguration of a capital for the European Union. It creates a mesh of complementary poles in terms of functionality and meaning as part of the identifier 'Brussels-Europe' as a system in search of its internal coherence.

/
/
Collective Equipment implantation in the Valley of Maalbeek
/
To improve the comfort of the urban habitat, adequate collective amenities must be provided. These also constitute opportunities for the different population groups in the district and in the adjacent municipalities to meet. The message of the new inter-district link (chaussée d'Etterbeek) will be reinforced by the presence of a series of collective amenities on the ground floor of new residential buildings and at the foot of existing buildings. By virtue of their visibility and accessibility, they constitute a response to the need to present a positive image of the facades of the chaussée and to effect the urban renewal of the district. In addition to the cultural centre and its different functions (community halls, exhibition and entertainment halls, European supermarket, etc.), there will be sports amenities, launderettes, local shops and childcare centres.
/
/
/
/
/
/
/
/
To mark the Festival, 130,000 m² of housing and shopping and leisure facilities were built in the valley.

/
/
/

/
/

To develop diversified and high-quality habitat: The objective is to create attractive and quality housing that meets the aim of winning the hearts and minds of the people who live in the district. By favouring stable housing, the existing pockets of housing and the inter-district connections will be reinforced. Quality housing requires high-quality and sustainable architecture, the kind of architecture that creates a strong sense of identification.

/

The upgrading of the European District is also an opportunity to create 'temporary' housing to reduce the pressure on selfcatering apartments in the neighbouring districts. Provided it is used in a positive way, this characteristic function offers the possibility of providing new types of housing and envisioning a new and interesting form of social and cultural mixity.

/
/
/
/
/
/
/
/
/
/
/

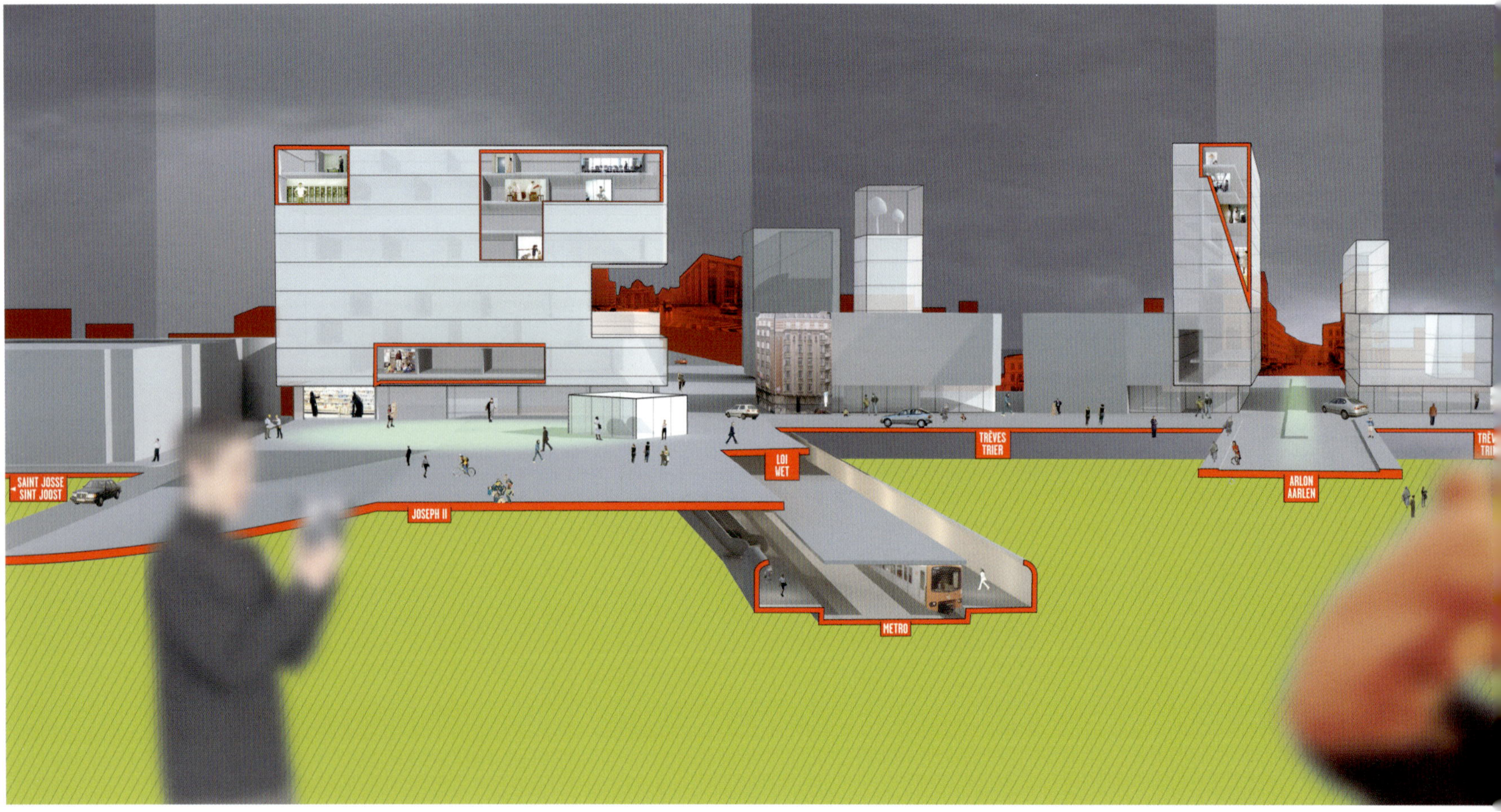

/
/
As a transitional area between the Léopold District and the Valley, rue de Trèves will be promoted as a variegated artery which brings diversity. In the long-term perspective, rue de Trèves will be injected with new potential as an element that stimulates connections with the neighbouring districts.
/
/
/
/
/
/
/
/
/
/
/
/
/
/
/
/
/
/
/
/
/

/
/
/
/
/
/
/
/
/
/
/
/
/
/
/
/
/
/
/
The use of temporarily vacant spaces. The mono-functionalism of the Léopold District leads to underuse of certain spaces at certain times. European experience in similar districts has shown that it is possible to use these spaces through specially selected activities. In Madrid a business district is used during the day for offices and at night for discotheques and clubs. Although these functions are an inconvenience in residential districts, they do not disturb anyone in the offices. The European District has similar potential.

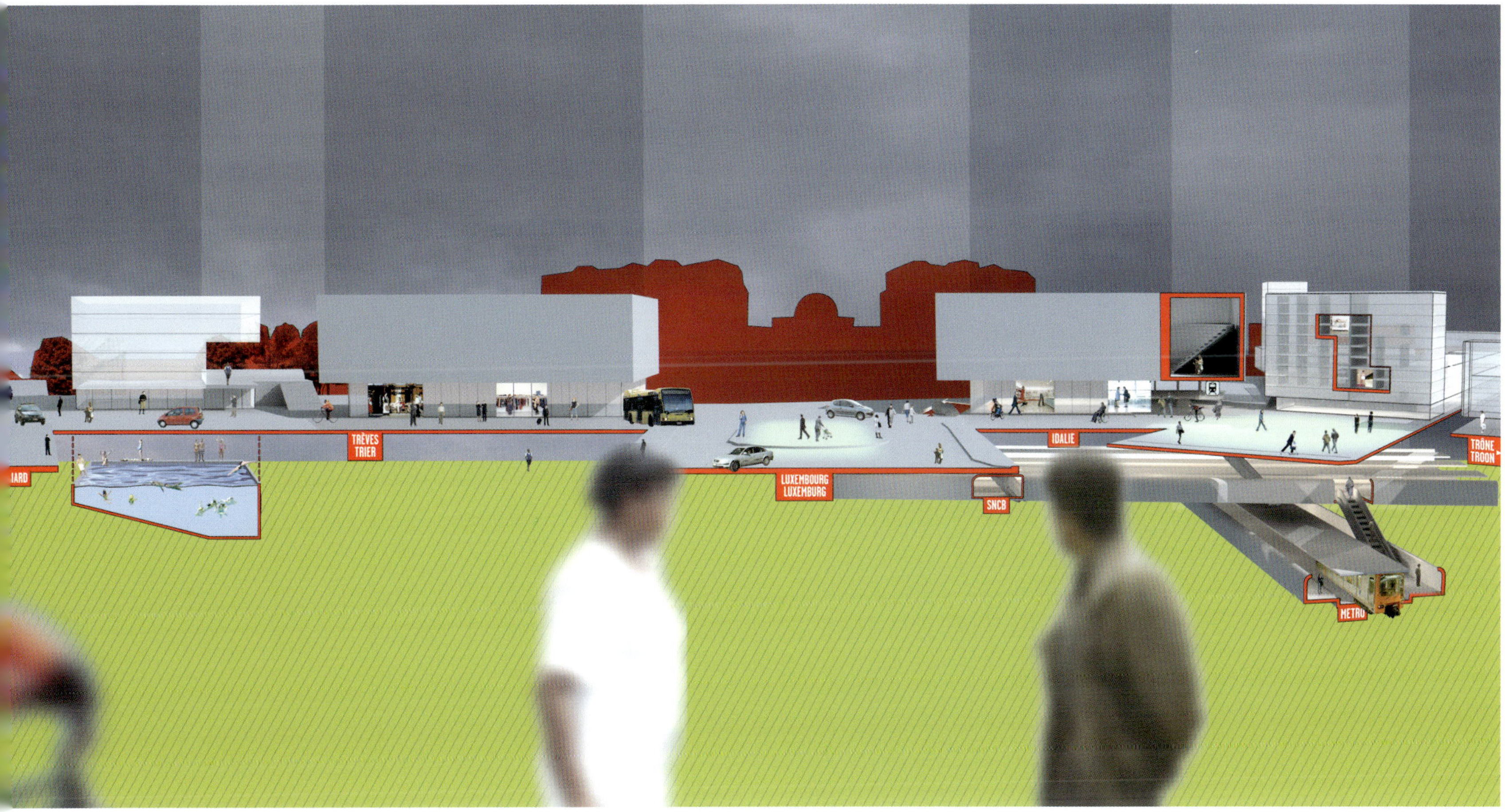
TRÈVES
TRIER
LUXEMBOURG
LUXEMBURG
SNCB
IDALIE
TRÔNE
TROON
METRO

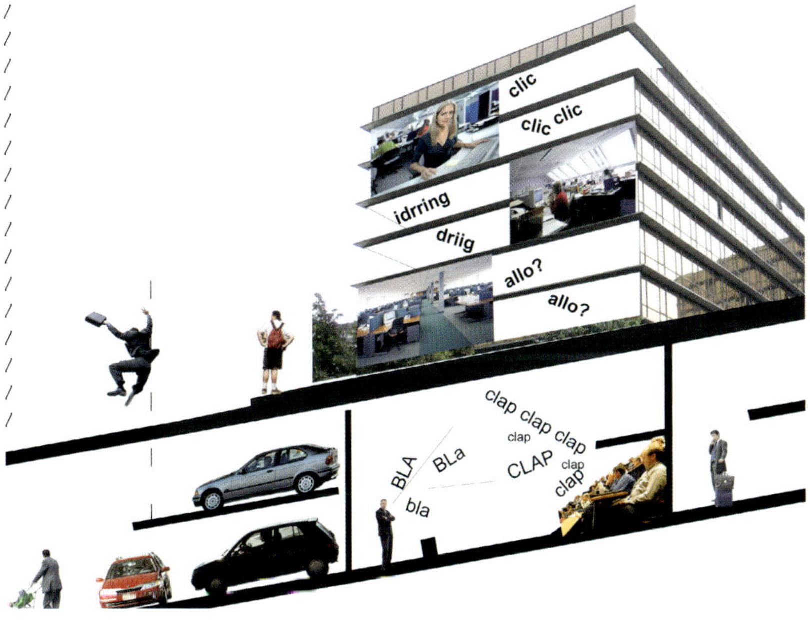
clic
clic clic
idrring
driig
allo?
allo?
clap clap clap
clap
CLAP
clap
clap
BLA
BLa
bla

pshiiiit
pshiiit
pshiit
WOOOOW
YE YE
YEAH
CHIC-BOUM
CHIP
CHIP
DELICATESSEN

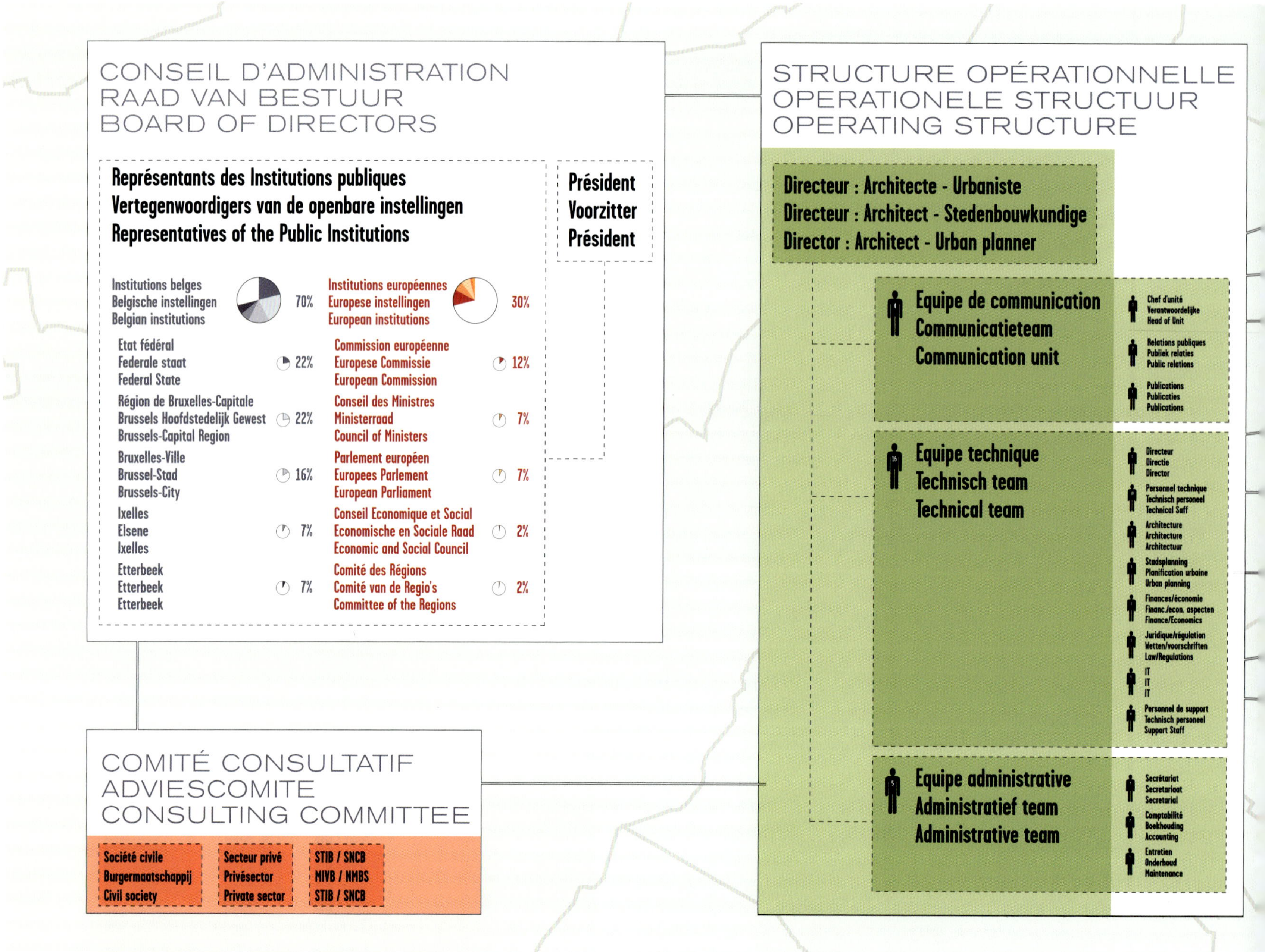

/

Setting in place an urban project coordination and management unit

The city planning of the European District calls for a coherent and integrated approach to the problems. Given the range of issues to be addressed, the presence of many interlocutors and the importance of the stakes involved, a body must be set up to tackle and manage all the issues raised. This coordination and management body or unit is referred to as the 'Partnership for the development of the European District' or, in short, the 'Partnership'. The Partnership is a body which, despite the fact that it involves adding an extra layer of decision-making, makes decisions more efficient and straightforward.

/
/
/

/

It is responsible for:

- the development strategy and the priorities
- the actions to be implemented
- the relevance of the actions in the context
- the implementation schedule
- follow-up of the implementation of the actions
- control of costs linked to the implementation of the actions
- exchanges between the actors (local residents, developers, STIB, SNCB, issuing authorities, etc.)
- communication of the project

/
/
/

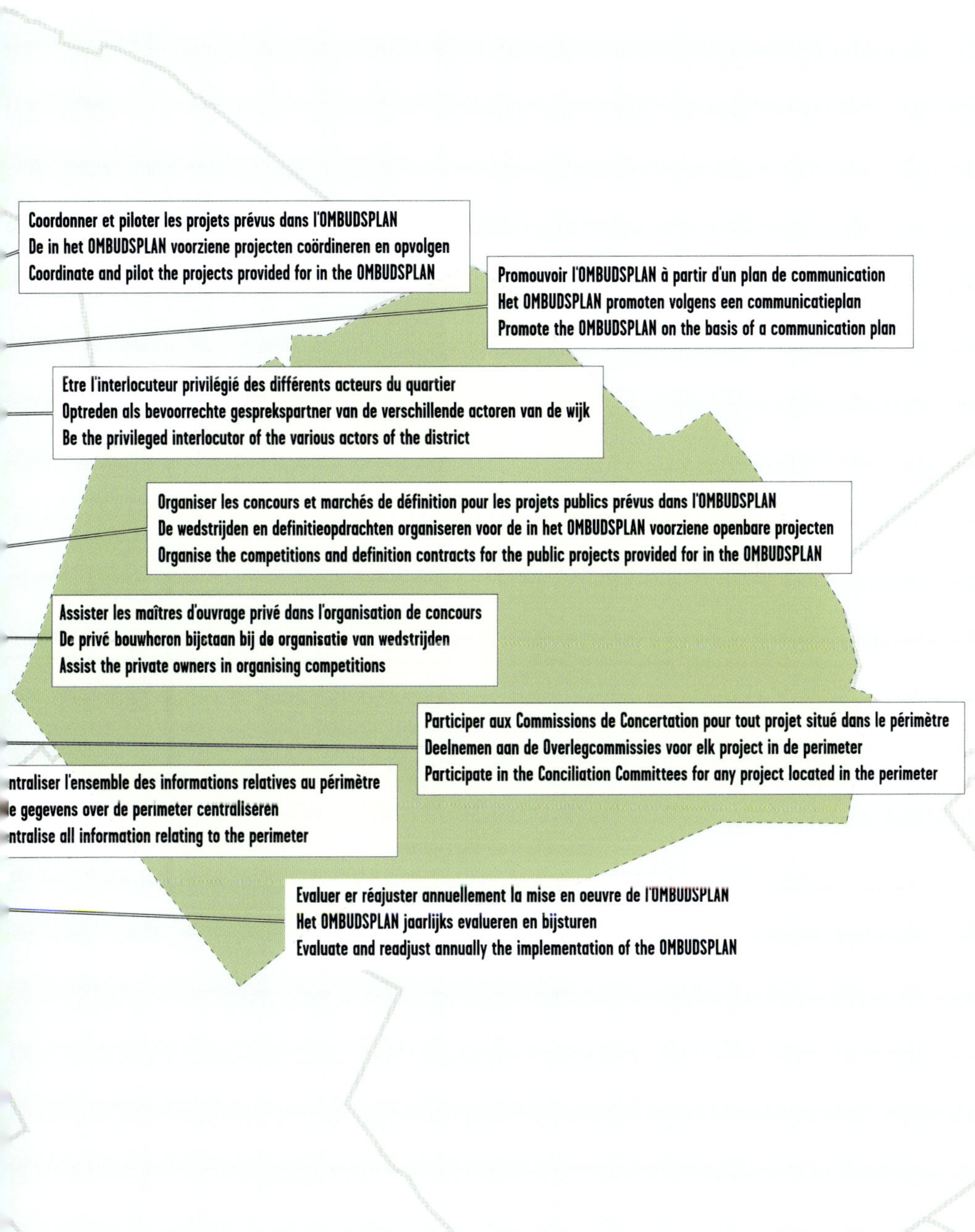
Coordonner et piloter les projets prévus dans l'OMBUDSPLAN
De in het OMBUDSPLAN voorziene projecten coördineren en opvolgen
Coordinate and pilot the projects provided for in the OMBUDSPLAN
Promouvoir l'OMBUDSPLAN à partir d'un plan de communication
Het OMBUDSPLAN promoten volgens een communicatieplan
Promote the OMBUDSPLAN on the basis of a communication plan
Etre l'interlocuteur privilégié des différents acteurs du quartier
Optreden als bevoorrechte gesprekspartner van de verschillende actoren van de wijk
Be the privileged interlocutor of the various actors of the district
Organiser les concours et marchés de définition pour les projets publics prévus dans l'OMBUDSPLAN
De wedstrijden en definitieopdrachten organiseren voor de in het OMBUDSPLAN voorziene openbare projecten
Organise the competitions and definition contracts for the public projects provided for in the OMBUDSPLAN
Assister les maîtres d'ouvrage privé dans l'organisation de concours
De privé bouwheren bijstaan bij de organisatie van wedstrijden
Assist the private owners in organising competitions
Participer aux Commissions de Concertation pour tout projet situé dans le périmètre
Deelnemen aan de Overlegcommissies voor elk project in de perimeter
Participate in the Conciliation Committees for any project located in the perimeter
ntraliser l'ensemble des informations relatives au périmètre
e gegevens over de perimeter centraliseren
ntralise all information relating to the perimeter
Evaluer er réajuster annuellement la mise en oeuvre de l'OMBUDSPLAN
Het OMBUDSPLAN jaarlijks evalueren en bijsturen
Evaluate and readjust annually the implementation of the OMBUDSPLAN

CERAU

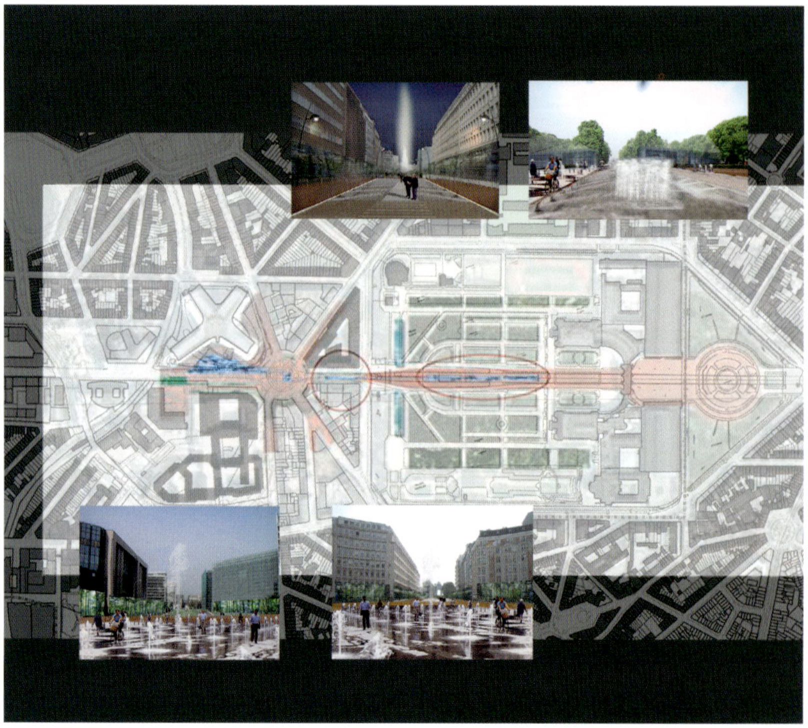

The European District

/

"It's no longer a question of empty words but an action, a bold action, a constructive action".

Robert Schuman
9th May 1950

/

The words of one of the founding fathers of Europe may have a double meaning here.
It seems that celebrating the 50th Jubilee in style is a Belgium tradition, just look at the Cinquantenaire arch, the park and the museum, or at the prestigious Palais du Centenaire in Heysel. In 2008, Europe will be celebrating the 50th anniversary of its foundation. What will be the symbol of that event?
This 50-year presence by the European institutions has had a marked effect on the city. The traces are present in the walls and public areas although they do not follow any real pattern, and that is a situation that has lasted for two generations. There have been studies, though none of them have ever been implemented, while the landscape of the valley of Maelbeek, from the Military Academy to the Royal Palace, the Cinquantenaire parks to the Léopold district have not been considered in an overall process of reflection by the state, the region and the local authorities concerned. There is nowhere in Brussels today that really belongs to Europe.
Where is Europe?

/

The first building used by the European organisation, the Berlaymont, was built at the foot of a major urban traffic hub, now set aside for the exclusive use of cars and buses. Is that an appropriate image for the largest community in the world?
Named after the founding father of Europe, Robert Schuman, the roundabout does at least have symbolic perspectives: in one direction the Parc du Cinquantenaire de la Belgique and in the other direction the heart of the Belgian capital, the seat of its institutions, the Royal Palace, the Chamber and the Senate.

While back in 1950 Europe founded itself on coal and steel, and while the economy and the currency may provide the cement that ensures a degree of solidarity, today Europe must turn towards the social aspects of the union: man and his environment, earth, water, air and light.

/

The fiftieth jubilee of Europe should be an image, that of a powerful link, a sort of identification between each European and these institutions, but should also be the attachment to these symbols, the new values to be defended.

/

The fiftieth jubilee of Europe could also be a place where Euro-residents and Euro-tourists can meet, stop, talk, a PLACE without cars, coaches or buses, where people are on foot like anyone else, a place where there is earth, water, greenery, stone:
- a walk next to water;
- a stream surrounded by greenery;
- the air calmed by the absence of traffic and noise;
- two pavilions in the park to house European projects, present them to visitors, hold meetings and concerts because Europe is, above all, cultural in its richness and diversity.

This process should spread gradually throughout the district. That is the challenge but who will take it on?

/

We are sure other places will be created to give a different perception of Europe in Brussels.
This is not a commemoration; it is the beginning of a more profound transformation, putting people back at the heart of the city where the tools of democracy and the decision-making bodies of the community are located.

/
/
/
/
/
/

/
/
/
/
/
/
/
/
/
/
/
/
/
/
/
/
/
/
/
/
/
/
/
/
/
/
/

URBAN STRATE MICRO-
/
Ti-Nan Chi/Luc Deleu & T.O.P. office/CERAU/Vincent Callebaut

GIES/
MACRO

ce/Vincent Cartuyvels/

Ti-Nan Chi

/

/

/

/

/

/

/

/

/

/

/

/

/

Micro-Urbanism in Progress

/

/

Subtle! Subtle! It approaches the formless.
Sun Tze, Art of War, 500 BC

/

/

Modern cities reached an unprecedented level of congestion and complexity in the 20th century. The formal structures of the city that we take for granted are gradually being blurred or erased by fast and unexpected development. Urban planning and design appear to be non-decisive and almost irrelevant when it comes to controlling urban conditions. Brussels is certainly one of the cities that is suffering from the dichotomy and that is looking for new solutions.

/

Today, the city contains patchworks of different physical structures and social-cultural situations. The experience, which should be a shared pleasure,

has already been lost, even in the old city. We blame thoughtless planning, but at the same time we do not know how to break this vicious circle. The hasty agglomeration of buildings continues in the blind pursuit of prosperity.
/
Examining the city on a macro level no longer makes sense, when current chaotic phenomena are often illegible using formal analysis, and probably very misleading. We have seen attempts to invent or resurrect dominant anaesthetics, to demonstrate sanitary surgeries, to tighten the bandages, etc., in order to fight the disease. On the other hand, attempts to simulate the complexity, whether by collage or computational generation, in favour of a seductive form of space are also futile to grasp what is actually going on inside this mess.
/
Micro-urbanism suggests there are internal realities to be investigated in order to describe how things interact and coordinate in the micro-scale realm, which manifest the true spirit of a city and its people. The inner reality comprises not only grass root activities, but also a plasma of conflicts and re-actions which is the everyday life that tests the limits of urban conditions. It is not a rational state and people still barely survive in this plasmodial mode of living.
/
Architects not only need to work within this inner reality, but also need to provide in-situ strategies and tactics to revitalise the self-organising possibility that has been forgotten and abandoned in the cultural politics of design. In Brussels, we see colonnades and steps connecting walkways to different levels of routes and open spaces that have developed gradually into micro-zones, which are themselves unique micro-urban elements in the city.
/
We propose to use a 4-meter grid as the general reference in which to allocate small elements that accommodate activities and structures. The small apparatus will be given qualities close to nano materials that are able to reorganise the urban fabric through the clever disposition of these micro-urban elements. The mechanism in the micro-zones is expected to contain free connections, multiple interactions, autonomous divisions, individualistic bunkers and extendible masses.
/
By deploying these tactical elements amid the existing urban landscape, political actions and communal exchanges are kept in places that are accessible to the general public. It is a question of how we want to treat the history of a city that never been single-faceted. Hidden corners and liminal areas must be uncovered and rejuvenated with care.
/
/
/
/
/
/
/
/

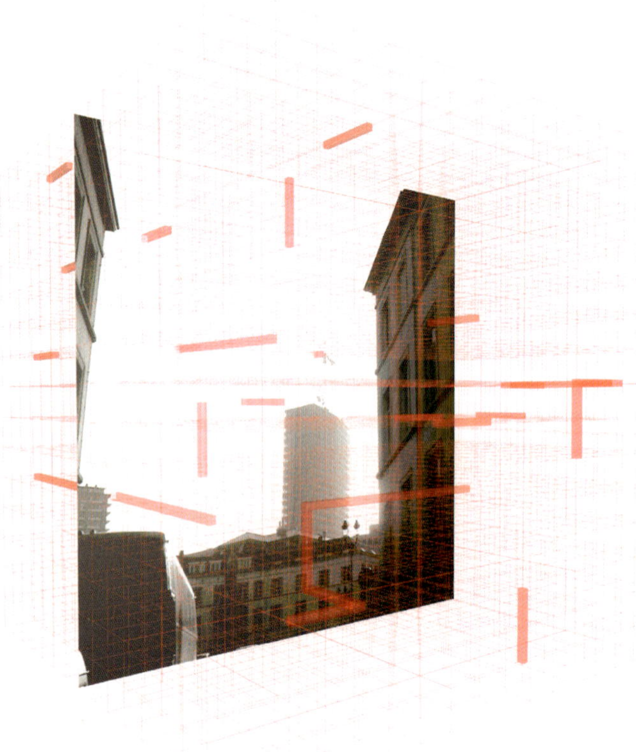

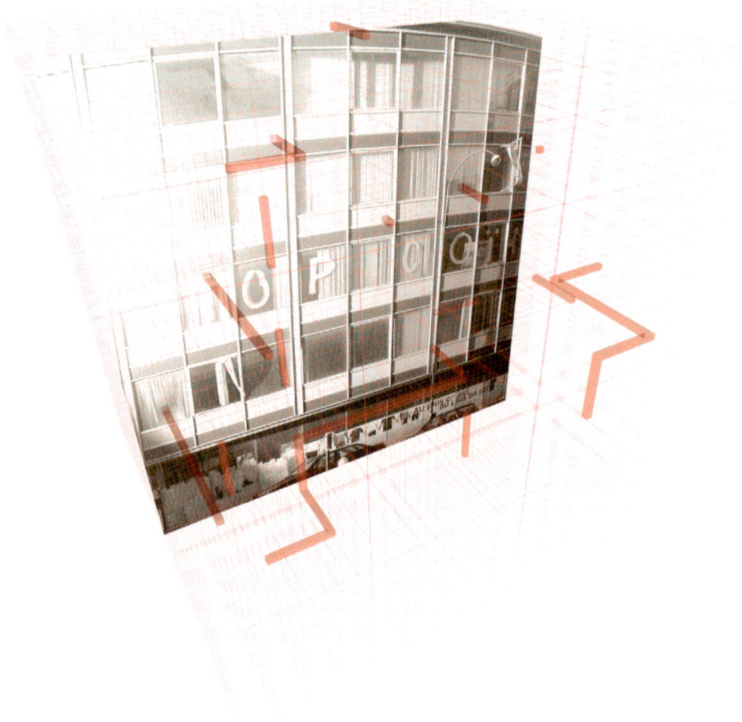

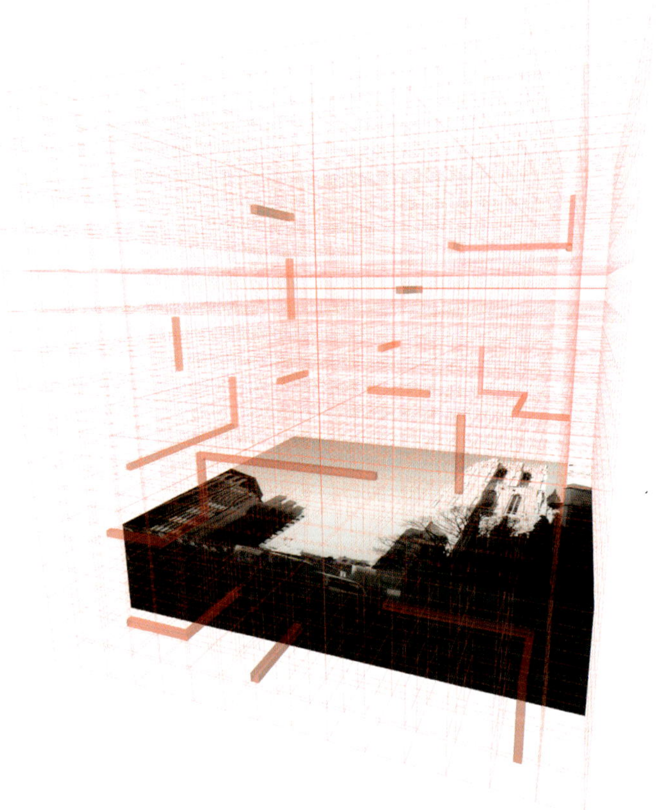

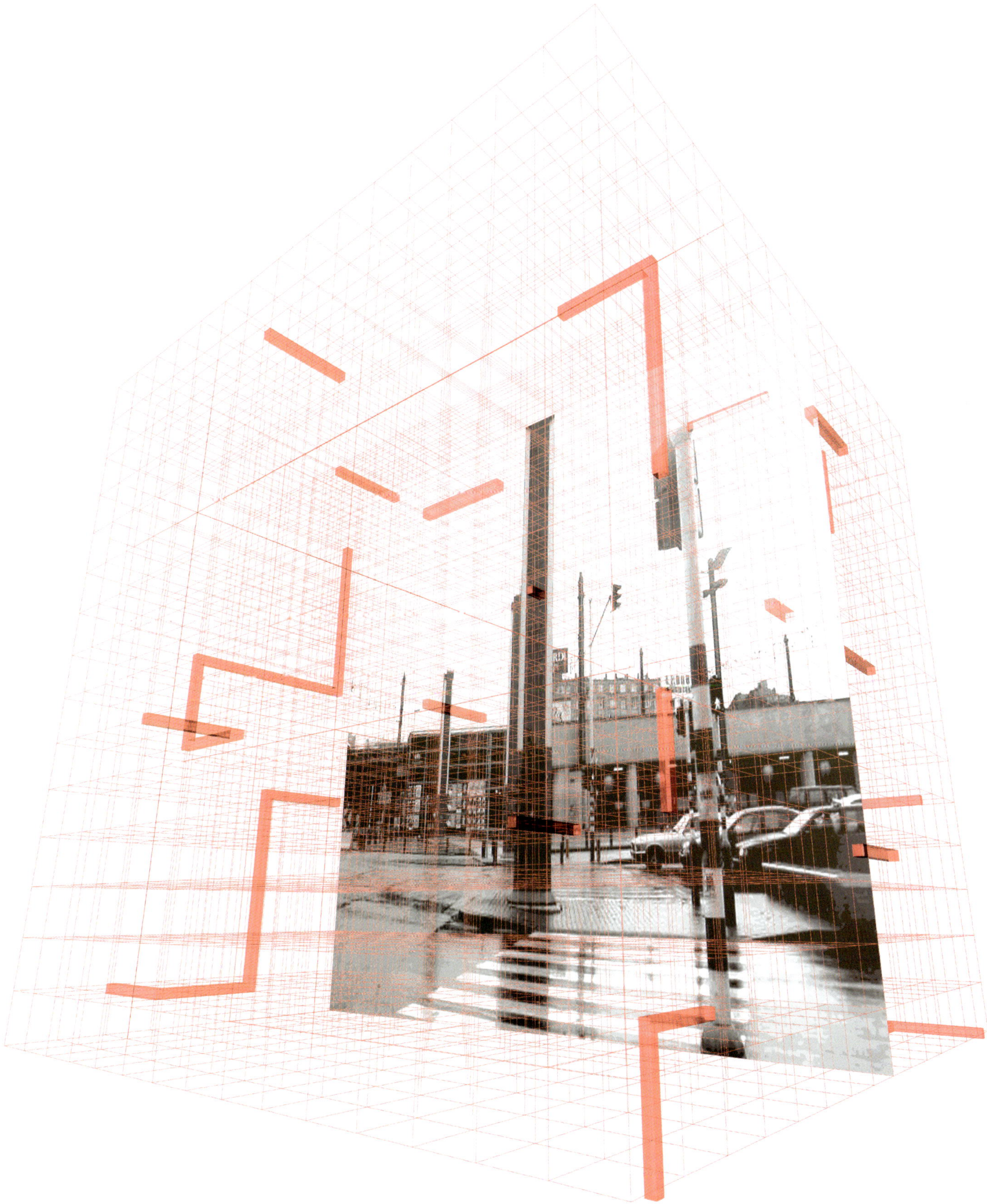

Luc Deleu & T.O.P. office

/
/
/
/
/
/
/
/
/
/
/

A nautical mile of amenities for 9,500 inhabitants, model, 2004
Photo: Steven van den Bergh

2 projects that will take your breath away

/
ORBANISM
/

I launched my project, which I refer to with the word orbanism, as early as 1980 - probably under the influence of Buckminster Fullers' poetic name 'Spaceship Earth' and having seen the first photos ever of the globe. The Earth is our spaceship, our mother and the home of all people. At that time, orbanism already referred to an [urban] design practice that was meant to be integrated at a planetary level and tried to consider the earth as the spatial and social context for cities and architecture. In this respect, orbanism strived towards a balanced organization of the Earth's space.
In other words, orbanism is the metaphysical and material arrangement of the world for the common weal, in the public interest. Orbanism aims to achieve a dynamic balance between order and chaos, between architecture and life, between culture and neo-culture... Orbanism is as environment-friendly as possible. Because we have to organize construction within an ever decreasing natural

space, ecology, in fact a global system, must always be the main structural principle of the ongoing orbanization or the conquering of nature by man.
/
Orbanism implies solidarity and the right balance. It is eco-centric, balanced and unique.
/
The more globalization is praised, the more a general view of our planet becomes not only obvious but also actually indispensable. We are evolving - at least we hope so - towards a world with global people and global institutions, subject to global rights and obligations and bearing global responsibilities.
/
/

URBANISM

/
Since CIAM, serious urbanism can be nothing else but planning for the benefit of all. Since then, urbanism became synonymous with the architecture of a house for society. Consequently, urbanism becomes much more complex and wants to include the many facets involved in the spatial organization of the entire city and even urban networks. At the height of its abilities, urbanism creates a flexible and sustainable system for all levels of society, during several generations and throughout the various models of society. At its best, [urban] architecture is a symbol of freedom for several generations and as such strives to achieve a certain degree of timelessness.
/
With its examples, design methods and strategies at a formal, spatial, structural and programmatic level, a conceptual urbanism wants to provide a stimulating framework. Ideas as an inspirational force are economic and efficient.
/
/
/
/
/
/

ARCHITECTURE

/
As urbanism takes place in an orbanistic framework, architecture takes place in the urban context.
/
In today's global village with its complex society, involvement at a planetary level can no longer be ignored in the current context of worldwide communication and information.
In art history and art criticism, the [realised] examples of architecture are nearly all objects of propaganda with which the client likes to manifest himself. He wants to sell a concept or an idea to society through architecture. The architect gives the building a metaphysical added value; he gives the building a soul and so elevates a building to architecture.
/
When the modernists began to include everyday programmes in architecture, a persistent, ongoing confusion arose between the terms architecture and building, and between house and architecture. Until today, these two completely different notions are seen and understood as one. However, architecture is a spiritual and cultural reality and by no means a valid pretext for building.
/
/

A CONTEMPORARY THEORY OF PUBLIC SPACE

/
Since the fall of the Berlin wall, globalization and deregulation are reflected in all aspects of our society and also in urban concepts and in the city itself. Public authorities are forced to share more and more of their power with private institutions and this means public spaces are gradually being privatized. Are the powers involved in the field of urbanism of our so-called democratic western world still controlled in a democratic manner and is it still possible to control them? Is public space still being arranged democratically and do we still believe that it can be shaped in a democratic manner? Although until today a narrow architectural vision refusing this

social and political debate continues to exist, a twenty-first century concept for the threatened public space could provide among other things a new ethical paradigm for private institutions that interfere more and more in public space and consequently - perhaps involuntarily - [will] have to assume public responsibility.

/

Democracy must exert its powers on the design and organization of public space, preferably on a permanent basis. The design and the protection of public space, the forum, should be controlled unconditionally by a public authority, in the interest of men, voters and safety, and should be considered as an urgent priority for urban architecture.

/

Now that the world is evolving so rapidly, a new and broader definition of our universal space is required. The communal space in general [our environment] requires a much finer differentiation and simultaneously acquires a global scope. There are several scales: the global communal spaces [the oceans for example], the national and regional communal spaces [landscapes for example] and urban communal spaces with their squares, streets and alleys. Our communal spaces can be forbidden sites, inaccessible or partially accessible areas. They can be easy or difficult to reach, they may be hidden, dangerous or safe, attractive or ugly, and so on, however, in their own special way they all require the specific attention of the political authorities. It is clear that an in-depth study, the designation and cataloguing of space types on [a planetary] scale will raise environmental planning to a higher level.

The urban scale covers a wide range of public and private spaces. The communal urban space begins with the surrounding landscape [usually a neo-landscape] which in certain cases is a small or large integral part of the city [views of the sea, a river, a panorama or skyline, for example].

/

The negative city, the city landscape, the form and spatial dimension of the city or the urban void are evidently universal. In this respect, the public space or the so-called forum is in addition a very specific part which in turn consists of different spaces which can each be located outside, indoors or covered. Furthermore, the city consists of an amalgam of communal spaces such as free spaces or residual spaces, infrastructure spaces, spaces for car traffic, for bicycles and pedestrians - together or separated - and also several pseudo-public spaces and semi-public and semi-private spaces. All these typical spaces, their mutual relationship and their relation to the private world are in my opinion an interesting programme for urban architecture.

/

/

DEFRAGMENTATION

/

The autonomy of the image is an interesting characteristic of the large scale. In nature, the small scale is chaotic while at a large scale nature always creates an image. From close by, a beach is an unstable collection of sand, shells, pebbles, rocks and plants, however, from the sea it is a wonderful, stable and autonomous image. Likewise, the large-scale pattern of the dynamic city, despite its ever-changing facets and its temporary, variable and unstable programme, is an image that deserves an architectural urban plan.

/

Societies of free people inevitably live in spatial chaos that requires a considerable amount of tolerance. However, major concepts, structures and interventions appeal to our sense of order and proportions and move us emotionally and intellectually. If they can satisfy us, they constitute the necessary counterbalance: 'large-scale order, small-scale chaos!'

/

Urban architecture in particular requires the ability to switch quickly and flexibly between scale levels, between large and small. Complexity and simplicity interact continually in the urban architecture design process. Analysis and synthesis alternate.

A nautical mile of amenities for 9,500 inhabitants, model, 2004
Photo: Steven van den Bergh

European Central Station, high-speed train line above Brussels, inside, 1986

Besides fragmentation, defragmentation must also be part of architectural urban strategies and resources. All man-made structures fragment and integrate simultaneously. The world is globalizing, regionalizing and atomizing simultaneously. A balanced urban space shows fragmentation and defragmentation. Ideally, cities should also be defragmented on a regular basis.
/
Designing from large to small or from the 'top-down' is fairly obvious and relatively easy. However, from small to large or "bottom-up" is not so evident, highly complex, difficult and confusing. The European Union is a good example! Nevertheless, both methods are important and have their advantages and disadvantages when designing a city. The first method is structuring, the second de-structuring. The first creates unity and tranquillity while the second creates diversity and commotion. The first is elitist, the second popular.
/
Developing the large scale from the small scale ensures a differentiated result because it takes into account peculiarities, exceptions and individuality: it is an essential guarantee for the conservation of individual freedom.
/
/
Luc Deleu, global urbanistic concept for the European District in Brussels, argumentation for nomination [August 6, 2002]
/
/
/
/
/
/
/
/
/
/
/
/
European Central Station, high-speed train line above Brussels, model, 1986
Photo: Wim Riemens

Vincent Cartuyvels

/

Daydream of a walker

/

/

/

/

/

/

/

/

/

/

/

/

/

AN ATTEMPT TO "CHANGE"

/

Why not tackle the essence of the syndrome? Perform surgery at the heart of the disaster, the fundamental paradigm of the phenomenon called brusselisation: the administrative complex.

/

The Cité is perched high above a useless and empty boulevard, on top of the railway junction, on a slab of concrete which is 13 metres high (= height of a typical house in Brussels). It is a concrete desert covering an area of six hectares, enclosed by a 300 m wall and with a 140 m tower. A modern-day Babel divides the city and creates a chasm.

/

This monumental confusion is simultaneously the centre and the summit of a much morc cxpansive void, a mono-functional zone of office-buildings which stretches from the canal to the European District; this urban diagonal, which has been totally deserted by its inhabitants, disrupts the urban tissue of Brussels over a distance of 3 km.

So how shall we move forward: reinvest in this strategic location and - by means of capillarity, rhizomes and contagion - introduce gradual fertilisation mechanisms to revive the barren environment: a so-called urban "reconquista"?

/

Too many "grand gestures" have fallen through in Brussels, where everything is dispersion, impertinence and slowness because in this country that rebels against authority, everything starts "at the bottom".

So why not try a more modest therapy and process: diversified, combinable, risky, unpredictable, popular and adjustable, based on sustainable development standards, inspired by life, using a magic wand.

/

/

/

/

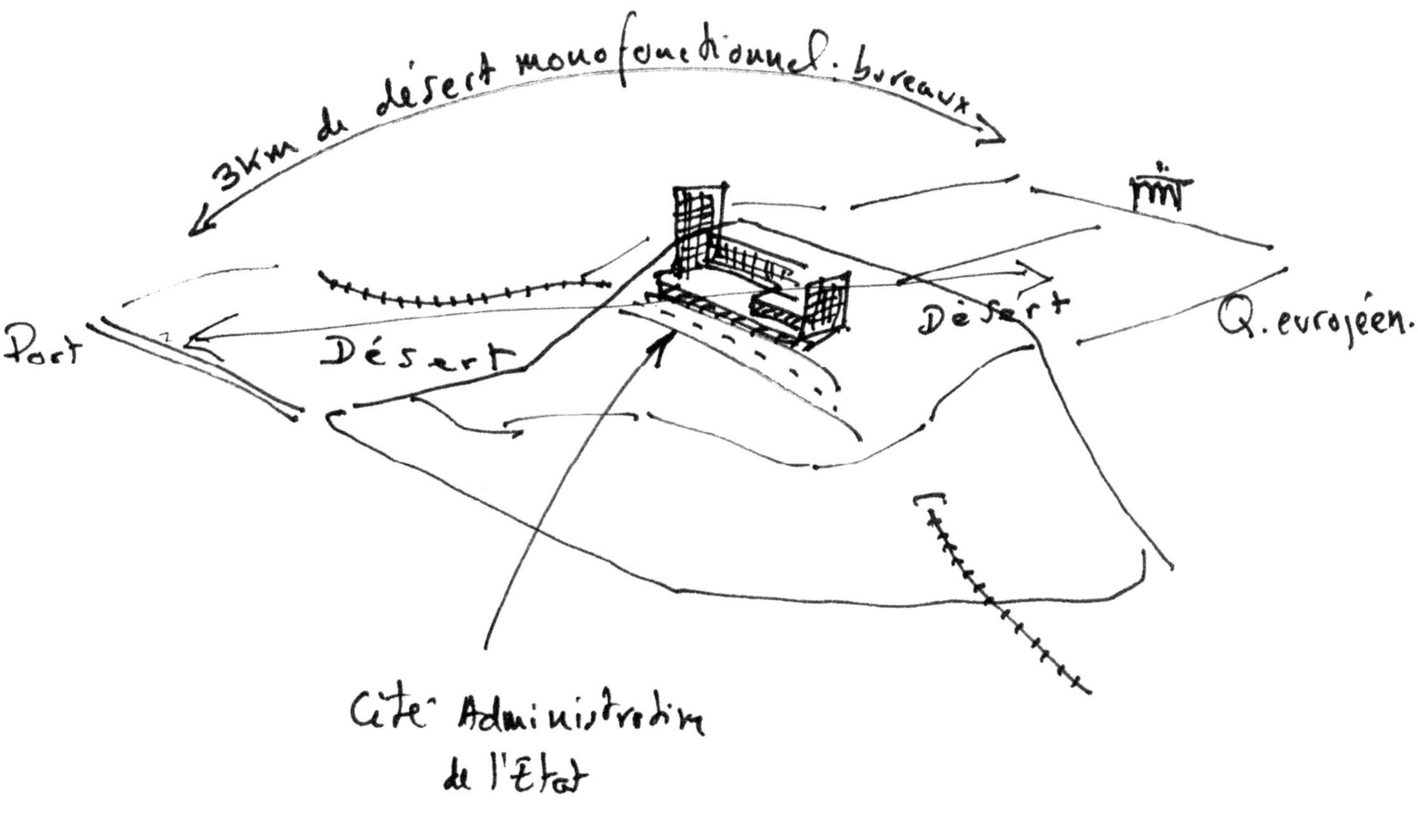

So mark, dig and move apart/ Water, irrigate/ Replant, graft, take cuttings/ Set up, import, enclose/ Connect, link/ Explore, interrupt, evaluate, correct/ Restart.
No matter which style is used, as long as it is contemporary, accessible and meaningful.
/
An ongoing mutation on a reduced scale would transform the landscape by means of micro-sites that relate to life instead of being the subject of just another megalomanic construction project.
/
The public authorities, who must be aware of the essential role of this urban laboratory, should orchestrate this pluralistic approach. They would ensure the simultaneous handling of all the problems that arise and manage the complexity of their relationships.
Thirty young architects[1] would be selected through a design competition, with Lucien Kroll as guest of honour, to re-invent this part of the city.
/
The slogan: liveable and alive.
/
No stars, please[2]

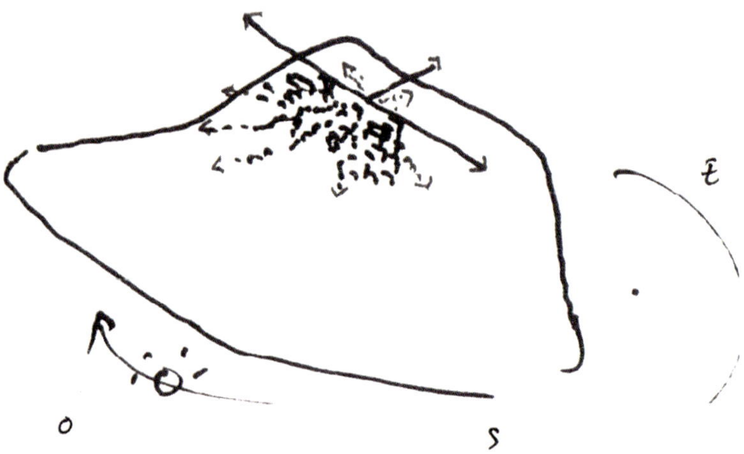

[1] One rule: none of these may belong to the group of six "major" Brussels architects.
[2] Or, on the contrary, as this was the case elsewhere, invite the "big names" to dominate the project and ask them to produce remarkable designs with reduced dimensions. A chain of architectural events shall serve as suggestions for the challenges ahead with Toyo Ito, Shigeru Ban, Spiegelhalter, Piano, Roche, Zumthor… And Gilles Clément, Dan Graham, Kawamata, Goldsworthy, Verschueren, Downsbrough, and many others…

Scenario: start at the bottom
/
As the top section is enclosed, start with the west side, which is open and more vulnerable, where the afternoon sun shines, protected from the north by the wall of the Finances building.

The fluid space of the Boulevard Pachéco, which is gigantic and useless, is transformed into a busy pedestrian zone between the Botanique and the cathedral.
/
Filling up: along the straight and diversified roads, provide green cells, small squares surrounded by dense social housing, shops and miscellaneous services. The "Ramblas Pachéco" with its spacious pavements would be the ideal location for café and restaurant terraces.
This al fresco design would be the first step towards winning the battle against the concrete.

centre
Botanique

The station today: a resource?

/

Today

/

Arriving and departing underground

The station, which is underground, is the entrance and the exit of the administrative maze which shuns the city and its light.

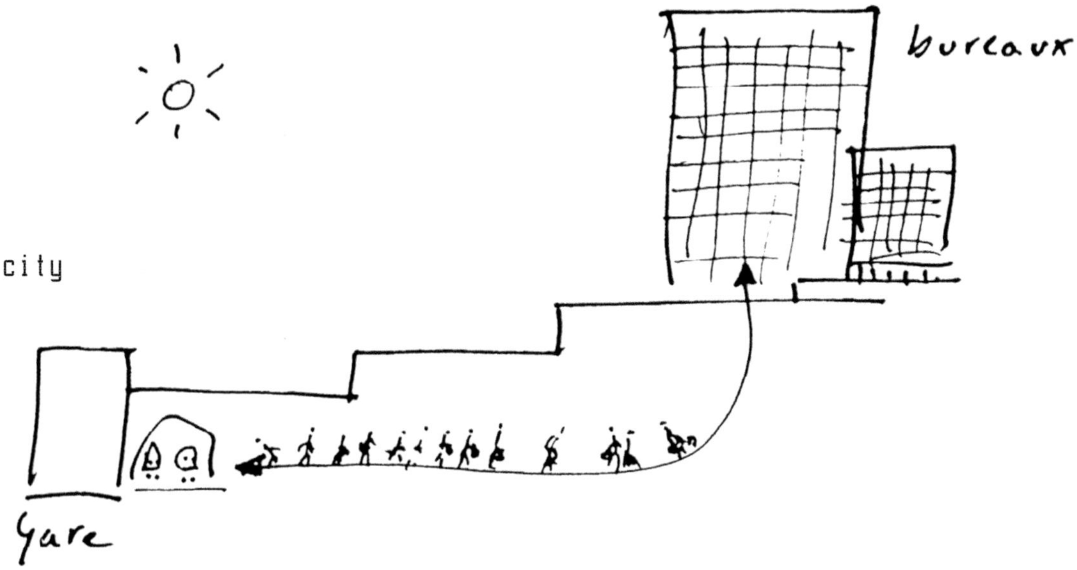

/
/
/
/
/
/
/
/
/

Tomorrow

/

An "energetic plot" irrigates with a flow of passengers the open Cité which is diversified and integrated with the rest of the city, and welcomes the afternoon sun.

/
/
/
/
/
/
/
/
/

Reinvent the paths

/

From these starting points, focus on hyper-diversity: diversify the networks, emphasise the multiplicity of needs and rediscover the principle of well-being.

/

To achieve this, bring together activities which are usually isolated: home and work and sports and culture, and balance private and public spaces...
Exploit the slope; bring back the water and plants on the terraces.

Work in phases which are self-fulfilling and serve as a critical base for the next phase.

/

Do not focus on security issues but stress softness as a fundamental factor for the tissue of the city and for the society of tomorrow.
Inventing the "hyper-liveable" city...

/
/
/

A museum of contemporary art
We shall avoid the use of the aristocratic "white box" and opt for a design tool that stimulates popular and multidisciplinary conception in the "public access" flows - visible day and night.
/
/
/
/
/
/
/
/
/
/

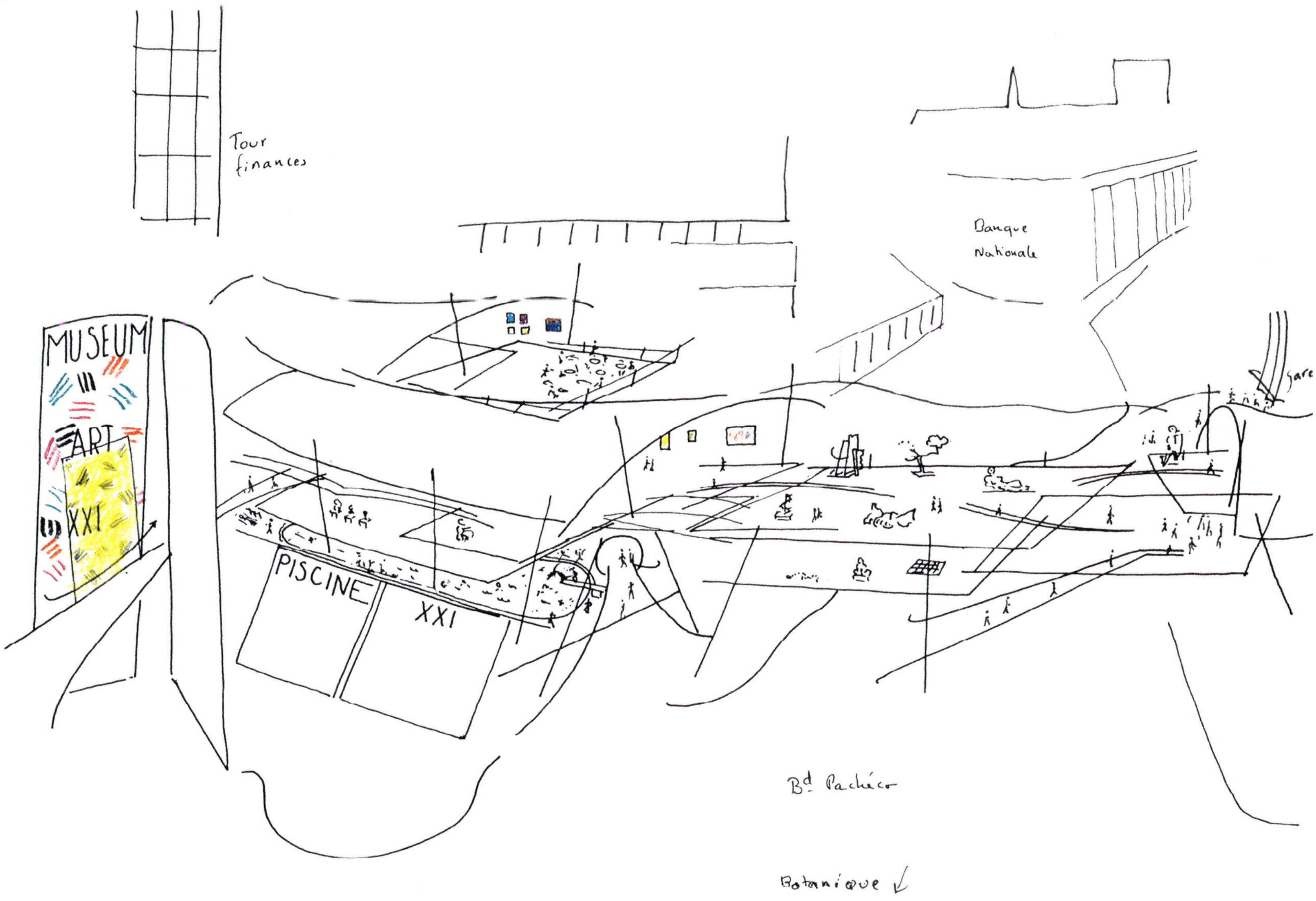

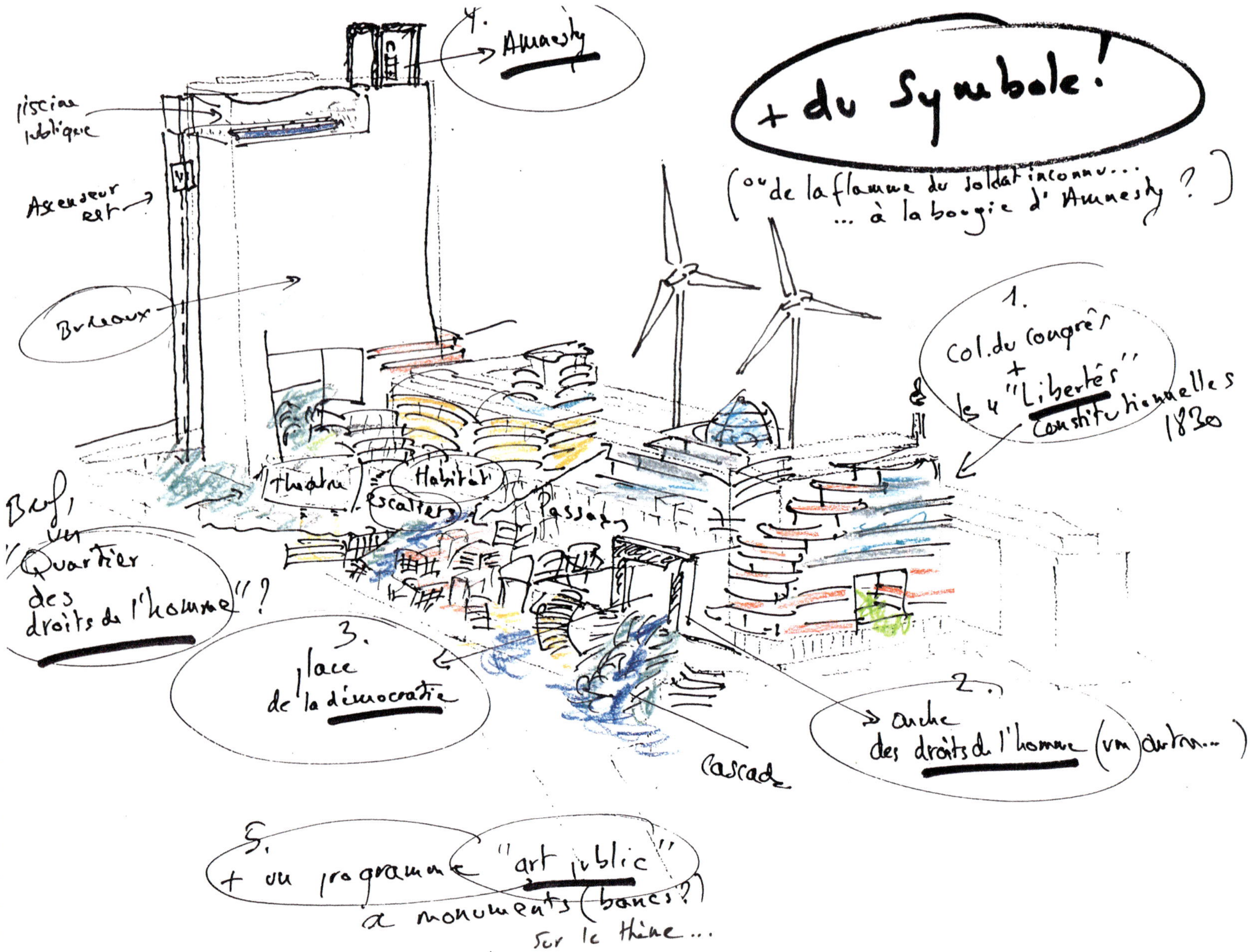
4. Amnesty
+ du Symbole!
(ou de la flamme du soldat inconnu...
... à la bougie d'Amnesty ?)
piscine publique
Ascenseur ext
Bureaux
1. Col. du Congrès
+
les 4 "Libertés" Constitutionnelles
1830
Théâtre
Habitat
Escaliers
Passage
Bref, un "Quartier des droits de l'homme"?
3. place de la démocratie
2. arche des droits de l'homme (ou autre...)
Cascade
5. + un programme "art public" et monuments (bancs?)
sur le thème...

A city that blends with the city: an article dated 7th June 2021

/

[...] Beyond the local supermarket, you have the gallery that leads to the exterior lifts of the Nausicaa aquatic centre which is located at the top of the tower [crammed during the weekends]; you hear the music of a John Cage concert as you walk to the atrium of the new museum of contemporary art; the transparent walkway [illuminated at night] is perched above the Ramblas Pachéco which is now inhabited. This atrium, which opens onto a very busy walkway that leads to the station [packed during the rush hour], is alive with a wide variety of eclectic music - managed by the adjacent multimedia library - and is effectively a melting pot of musical styles every evening from 5 to 7. At the weekend, concerts are held as you leave the cinemas whose projection rooms are located underground in the space where the old car parks used to be.

/

At the back, you can find a laundrette, playing facilities for children and Chez Nouredin tea room, a student haunt. The students live in the studios above the steam baths and cyber café on the ground floor. New apartments with two terraces have been provided for families and rise floor by floor to the level of the esplanade which has been redeveloped. The Colonne du Congrès interacts with the Arche des Droits de l'Homme [R. Serra] which dominates the square and the park with the same name [cascades].

A semi-circular street leads up the slope: cars use this road [at 20 km/h] to cross the Cité and reach the Rue Royale. It follows a green pedestrian zone bordered with staircases, varying levels and numerous cafés where you can enjoy the afternoon sun.

A funicular railway [Calatrava] joins the Ramblas and the Square of the Independent Press lower down, or the Place Chico Mendes above, at the foot of the wind generator that can be seen from the Porte de Hal.

/

The geode from the experimental bio-dome [F.H. Jourda] still has to be provided by the museum of natural sciences and the university as well as the planet observatory with educational rooms for schools and the general public.

/

A vertical garden [Patrick Blanc] now grows on the walls of the deserted car parks. The local residents' group H. Arendt, which was consulted for the third phase of the "fertilisation", fiercely oppose the demolition: they would like the primary school to have this stretch of green incorporated into their plans for the extension of their sports facilities [a climbing wall] and for the installation of sun panels which were requested some time ago.

/

The following notice is displayed everywhere:

/

83rd meeting of the City of Human Rights
Agenda:
Critical analysis of the functioning of the new installations
Evaluation of the requirements for the next phase
Presentation of the projects for walkways to the Botanic Gardens Winners: Bureau Greisch, Calatrava, to be decided
Presentation of the projects developed by 12 architects for 73 modular homes, the clinic and the offices of the EU which is decentralising[3].
Please attend this meeting! The city can only be built with the help of its inhabitants!

/

/

With reference to "CHANGE no. 2"...

/

/

/

/

[3] In fact, the European district was also reinvested. The partially demolished D4 and D5 were reconverted into housing and the D3 was entirely remodelled by Piano and Benisch.

CERAU

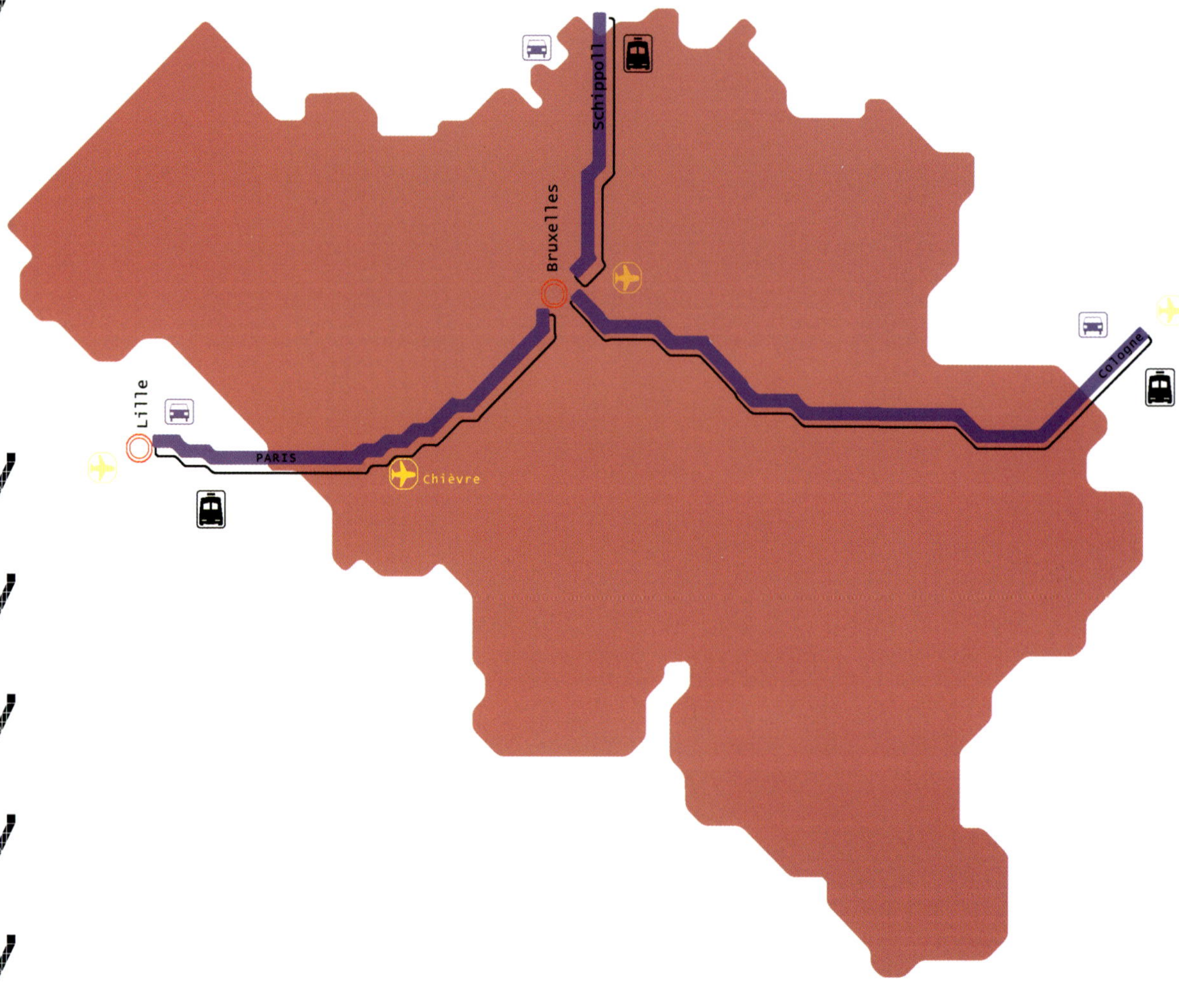

Towards a new National Airport?

/

Brussels National Airport is already an airport with a past. Everything was going along nicely until Brussels's plodding growth gradually started picking up speed and no measures were taken to restrict occupation of the land around the airport and the traffic landing and takeoff cones.

/

On the contrary, the low cost of land due to the noise pollution prompted people living mainly in the north of the country to move to Brussels and set up home in the Flemish area, on the outskirts of the capital. This phenomenon has not been curbed in any way, especially as the Flemish authorities are actually rather pleased to see the Flemish population moving to Brussels and its immediate surroundings.

/

Once firmly established, this very same population group demanded that the noise pollution be shared equally with its neighbours by creating new flight paths that would then disturb residents in areas which had never heard an aircraft before.

/

However, that is not what led us to carry out a study and look for an alternative site for the national airport, but two different reasons, which were later joined by a third.

/

The first was the observation prior to 11th September 2001 of constant linear growth in the annual number of flights. Zaventem airport and its extensions could obviously cope with that growth in traffic but the noise, on the one hand, and, on the other, the objective danger of increasing numbers of flights over a city which is expanding and becoming more dense is no longer compatible with the location of the present facilities, despite the communication benefits they offer in terms of closeness to the city.

/

The second reason is the demand from Lille and its hinterland, which is unable to develop the airport at LESQUIN for national strategy reasons [there is one in France] and which would very much like to see an international passenger airport 20 minutes from the city centre.

/

Another new factor is the arrival of large aircraft on the travel market, including the A380 with its 840 passengers, which has completely overturned the current concept of access, entry, and controls.

/

Air traffic policy in Belgium, if we can call it a policy, has a tendency to allow each of the airports to try to develop at the expense of the others without any concern for overall consistency which could benefit everyone.
By way of example, it is hard to imagine Charleroi or Bierset becoming large international airports, which would require a certain number of ingredients that they do not possess.
But why not earmark these airports for a particular purpose [like TNT at Bierset].

/

Our idea from the outset was to force decision makers to reflect by pointing out that it takes 25 years to build a new airport and there are many examples, including Munich, Tokyo and Hong Kong. Therefore it is urgent to find an appropriate area, today and freeze development during the period of reflection about the real needs.

/

We have already studied several sites, first of all between Brussels and Liege straddling the linguistic boundary, which also corresponds to a crest line in the form of a relatively unpopulated plateau.

/

Four sites are perfectly suited with a preference for Beauvechain, which is closest to Brussels, and

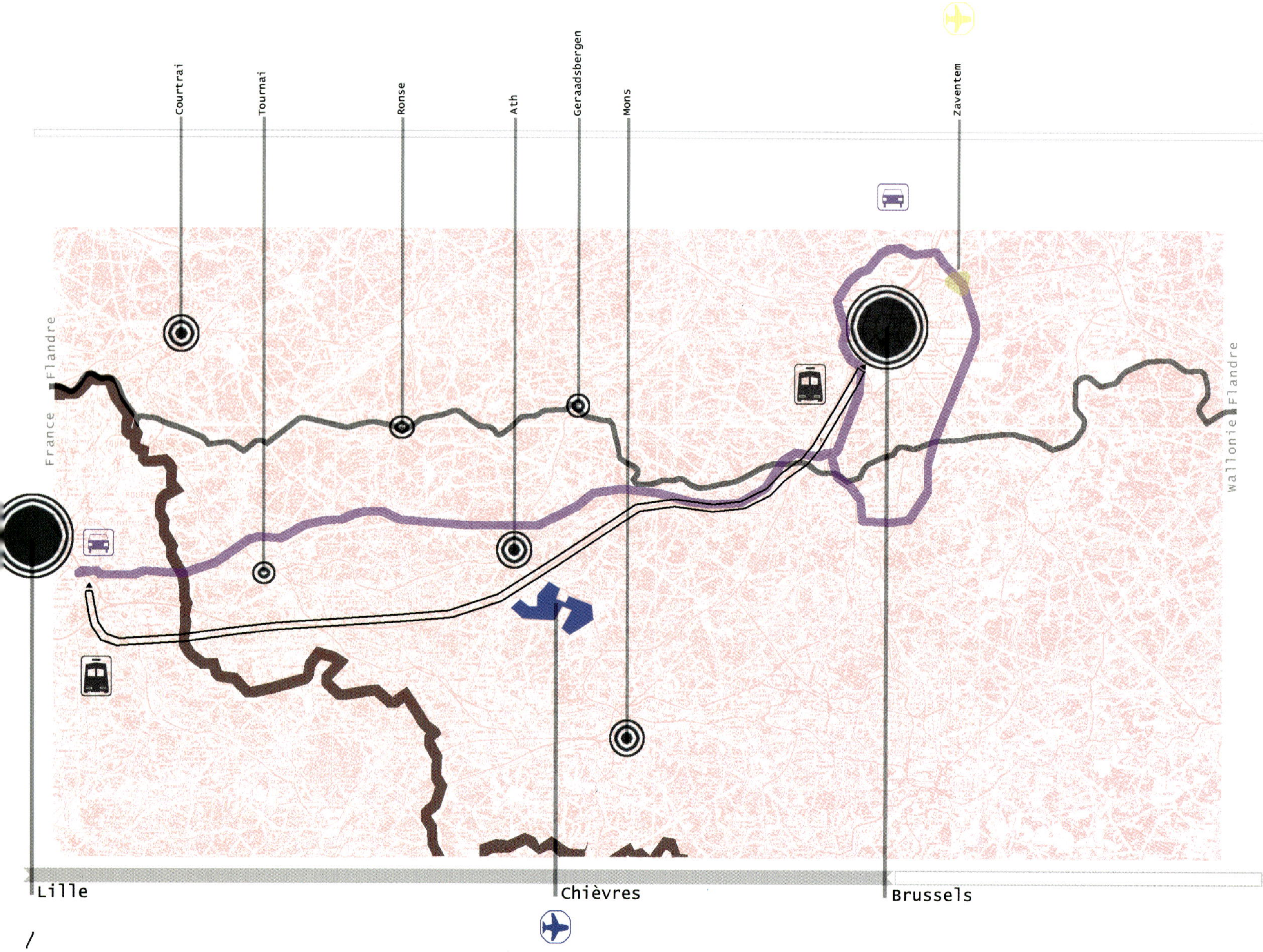
Courtrai
Tournai
Ronse
Ath
Geraadsbergen
Mons
Zaventem
France
Flandre
Wallonie
Flandre
Lille
Chièvres
Brussels

/
/
/
/
/
/
/
/
/
/
/
/
/

already has an infrastructure and restricted urban development due to the current noise pollution. That was the case back in 1994; 10 years have already passed since then.

/

The interest shown by Lille led to a second search to the southwest of Brussels which almost spontaneously revealed the appeal of the site at Chièvres which is also an existing airport. There are many advantages, with an existing motorway and high-speed train line, a region that is weak from an economic viewpoint and could certainly benefit from economic development, a site close to the linguistic boundary which would allow the economic development to be shared between the regions, as always happens with airport zones. This is an area with a relatively low population density where agriculture is not particularly viable. The catchment area of potential users is expanded by the appeal that this airport could have for the whole of northern France and its location midway between Charles de Gaulle and Schiphol.

/

What about Brussels national airport? The site could become a giant land bank or retain its airport function, sharing the flights between European flights and those outside Europe, but it would probably disappear in the long term. The recent extensions will have largely paid for themselves by the time a new airport is operational if all the necessary steps are taken today, but in Belgium who can take decisions about major projects?

/

If Brussels wants to retain its role as capital of Europe, it cannot afford a stalemate when it comes to the question of an international airport. Surely that is currently one of the weaknesses of Strasbourg?

/
/
/
/
/

Vincent Callebaut

/
/
/
/
/
/
/
/

THE URBAN CORSET
A hybrid intermediary
Porte de Namur

/
/
/
/
/
/
/
/
/
/
/
/
/
/
/
/
/
/
/
/
/
/
/
/
/
/
/
/

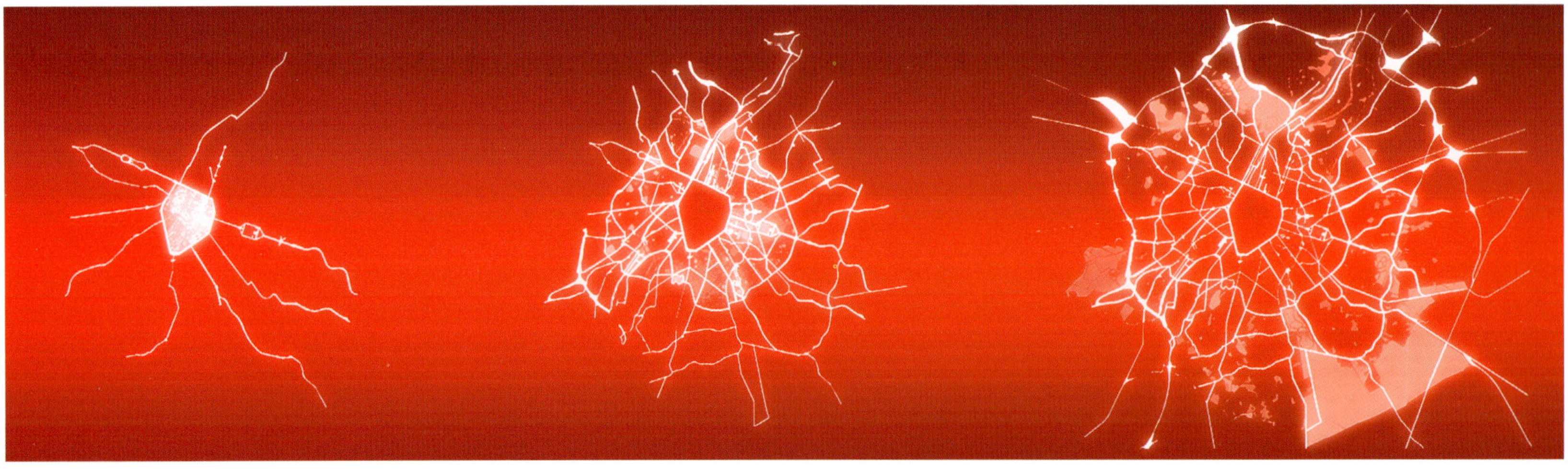

A city of paradoxes. In no other European city are the contrasts as apparent as they are in Brussels. It is a city where the banal is found side by side with the most unexpected, where the most beautiful is combined with the most derelict. The singular appeal of Brussels is probably due to this strange blend. Within the city, the urban planning chaos of the Porte de Namur has the appearance of an experimental playground alongside the Brussels inner ring road, the site of the former mediaeval fortifications converted into a ring road.
/
It is the product of a transient, surreal eccentricity. A ramp used by cars, trams, metros and passengers. Aerial and underground movements. Diffraction into programmed sequences. Any space that can be built up is built up. The boulevards of the "petite ceinture", the inner ring road, are growing into the new landscapes of the "in-between". The city must forget its boundaries and accept the new paradigms of nomadic urbanity. The "Corset Urbain" project proposes to build this intermediate space on the basis of a new specific development plan, revised and corrected according to a stratification of the city that is not only horizontal but also vertical.
/
The 4 intentions of the project are:
/
1. To free up the ground level by managing flows
/
The Louise and Trône tunnels will be connected to make a single tunnel. Road traffic will then pass underneath the Porte de Namur parallel to the Simonis-Clémenceau metro line. Ample cycle paths will be laid out. Local residents will be able to move around using a minimum number of secondary roads, and peripheral car parks will be built to relieve congestion in the city centre.
/
2. Mixing the communities
/
This bastion of the car will make way for a large, open square that will expand the interstitial spaces of the Square du Bastion and Chaussée d'Ixelles. A new place for meetings and human interaction will bring together the many communities living in the area, and reorganise their various uses of the space, encouraging contacts.
/
3. Expanding the built-up area and increasing its density
/
The Porte de Namur is a place of work, shopping and leisure, and above all a place of transit. New modular and flexible residential spaces will be introduced in the interstices of the crossroads, behind the walls of the tunnels connecting the Toison d'Or and on the roofs of the existing buildings, in order to ensure balanced amenities. A second structural lattice of construction, offset and with support inside the islets, will be placed on the roofs of the city, which will become its main floor. Thus, the skyline will become its bottom line, and plants will take over the space.
/
4. Connecting the strata and the network
/
The land-use plan of the City of Brussels will make way for a three-dimensional urbanity that will develop both horizontally and vertically. The successive strata of the city from the tunnel and the metro up to the tops of buildings will be interconnected by a network of vertical circulations. The mix of amenities, developing like an immense origami, will be encompassed by an immense urban roof creating an indoor microclimate. This "hot" roof, coloured red and gold and with millions of photovoltaic cells, will have its roots in the basement at the foot of the "Sign of light" sculpture and convert solar energy into electricity and urban heating.
/
/
/
/
/
/

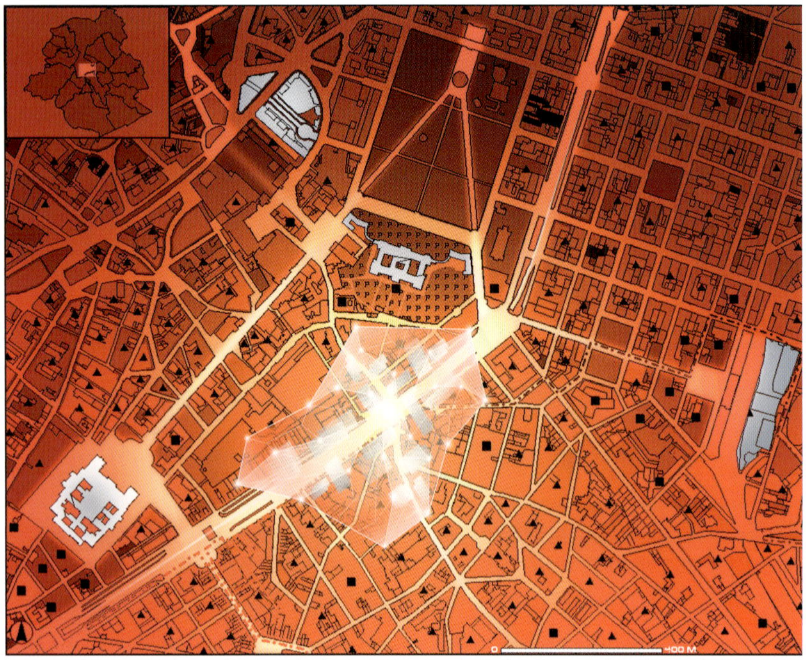

/
/
Like a corset holding together the residential fabric of the Porte de Namur, this self-supporting roof will unify the diverse typologies within a powerful identity via the temporal morphing of urban histories. It is a real prototype of urban development laid out in tiers of amenities whose intention is to increase the density and mix together the intermediate spaces generated by our civilisation of flows. Quite a challenge!
/
/
/
/
/
/
/
/
/
/
/
/
/
/
/
/

TOISON D'OR

HOTEL
Chambord

Avenue Louise
Louizalaan
Place du Trône
Troonplein

CUSTOM

/

Dominique Perrault Architect

/

/

/

/

/

/

/

/

ISE

Dominique Perrault Architect

/

/

/

/

/

/

/

Brussels Fashion Show

/

/

Brussels is a city that is open to trends and cultures. The composite and fragmentary character of its fabric is evidence of its cultural cross-fertilisation. Our proposal attempts to express the qualities of this urban diversity. Brussels fashion show raises the idea of an "haute couture architecture": architecture expressing a cycle and renewal, architecture which is FASHIONed in keeping with the times, which is created according to the expression of the artistic trends which are changing Brussels from one season to another.

/

Like models in a fashion show, Brussels' modern buildings are clad in works by great designers. They are draped in motifs, materials and fabrics - and they are paraded like proud models with sensual and ephemeral charms. They take part in the superficial and transient game of fashion and ceremony.

/

This makes Brussels the stage for an architectural fashion show. It has a catwalk on an urban scale. Its highest buildings are becoming fashion buildings, similar to the ultra designed buildings in the centre of Tokyo. Their localised density is accompanied by a graphic and architectural identity. Their silhouette acquires a new seductive power which attracts crowds and changes the temporary structure of the city by creating new landmarks and new urban concentrations.

/

The meaning of the towers is changed radically. The irregular skyline of Brussels is no longer the symbol of town planning set in stone, blind and authoritarian, but instead the sexy and versatile expression of the immense dynamism which drives its districts. Brussels' modern architecture reveals its positive energy and all its potential for investment and the regeneration of the urbane fabric. This is an argument in favour of the radical and heroic architecture of the 60s, which admittedly created a break with the historic fabric of the city, but which also introduced new open and symbolic spaces. Brussels' modern buildings are part of its heritage. They contribute to its memory and its identity. Brussels Fashion Show calls on people to go along with this, and accept the breaks, the fragments, the events, the differences and the exceptions which now make up the urban identity of Brussels. The City's modern architecture is no longer a handicap but a positive reality which must continue to be changed and compared with contemporary fashions and trends.

/

Dominique Perrault, Gaëlle Lauriot-Prévost, Gilles Delalex, Anne Speicher

/
/
/
/
/
/
/
/
/
/
/
/
/
/
/
/
/

Our thanks to the Maison Paco Rabanne
Bruno Pellerin, photographer
Malin Persson [NEXT modelling agency] and Euguenia Volodina [VIVA modelling agency], models

/

For the pages 258 - 260 to 264

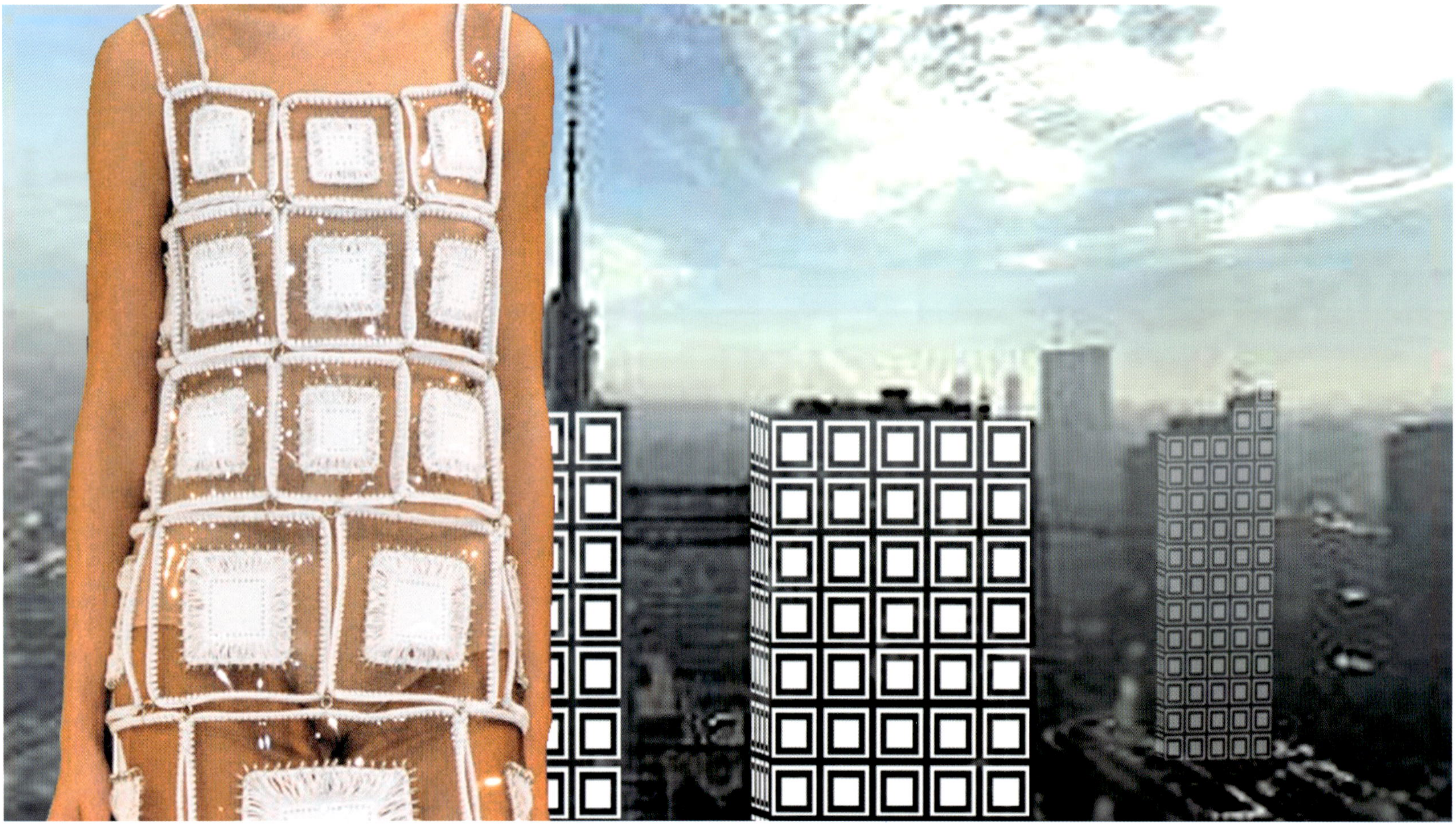

/
/
/
/
/
/
/
/
/
/
/
/
/
/
/
/
/
/
/

/
/
/
/
/

/
/
/
/
/

/
/
/
/
/

/
/
/
/
/

UNIVERS METAPHO

/

Massimiliano Fuksas/Joël Claisse
Philippe Samyn/André Jacqmain

/

/

/

/

ALISE

RISE

Vincent Callebaut/

Massimiliano Fuksas

/

with Fabio Cibinel
and Agostino Ghirardelli

/
/
/
/
/
/
/
/
/
/
/
/
/
/
/
/
/
/
/
/
/
/

NOISE IN BRUSSELS, THIS IS NOT A PROJECT

/

Brussels has a weak urban morphology;

/

we would like to build up a trace, a new urban geography that,s gives a leading scheme to the city,s development.

/

We would like to claim
Brussels city of lakes,
Brussels city of mountains,
Brussels city of forests,
Brussels city of rivers.

/

Green clouds, the town is below and is transformed: a crater, then a lake surrounded by rocks, then mountains. The city is going to be oriented, it has a pivot, a reference point.
A torrent that scours the earth ; some gorges are created under the corrosive water action ; the urbanity is the textile: an indifferent pattern.
A new river, excavated, flows through the town that becomes a new natural infrastructure.

/

Some hills, a new system : a new territory.

/

By these images, by these dreams we start working towards the city of tomorrow.

/
/
/
/
/
/
/
/
/
/
/
/
/
/

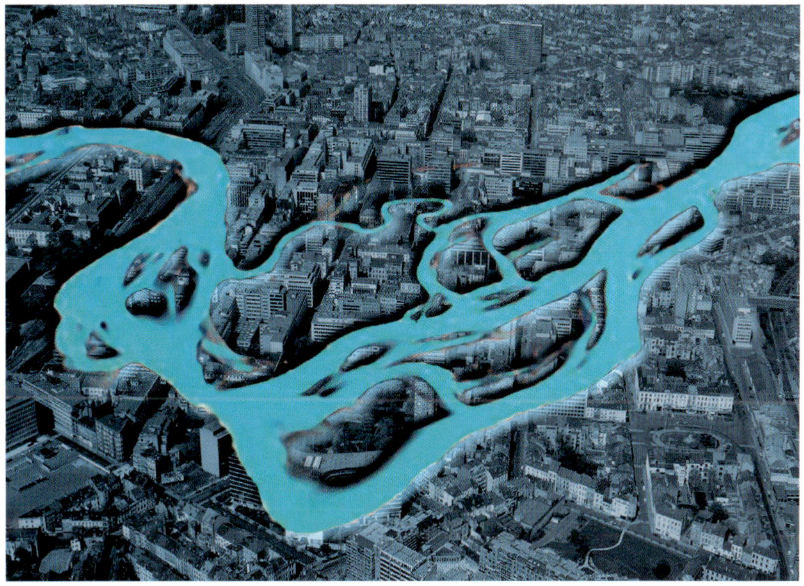

/
/

/
/
/
/
/
/
/
/
/

Joël Claisse
Vincent Callebaut
/
/

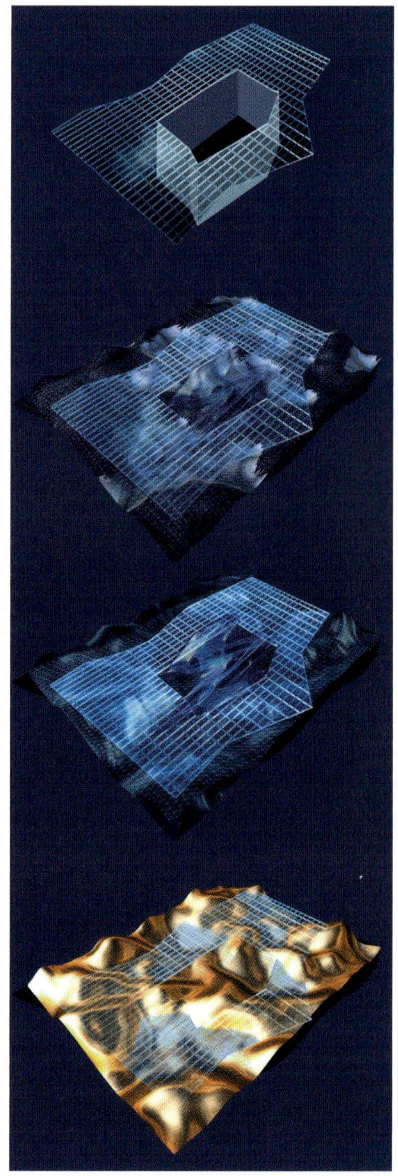

INTERACTIVE DEMOCRACY

/

/

2036, the Internet is 50 years old! Democracy has spread in real time and knowledge is within everyone's reach. Lies by the State and condoned genocide are no longer possible. We are moving towards world peace. Information and communication technologies have considerably modified the layout of public spaces, the consumer society of the 20th century and citizen movements. The economy of this cyberdemocracy is no longer based on money, but on the intangible exchange of information.

/

But what is a human being?

/

All concepts of frontiers have been abolished, and Man has become his own territory. Therefore, the haptic space is only an extension of his body. A nomadic autobionic mutant, he is seeking to eliminate any material interference between him and the world, to rationalise energy consumption and limit loneliness.
The search for happiness via hedonistic pleasure remains the key value. Clothes have become the main interface between the real and virtual worlds. Cybernetic technofibre regulates the body directly, and propels the mind into the virtual world by telepathic pulses. Chains of molecules with shape memory create the new private clothing sphere.

/

The world is shrinking

/

Physionic ergonomy is attempting to reproduce the body in virtual space using simulation software. This modern desire for infinite freedom and easy living is the result of the omnipotence of the city-world. There is no point in moving to trade, money has been abolished. The polycentric society has turned manual workers into decision-makers! In fact, the autonomous individual is on the way to replacing decision-making organisations.
The open-mindedness that has arisen from this knowledge society now enables the various cultural breeding grounds to be preserved, respected and incorporated across the generations, while allowing new societal rituals to be created.

/

Internet 3d

/

Multisensory sensors, techno-logical fabrics, textiles treated with electrical pulses, carbon or kevlar stretch fibres, microencapsulation, anti-wave polymers, chains of molecules with shape memory, dynamic bio-design are all new materials to be exploited for this virtual trans-nomadism! The bionic body is now replacing the computer. All the senses are orchestrated and transmitted by three-dimensional projection. The children of speed and the instantaneous, we travel at the speed of light, while we seek to immobilise light so as to make architecture produce energy sources and react to it. Photovoltaic cells, luminescent holograms, microcrystalline glass, X-rays of the electromagnetic spectrum, quantic computers and laboratory black holes are the means used. Now, cybernetic three-dimensionality is optimising space via the essence of the void, reducing physical contingency.

/

Light at 0 km per second

/

Basic research has succeeded nowadays in stopping light dead, using magnetic fields. In slowing from 300 000 km/s to a complete standstill, light is lost but its passage leaves a trace, a sort of print. A high density of magnetic pulses traps the light rays and forms a black hole with a quantic memory. Through digital manipulation, this stabilised light can be parameterised according to sensory and statistical data. So, an infosphere with deformable architecture, like a muscle

responding to movement of the body, develops in a three-dimensional space, a new matrix of an interactive democracy.
/
/

Digital landscape and historic impetus

In this dynamic and elusive reality, we are contemporary explorers seeking to find our bearings via landscapes - not always physical landscapes - in a situation of constant change and simultaneity between different scales. The reconquest of the historic city and the qualities of mutability and instability of its interstices fascinate us. Absence, deficiency and distortion mean that the city is no longer a linear and homogeneous system, but a morphing of trajectories and processes of expansion, inversion and contortions. In 2036, the urban population of an estimated 12,000,000 000 citizens lives in a synchronous space-time continuum; architecture has finally incorporated time as a malleable and measurable component enabling a multiplicity of experiences through a typology of interconnected networks.
/

La Grand-Place de l'O.T.A.N., Brussels

/
This innovative response reflects the needs of the alliance in terms of dynamism, flexibility and transparency. A modern, efficient organisation, NATO has taken on the mission of managing crisis prevention. Our architecture for an interactive democracy proposes a project for humanity, on a planetary scale, using new technologies. "Push forward communication to push back violence", this is the eloquent slogan of a new spatialised democracy in a real/virtual dialogue. The Grand Place in Brussels, in the heart of the capital of Europe, would be home to the headquarters of this institution, under an anamorphosis reacting to the constant flows of the Internet, a real world forum. Each human being would be a player in a socio-political anti-system, and the world would move towards becoming responsible!
/

FORCE

/
/
/
/
/
/
/
/
/
/
/
/

Philippe Samyn

/

Illustrations
David Mileikowsky

/
/
/
/
/
/
/
/
/
/
/
/
/
/
/
/
/
/
/
/
/

THE PARADOXAL SLEEPINESS OF THE ARCHITECT

/

/

Democracy and humanity

/

We are in the year 2040: every country in the world is a democracy, there is world peace and all men and women are free and equal. We could never have imagined this at the turn of the century. It is the result of the eradication of illiteracy and the consequence of our efforts to share drinking water and energy fairly with all people which was finally accepted by the rich countries following a devastating period of terrorist attacks.

/

The planet has been demilitarised, with the exception of security troops which are controlled by the parliaments and practically all weapons have been destroyed. However, the possession of rifles and guns, and galleries for shooting practice has continued to be tolerated for certain groups of the civilian population. These groups are isolated in large reservations which are carefully barricaded and guarded and which you can only enter at your own risk.

/

Death by violence in the year 2000 was caused by firearms in 18.6% of cases , 31.3% by homicides and 49.1% by suicides which today account for nearly all such deaths. This subject is worrying and is being investigated in numerous research programmes.

/

The eradication of malnutrition and epidemics caused by poverty, as a result of ongoing progress in medicine, have increased our life expectancy considerably.

/

/

/

/

Higher education is now available nearly everywhere and the quality of these schools is similar. Discoveries, inventions and artistic creations continue to appear and are quickly disseminated.

/

The world is highly intellectualised and the ongoing acquisition of knowledge, as a result of revisoting university at regular intervals, for example, has become commonplace. Unemployment no longer exists.

/

Individuals cultivate, write and speak their mother tongue in which intentions can be communicated effectively, however, they also speak other languages for intellectual satisfaction and to facilitate meeting others.
They are educated to improve language and to search for the roots but at the same time to propose new words and expressions.

/

Since the beginning of the century, computer translation software has begun to integrate all available vocabulary and grammatical rules and their subtle nuances in such a way that everyone can now immediately read a true translation of a written text in a different language.

/

/

/

/

/

/

/

/

/

/

/

/

Communication, traffic and the city

/

The global population has stabilised and is concentrated in urban zones so that nature can go its own way in the hostile zones which were abandoned in the 20th century: the zones liable to flooding and those with an unstable geotechnical balance.

/

Since 2025, all vehicles, from the smallest car to the largest truck, can be controlled electronically from a remote location anywhere on Earth and without the use of a steering wheel. They no longer crash or collide with other objects such as pedestrians or cyclists or run over dogs. They consist of modules and exchangeable parts whose raw materials can be recycled with low use of energy. The quiet engine runs on clean energy and does not release odours or dust.

/

At night, remote-controlled trucks transport the goods to their destination where machines load and unload them automatically.
Lifting equipment and manufacturing and maintenance machines are all automated to a certain degree and make sure no one is injured at work.

/

Now that most vehicles from the beginning of the century have disappeared from the roads, urban traffic can move in a continuous flow along a network which is much smaller than it used to be.

/
/
/
/
/
/
/
/
/
/
/
/
/

In the cities, small vehicles have replaced taxis and public transportation. They cost the authorities less, enable free movement even for the less-fortunate and they are large enough for your groceries, small furniture and even a bicycle.

/

These small vehicles can be parked at special terminals which are located conveniently to ensure fast transfers without waiting. With your personal communication module, which is derived from the outdated mobile telephones of the previous century, you can call your vehicle of the day to your doorstep.

/

The urban zones have also been redefined to offer uncanny simplicity, among other reasons to organise traffic efficiently, in units of 30,000 inhabitants, communes or small towns.
With a gross average density of 100 to 120 inhabitants per hectare, the area of each unit is between 2.3 and 3 km and can be contained in a square of 1.5 by 1.75 km with a dense network to provide access and provide a way out of the unit: the streets.
Four communes linked by their streets, are grouped around two orthogonal avenues to form a city with 120,000 inhabitants.
Four cities linked by their orthogonal streets and avenues at a distance of 3 to 3.5 km are grouped around two orthogonal boulevards to form a large city with 480,000 inhabitants.
In turn, four large cities, linked by their orthogonal streets, avenues and boulevards at a distance of 6 to 7 km are grouped around two orthogonal main roads to form the metropolis with 1,960,000 inhabitants.
And finally, four of these metropolitan centres, linked by their orthogonal streets, avenues, boulevards and main roads at a distance of 12 to 14 km can be situated around two main roads to form a regional capital with 7,680,000 inhabitants.
The few urban agglomerations with even more inhabitants than existed at the end of the last

century have been divided into sections and separated by farming zones or wastelands which are at least 10 km wide.

/

The major road network that links the urban units is inherited from the past but many of the roads no longer need to be as wide as they used to be.

/

/

/

High-speed trains and the new ultra-high speed trains run on electromagnetic rails: the UHST travel at 800 km/hr and they are gradually replacing aircraft for continental flights as well as trucks for long-distance transportation of goods. The tracks generally follow the path of the old motorways which provide a sufficiently dense network. A HST station every 200 km can serve an area of 17,300 km^2 or a population of one to four million inhabitants while an UHST station every 800 km can serve a catchment area of 276,000 km or 16 to 64 million people.
They are all equipped to load and unload personal cars as well as a variety of goods very quickly.

/

/

/

/

/

/

/

/

/

/

/

/

/

/

/

/

/

/

/

/

Airports are only used for intercontinental flights and flights above large uninhabited zones, and are now mainly situated along coast lines, near the ports, every 400 to 800 km. These hubs that combine sea ports and airports also have UHST stations.
Flight paths have been remapped so that planes only fly over oceans, seas or deserts and outside populated areas.
/
Waterways are only used for exceptional transportation. They have all been redeveloped for leisure and entertainment. All the embankments in urban areas have become busy social meeting places and accommodation there is in high demand.
/
For about twenty years, the trading and transportation of soil-polluting products has been forbidden.
In this respect, the exploitation of quarries has been discouraged and Brazilian stones are no longer transported by sea to Europe. Vehicles must be manufactured and recycled locally, on the spot, and this enables users to pick up a new vehicle when they decide to get rid of their old one.
/
These regulations have greatly stimulated paid transportation of immaterial goods such as data, ideas and concepts and there is no longer interest in moving goods from one remote location to another because practically all products can be manufactured locally.
/
/
/
/
/
/
/
/
/
/
/
/
/

In towns and cities, increasing numbers of bicycles and other human-powered vehicles have given rise to the general availability of cycle paths with vital traffic lights; the latter are no longer necessary for the remote-controlled vehicles.
The cyclist pressure groups have even succeeded in obtaining cycle paths which are sheltered from the rain and wind. These paths often pass under road junctions and through small tunnels.
The number of accidents has risen faster than the number of bicycles and as a result, a rider's licence for cyclists is obligatory from age 10.
Mopeds and motorbikes which proved to be quite useful in the last century are no longer in use, except for entertainment purposes; this is also the case for horses.
/
The structuring of motorised vehicle traffic has also allowed planners to transform quite a lot of road sections into pedestrian precincts.
/
All the old car parks - public and private ones - have been renovated: most of them are now ventilated and lit naturally.
/
Parking on the public highway is no longer allowed and the necessary additional car parks have been built to ensure that sufficient parking space is available at regular intervals.
/
Footpaths are now very wide and numerous canvas or glass awnings provide shelter from the rain so that pedestrians can stroll along past buildings and all sorts of shops, or sit at outside restaurant patios. Lawns and even expanses of water with fountains embellish certain areas.
/
Trees have been planted along most of the streets to capture the dust, moderate the climate and reduce ambient noise.
/
Urban signage which had proliferated inefficiently and polluted the urban landscape is currently organised more rigorously thanks to its universal character. This had gradually developed in the old airports which had been built in large quantities everywhere around the world at the beginning of the century. The urgency of a clear message that people would understand immediately had resulted in a structured system of coded pictograms which everyone understood.
/
Individual communication modules are able to read and decode immediately the signs which are read or heard in foreign countries, in the cities and towns which have rediscovered their charm and identity in their street names, concert programmes, spoken commentary, labels in shops, drug instructions, etc.
/
Buildings constructed at the beginning of the century had smooth surfaces to keep them clean in the polluted and dusty environment that existed at the time. They were sealed hermetically and insulated thermally and acoustically from the adverse effects of the outside world. In today's new environment where air is purified and calm, the façades are opening up with sliding windows and balconies.
/
Historical sites are treated like immense inhabited museums and just about anywhere buildings can be found which are listed for their heritage value. The numerous and complex building regulations which were determined by formal and conceptual requirements continued to increase until the beginning of the century and could subsequently be replaced by universally accepted rules based on common sense and safety.
Architects/citizens can now experiment with construction within this new framework, however with ample freedom and safety because most of the components are modular.
Cladding is possible in a variety of fashions and can change in accordance with personal wishes - like choosing clothes.
/
/
/

Special efforts have been made to increase green areas at all costs: roof gardens which can be easily laid out on old concrete buildings or plant façades which the city of Paris successfully experimented with forty years ago.
/
/
The workplace
/
Administrative buildings in concrete, which nearly all had eight storeys and were constructed between 1960 and 2010, gradually replacing the patrician houses and mansions with three to four storeys which had been built between 1890 and 1930, and forming clusters of concrete islands, have been reduced in height and depth to create new green areas.
/
New buildings are much more slender and elegant towers of 20 to 30 storeys are now positioned harmoniously in the urban landscape. The end of the ban on high-rise buildings has resulted in more green zones in the city centre and the return of luxury accommodation which had not been seen there for more than a century.
/
Industrial production and crafts do not necessarily require manual labour. The latter is considered as a form of entertainment like sports and travelling.
/
Work has become an intellectual activity which is organised in accordance with individual abilities and can be performed at any location. The need to meet other people has however led to the regrouping of places for working and networking near the stations. Here you will often find many buildings which are very high so they can accommodate large numbers of people without occupying too much land.
These imposing buildings are gigantic, spatial structures of 50 to 150 storeys which are interconnected and offer a useful surface area of 3 to 12 million m for between 300,000 and 1.2 million people in the HST stations and at least ten times more in the UHST stations. Even though

Le 44, c'est juste derrière le petit mimosa à gauche des Tulipes vous contournez la glycine et quand vous sentirez le citron c'est que vous y êtes.

they are very high, these structures occupy the area of a commune or even a city.
/
The high-rise buildings of the turn of the century were dense and slender and had quite a rigorous structure which was heavy and expensive in order to cope with stress factors caused by the wind. By contrast, the high buildings we see today are up to four times wider than their height in order to reduce their weight. They are extremely open so that natural light and ventilation can enter into all rooms and public spaces at all levels. The ramps and smooth slopes are not steeper than 8% to ensure they are accessible by bicycle and they all lead to public spaces.
The lifts are glazed and have natural lighting which makes them quite pleasant for moving around.
/
In the 19th and early 20th century, factories and other industrial production facilities, warehouses and distribution centres were often housed in structures of 4 to 5 storeys in the heart of the towns and cities. They subsequently moved to single-storey structures, initially in the immediate vicinity of towns and near railways and waterways, and later in vast industrial zones out in the country and near the motorways. The buildings were islands in a sea of asphalt which was necessary for the trucks and cars.
/
The inconvenience caused by the high cost of installing and maintaining these infrastructures and in particular the necessary facilities for the distribution of water, energy and information as well as drainage systems, ultimately outweighed the advantages resulting from their economic construction and easy access. The increasing use of robots for industrial production has practically made human presence redundant in these production plants which are now monitored by remote surveillance systems.
/
Today, factories are being built with several storeys once again and the outer shell is usually a cube or a hemisphere. They are no longer surrounded by expanses of asphalt thanks to the structuring of traffic as discussed above. The amount of land occupied by production zones is gradually falling and this means that more countryside can be restored.

– un dimanche à la Campagne –

Habitat

/

The majority of the inhabitants of the rich regions already had decent accommodation at the beginning of the century and these only need to be transformed and improved.

However, between the poles and the tropics the necessary reduction of energy consumption requires the reconstruction of many homes.

/

A different approach is used for the formerly deprived regions of the planet. The logical and harmonious construction of complexes of individual houses or groups which are integrated perfectly by means of urban redevelopment plans, has captured the imagination of architects. Their creativity has been unleashed and they are also inspired by the great traditions of the crafts, which are now performed by robots, and the originality of the local culture and materials.

/

Houses are mainly designed and built by the inhabitants and the services of an architect are not always employed.

/

The countryside and nature

/

Expansive zones which have been cleared as a result of the restructuring and compactness of the industrial zones and communication infrastructures have been redeveloped and transformed into forests and vegetable allotments.

The timber industry is booming once again.

Landscaping is also very popular.

/

Contextuality

/

At the beginning of the 20th century, interested travellers could still discover or discern the diversity of foreign cultures which could enhance everyday life. These influences naturally had an effect on life at home.

/

/

/

By the end of the century, mass products had been distributed to such an extent that all local cultural details were lost and their richness was rapidly forgotten. For example, outside Europe, hurried travellers would only find identical and sterile hotels which were decorated in a nearly caricatured style: a mixture of odd objects and furniture influenced by a variety of cultures but always the same in all hotels - a mediocre pastiche of refined period objects. Travelling lost a lot of its charm and was only done to discover the natural beauty of these regions.
/
Artists, who have been stifled for a long time as a result of this globalisation, are gradually rediscovering their cultural roots.
The intelligent tools of industry and the crafts have made it possible to produce unique works at the same price as mass-produced articles.
On the other hand, now that local culture is being revived, it is possible to select the best of these material riches and identify the best objects whose use was previously too local to enjoy universal distribution.
/
/
/
/
/
/
/
/
/
/
/
/
/
/
/
/
/
/
/
/
/

Shiefs
Ca doit etre moi Le chef !
C'est moi Le chef !
Non ! Pas du Tout c'est moi Le chef

The lampposts in steel and concrete for public lighting which were installed practically everywhere and were very heavy and expensive, have gradually been replaced by light metal grids which were already used in Sweden at the beginning of the century.
/
The typical bollard lights made of steel, concrete, stone or wood that used to line the roads and pavements of public spaces have nearly all been replaced by "Panettone" lights which were designed in Italy by Enzo Mari. These dimension stones or concrete blocks consist of a cylinder of 40 cm diameter and height and end in a hemisphere and a vertical cylindrical cap with a diameter of about fifteen centimetres; they can be installed on the ground easily and moved around without losing their protective function.
/
The lightness of material
/
The widespread development of knowledge and skills in the field of manufacturing and construction have made it possible to create objects and constructions which are lighter.
Intellectual effort and the amount of work for a unit have replaced the consumption of material. This has resulted in substantial savings of energy. This is also the case for transportation and production resources as well as for the operation of buildings.
/
The lightness of new constructions and the objects inside them has made them much more resistant to seismic shocks.
/
The standardisation of small components and the standardisation of the compatibility process also contribute to the possibility of producing and constructing in a fashion which is more appropriate for the cultural context of the site. This context was lost at the beginning of the century and has been revived as a result of the local availability of the necessary materials.

Wood for example, has regained its natural place, in particular for the frames of windows and doors. Aluminium profiles were recycled for more pertinent uses long ago. The recycling of raw materials has also given rise to the gradual reduction of mineral production.
/
This also implies the application of the principle of implementing reusable and even modular construction elements, which complements the lightness aspect.
/
Mortar for walls in brick or stone is flexible again and weaker than the elements that it supports.
Reinforced concrete is still in use, however, only in accordance with very strict regulations and for structures whose need for a long life have been carefully considered.

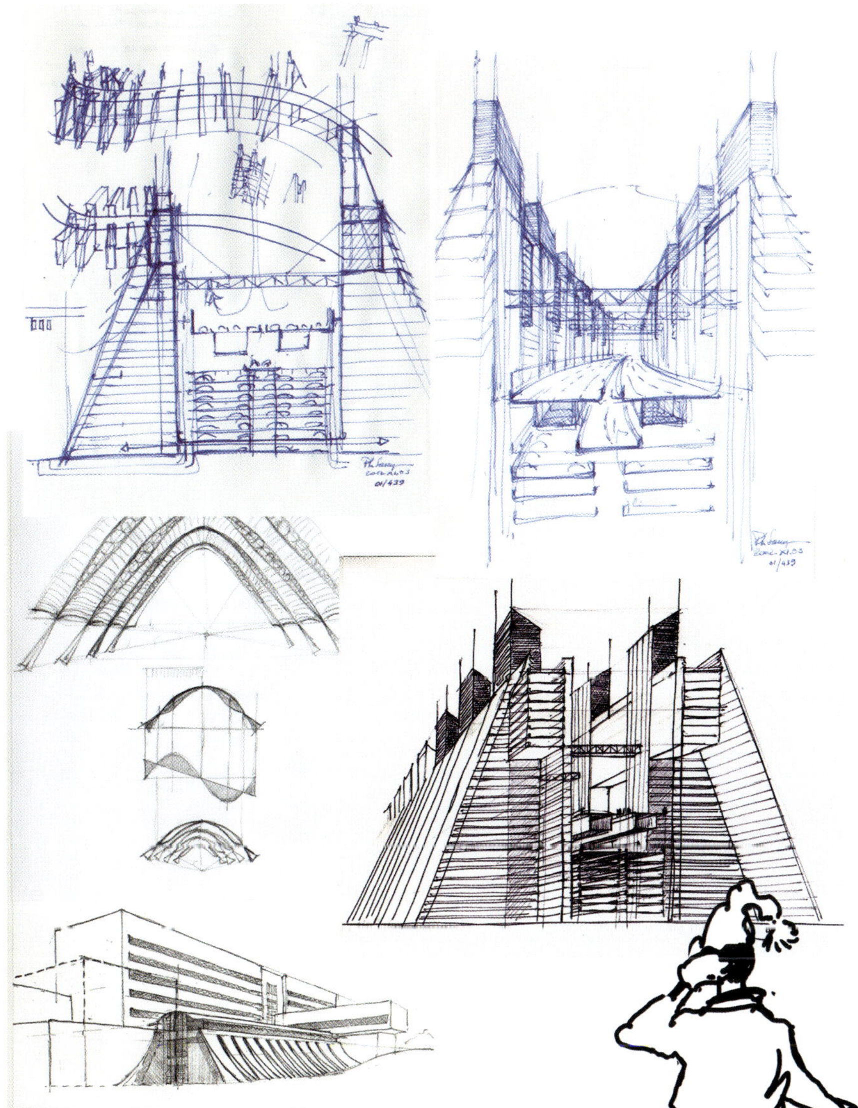

Les maisons sont de
plus en plus legères

cherie, viens un peu m'aider
JE ne comprend Rien à CE
que j'Ai REVE. hier soir

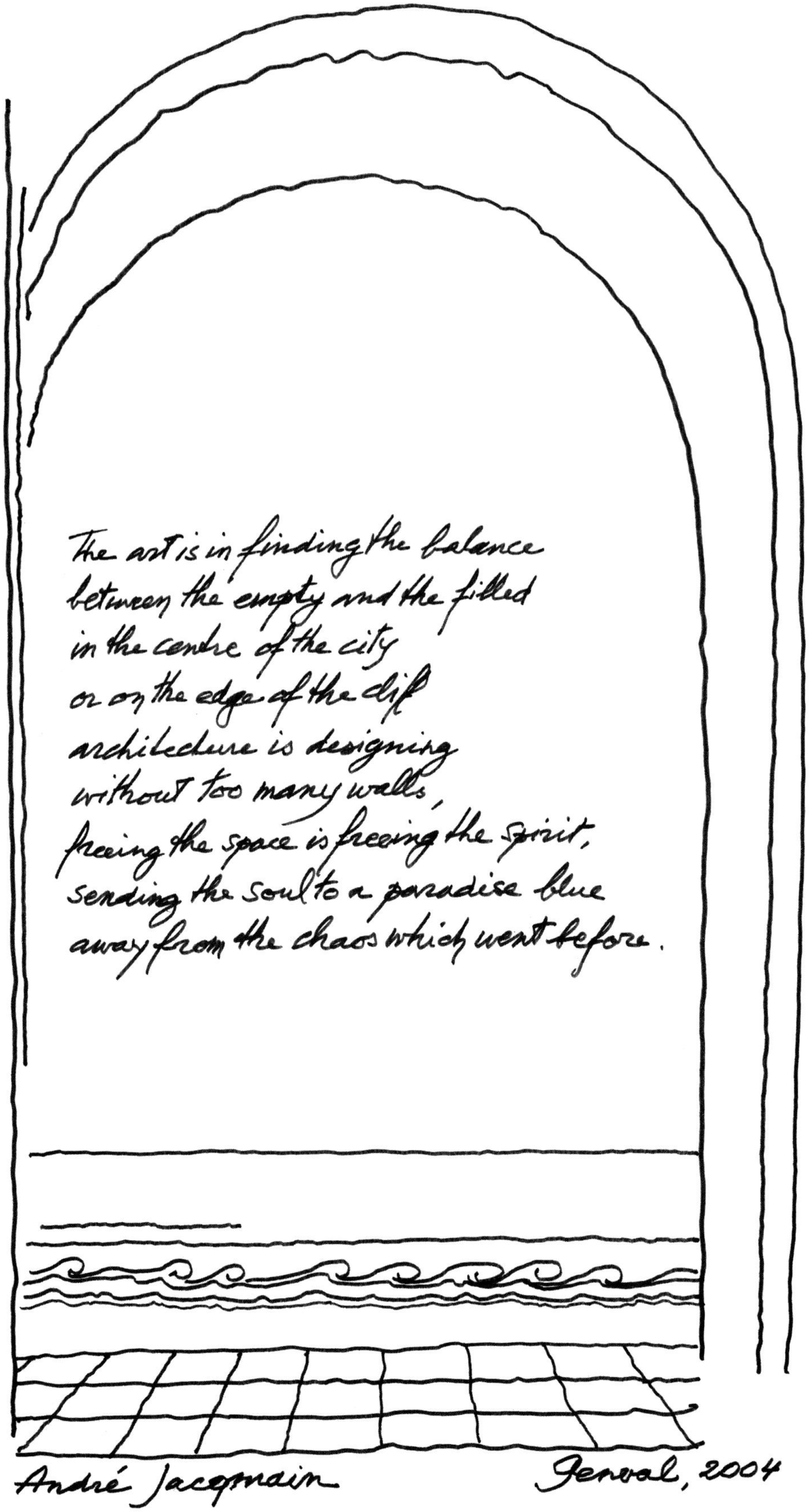

André Jacqmain — Genval, 2004

CONCLUSION

/

/

Atmospheric images, statistics and historical accounts served as an inspiration for the projects that we received. We are delighted with the diversity of the projects, but it only reflects part of the contemporary proliferation. We want their energy to change the culture of our decision-makers, through the plurality of positions. The age of certainties is over! Any city, by definition, is a place of myriad ideas and divergent practices. This vision of urbanity applies even more so to Brussels, which is the very model of multiplicity: of legal frameworks, institutions, communities and cultures. In this capacity, it is an example for the cities of the future. A fine challenge for the capital of Europe…

/

This book is only a starting point. It makes an appeal to architects as well as to artists, cultural players and to ordinary citizens: we want them to react to these initial outlines, criticise them and reinvent them in a second manifesto for different models of a city with a real quality of life.

/

/

Joël CLAISSE, architect, in cooperation with Pierre Loze, writer, Vincent Cartuyvels, art historian and the authors.

/

/

/

/

/

/

/

/

/

/

/

Metapolis - project 972
Frédéric Flamand/Zaha Hadid
Charleroi/Danses - Plan K
© Pino Pipitone Photographer

AUTHORS

/

/

Gilbert Fastenaekens

Belgium - Photographer
2003: Personal exhibition, Les Filles du Calvaire Gallery, Paris - France
2003: « Wiels ! » Exhibition for the future «Centre des Arts Contemporains», Brussels - Belgium
2002: « Perret - la poésie du béton » Palais de Chaillot, Paris - France
Since 1992, Gilbert Fastenaekens has been working as a publisher, specialising in the landscape in contemporary photography as editorial line [ARP Editions]. He currently teaches at the «Institut Supérieur Libre des Arts Plastiques» [ERG] in Brussels.

/

Marie-Françoise Plissart

Belgium - Photographer and video maker
2004: «Kinshasa, Imaginary City» with the curators Koen Van Synghel and Filip De Boeck. Golden Lion at the 9th International Architecture Exhibition, La Biennale di Venezia.
2001: «L'occupation des sols» 26-minute video, co-production Arte/RTBF/Michel De Wouters.
1998: «Bruxelles Horizon Vertical» texts by Benoît Peeters, Prisme Editions.
1985: «Droit de regard» reading of Jacques Derrida, Editions de Minuit.

/

Pierre Loze - Belgium

Pierre Loze is an art historian and journalist. He writes about all periods of art in Belgium, music, sculpture and contemporary architecture included. He works as a researcher at the "Association du Patrimoine artistique" ASBL.

/

Vincent Cartuyvels - Belgium

Art Historian - Teacher - Lecturer
La Cambre - ENSAU - Institut Victor Horta
Coauthor of the film «La cité dans tous ses états» RTBF + CVB 2000

Pierre Laconte - Belgium - Coauthor of the project for the town planning scheme of Louvain-la-Neuve.

Vice-President [1999-2007] of the International Society of City and Regional Planners [www.isocarp.org].
His work «Mutations urbaines et marchés immobiliers: le développement des immeubles de bureaux à Bruxelles» received the law-economy Prize 1974-1978 from the «Crédit Communal de Belgique».
www.ffue.org

/

Lucien Kroll - Belgium - Architect

http://homeusers.brutele.be/Kroll

/

Carola Hein - USA - Assistant Professor

Assistant Professor at Bryn Mawr College in the Growth and Structure of Cities Program.
She has published and lectured widely on topics of contemporary and historical architectural and urban planning in Europe and Japan.
She co-authored the volume "Hauptstadt Berlin" and co-edited "Rebuilding Urban Japan after 1945" [2003]. Her book "The Capital of Europe. Architecture and Urban Planning in the European Union" was published in 2004.
www.brynmawr.edu/cities/CHein.htm

/

Francis Rambert - France - President of the «Institut Français d'Architecture»

www.archi.fr/IFA-CHAILLOT

/

ACTAR Arquitectura - Spain - Architects

http://arquitectes.coac.net/actar

/

ARIES / MSA [Moritz & Simon architectes] / IDOM - Belgium - Architects

www.ombudsplanmediateur.be/noflash.htm

/

Vincent Callebaut - Belgium - Architect

www.vincent.callebaut.org

Casagrande & Rintala - Finland - Architects
www.casagranderintala.com
/
CERAU - Belgium - Architects
www.cerau.be
/
Ti-Nan Chi - Taiwan - Architect
2002: «URBAN Flashes» publisher: Chaio-Yin Huang, Taipei - Taiwan
2001: «The Turn of the Dragon Tail» project for the Capitol Core Plaza competition, Taipei, Taiwan
/
Joël Claisse Architectures
Belgium - Architect
www.claisse-architecte.be
/
Odile Decq Benoît Cornette
France - Architects
2001-06: «MACRO» [Museum of Contemporary Art] Rome - Italy - under way
2005: «Flaying horse or the rolling stone» Villa, Nanjing - China - under way
2005: «LIAUNIG Collection Musée» Neuhaus Austria - under way
/
XDGA Xaveer De Geyter Architecten
Belgium - Architects
www.xdga.be
/
Luc Deleu & T.O.P. office
Belgium - Architects
http://home2.planetinternet.be/topoffic
/
Massimiliano Fuksas - Italy - Architect
www.fuksas.it/html/index.html
/
MVRDV - The Netherlands - Architects
www.mvrdv.nl
/

Dominique Perrault Architecte
France - Architect
www.perraultarchitecte.com
/
Philippe Samyn - Belgium - Architect
www.samynandpartners.be
/
WEST 8 - The Netherlands - Architects
www.west8.nl
/
André Jacqmain - Belgium - Architect
Atelier d'architecture de Genval
/
AIRPRINT - Belgium - Aerial photography
www.airprint.be
/
Frédéric Flamand - Belgium - Choreographer
Collaboration with the architects Zaha Hadid, Jean Nouvel, Thom Mayne [MORPHOSIS], Diller + Scofidio
2004: Appointed manager of the «Ballet National» and «Ecole nationale supérieure de danse» of Marseille.
/
/
/
/
/
/
/
/
/
/
/
/
/
/
/
/
/

The editor would like to say a heartfelt thank you to the authors, his colleagues and all those who, in some way or another, have contributed to the publication of this book.
/
PRISME EDITIONS
www.prisme-editions.be
Liliane Knopes
Editor
Vehap Shehi, Jenny Provost, Véronique Wilmot,
Contributors
/
BASE
Graphic Design
www.basedesign.com
/
PRODUCTION SA/NV
Translations
/
DEREUME PRINTING COMPANY SA
Printers
Paper: Artic Silk 170 gr
/
CREA
Lenticular
/
PRINTED in Brussels - Belgium
D/2004/7555/1
ISBN 2-9600103-8-8
/

FORTIS

Glaverbel

FEBELCEM

TEIN TELECOM

CCIB KHNB

Port de Bruxelles
Haven van Brussel

détrois

PRO

DELHAIZE